CHARLES THE SECOND'S
FRENCH MISTRESS

The Real Francis Bacon
I was James the Second's Queen
King James the Third of England
Nell Gwynn
The Great Seamen of Elizabeth I

Charles the Second's French Mistress

A BIOGRAPHY OF LOUISE DE KEROUALLE
DUCHESS OF PORTSMOUTH, 1649–1734

Bryan Bevan

ROBERT HALE · LONDON

© *Bryan Bevan 1972*
First published in Great Britain 1972

ISBN 0 7091 3418 5

Robert Hale & Company
63 Old Brompton Road
London, S.W.7

115796

PRINTED IN GREAT BRITAIN
BY EBENEZER BAYLIS AND SON LIMITED
THE TRINITY PRESS, WORCESTER, AND LONDON

CONTENTS

ILLUSTRATIONS

ACKNOWLEDGEMENTS

To the Trustees of the Goodwood House Estate for so kindly giving me permission to use in my book the interesting letters which are among the Goodwood MSS in the County Record Office, Chichester.

To His Grace the Duke of Richmond and Gordon for encouraging this venture and for his assistance.

To Lord Clifford of Chudleigh for kindly showing us the original copy of the historic Treaty of Dover, the Clifford MSS, and his valuable collection of portraits.

To my wife for her help in typing the original manuscript and for encouraging me in numerous ways.

To the Directors of the Archives in the Ministère des Affaires Etrangères, Quai D'Orsay, Paris, for allowing me access to the voluminous correspondence of French Ambassadors in London.

To Father Edwards for kindly allowing me access to the Archives of the English Province of the Society of Jesus at 114 Mount Street, London.

To the London Library for their courtesy at all times, their general helpfulness, and for allowing me to retain books long after the permitted period.

To my publishers, Messrs Robert Hale, for their continued confidence in me and for their help and co-operation.

To my sisters—Gwen for her helpfulness, Penny for her constant encouragement, and Win also for her helpfulness.

ONE

MAID OF HONOUR

Louise-Renée de Penancoët de Keroualle, who was to acquire more influence and power than any of Charles II's other mistresses, was born in Brittany. She first saw the light in September 1649 in the ancient Château de Keroualle, which lay in the Breton countryside about a mile from the sea-port of Brest, where the waves dashed themselves against the rugged coast. Her father, the Comte Guillaume Penancoët de Keroualle, came of a noble but impoverished family. By profession a soldier, he had served with some distinction in the French wars, and had taken part in the sieges of Hesdin (1639) and of Arras (1640) where he was wounded. The Bretons have the reputation of being brave soldiers. Madame de Sévigné once wrote to her daughter: "The Lower Bretons are a strange people; I cannot conceive what method Bertrand de Gueslin [a famous Breton warrior] took to make them in his time the best soldiers in France."[1]

The Comte de Keroualle was a man with rather rigid, bigoted opinions. Though he lacked the courtly graces yet he was a loyal friend. Louise's mother, Marie-Anne de Ploëuc, was a handsome woman, as is evident when we look at her portrait at Goodwood painted by Henri Gascar. Her family was as aristocratic as her husband's. Her father was the Marquis du Timeur, and her grandmother a de Rieux. Louise's great-grandfather, Jean de Rieux, was Marquis de Sourdeac, second cousin to King Francis I.[2] It is proper to stress Louise's natural pride in her birth, for she was later mocked at Charles II's court for her alleged insufferable snobbery. It is significant that King Louis XIV often addressed her in his letters as "*Ma chère Cousine*". She was a distant cousin both of King Louis and King Charles II.*

The Keroualles had married in 1645, and Louise was their elder daughter. She had a younger sister Henriette, and a brother

* See Genealogical Table, pp. 192–3.

Sebastien. Louise's family name of Keroualle has been spelt in so
many ways that it is sometimes confusing. The French genealo-
gists refer to it as Keroual, while the English often call her
Querouailles. The distinguished contemporary philosopher and
author, the Seigneur de Saint-Evremond, once addressed her as
Mademoiselle de Queroualle in a letter, while Colbert de Croissy,
the French Ambassador in London, wrote her name Queroel.
Old family papers describe the name as Keroualle, so I shall keep
to that.[3]

We know that Louise was baptized at Guiler or Guylar, a
village near her home, and that her mother, who was extremely
devout, sent her to be educated at the Ursuline Convent at
Lesneven, a small town near Brest. Madame de Keroualle liked
to appear as *marraine* (god-mother) at the conversion of Huguenot
soldiers at Brest. Louise grew up a pretty child with her curly
dark hair in ringlets, her dark brown eyes and her exquisitely fair
skin. She was already envied by her companions. In this quiet
countryside Louise's character slowly developed. The Breton
influences were very marked, particularly her stubborn pride,
which bade her that she was descended from a noble family. She
was a sensitive child, always prone to tears, and her cunning and
acquisitive sense were later to be characteristic of the people of
Brittany.

At this period the young King Charles II was a homeless exile
in Europe, and Brest, rapidly becoming France's foremost sea-
port, was full of English refugees. The King's resident at the
Court of France since 1641 was Sir Richard Browne,* a distinguished diplomat and staunch Royalist. Between 1652–1654
Browne was often in Brest and Nantes, engaged in his official
duties, and it was then that he formed a sincere friendship with
the Comte and Comtesse de Keroualle. It is evident that Browne
never forgot the courtesy and hospitality he received from this
family, for he was to return it in later years. Sir Richard's wife,
Elizabeth, was daughter of Sir John Prettyman, a Gloucestershire
squire. Their daughter Mary later became the wife of John
Evelyn, the diarist, who was to write so uncharitably of Louise de
Keroualle. Louise's parents, despite their slight frigidity, were
kindly to some of the noble exiles in Brittany. Important people
at Louis XIV's court spoke warmly of the Keroualle's hospitality.
On one occasion Sir Richard sent a present of some wine—a butt

* Only son of Christopher Browne of Sayes Court, Deptford. Born in 1605.

of Canary—to Charles II, committing it to Thomas Killigrew's care. Since Killigrew was unreliable, however, it was hardly prudent to charge him with such a mission.[4] Charles I and Charles II were certainly fortunate in some of those who served them, though political corruption became a fine art after the Restoration. The correspondence between Sir Edward Hyde, later Lord Clarendon, and Sir Richard Browne illustrates how valued his services were.

During those early years in the Château de Keroualle, Louise learnt the bitterness of poverty, and a gnawing hatred of the necessity of doing without beautiful things. Although she already craved for rich, splendid dresses, she had to be content with plain clothes. Sometimes she sat demurely in the vast draughty salon, gazing intently into a log fire, which crackled and spluttered. No doubt she was dreaming of being loved by a rich man, who would spoil her with gifts of priceless jewels, of exquisite tapestries and pictures, silks and satins. She was plagued by the longing of any young girl without a dower. Sometimes she longed to leave the oppressive atmosphere of her home and to travel to Paris or Versailles, for she had already heard something of the splendour of Louis XIV's court. Stories of the triumph of Louis XIV's favourite, her namesake Louise de la Vallière, had reached her parents' home. At all costs she, too, must find her way to court. Perhaps she would attract the interest of the King, or at least find a rich husband, for the furtive glances of admiration of the young men in her neighbourhood fed her vanity and told her that she was desirable. Yet she realized in her stubborn way that the only way to achieve her desire was to be appointed a maid of honour. Indeed the most significant event in Louise de Keroualle's early life—she was nineteen at the time—was her appointment as maid of honour to Henrietta-Anne, Duchess of Orleans, youngest and favourite sister of Charles II. She had been born at Bedford House in Exeter at the height of the Civil War in 1644, and the infant Princess attended by her governess Lady Dalkeith had managed to escape to France. In 1661 she had married the effeminate Philippe, younger brother of Louis XIV, a corpulent little man who wore shoes with heels so high that he seemed to be on stilts. He had a kind of waspish intelligence, and an amusing, spiteful tongue. He often rouged his cheeks and used perfume.

It is related that it was owing to the influence of the Duke of Beaufort, Chief Admiral of France, an intimate friend of the

Keroualles, that Louise became a maid of honour to the Princess with a salary of £150 per annum.[5] Monsieur de Chaulnes, Governor of Brittany, also recommended her for this position at court. Even when a young girl she was extremely adroit in gaining the good will of those who could be of use to her. She carefully cultivated the art of pleasing influential people, though she was really a minx. By a subtle kind of coquetry she knew how to flatter an old man such as the Duke of Beaufort. At court Sir Richard Browne told the Duchess of Orleans that the Keroualles had done much to soften the exile of the Royalists.

Saint-Simon, the contemporary French historian, accuses her parents of a design to obtain the post of maid of honour for Louise so that she might attract Louis XIV's attention, and even become his mistress.[6] This seems most unlikely when we consider what we know of the Keroualles character. It is certain that they later strongly disapproved of their daughter's liaison with Charles II. They probably hoped that whilst serving in the household of the Duchess of Orleans that a wealthy Frenchman would seek her hand in marriage.

At nineteen Louise was still unattached, though Forneron in his biography states that the Comte de Sault, son of the Duc de Lesdiguières, a debauched courtier, was in love with her.

At this period towards the end of 1668 when Louise became a maid of honour to Henrietta-Anne, Duchess of Orleans, France dominated Europe. It was a great age in French history, a period of expansion when the naval ports flourished, ships were built, and the French colonial empire prospered. Louis XIV wrote in that year:* "My dominant passion is certainly love of glory [*gloire*]". A wonderful epoch also from 1668–1672 for French literature and art when Molière was delighting audiences in the theatre with his wit and genius, La Fontaine published his *Fables*, and Racine triumphed with *Andromaque*.

Venetian diplomats had written of Louis XIV:

His constitution is sturdy and his appearance majestic: his face is at once open and imposing, his manner courteous and serious ... the King's heart is constantly ablaze with two consuming subjects: one is jealousy of his own greatness, which rules out any favourite ... the other is the desire to surpass, with acts of true magnificence, the finest examples that present themselves for his emulation ...

* He was born in 1638.

But his soul glows with a feeling of humanity. The King loathes all severe and, *a fortiori*, cruel actions . . .[7]

That might be so, but Louis was capable of treating his wretched mistress Louise de Vallière with cruelty and inhumanity when he was tiring of her.

On 18th July 1668, only a few months before Louise de Keroualle joined the Duchess of Orleans' household, Louis XIV had given a magnificent *fête* at Versailles, which had caused an enormous sensation. Its ostensible object was to celebrate the conclusion of the Peace of Aix-la-Chappelle, but it was really designed to do honour to the new royal mistress, the arrogant, sensual and beautiful Madame Françoise-Athénaïs de Rochechouart—Marquise de Montespan.

Madame de Sévigné has described its splendour. The Sun-King in a setting worthy of a great monarch. There in the celebrated grotto of Thetis "an enormous bas-relief cut in the rock, a golden sun, the King's favourite device, was seen setting in the waves of the sea, surrounded by Tritons and Sirens that gushed with streams of water, while life-size statues of Apollo and the Muses adorned the sides of the grotto."[8]

Louise de Keroualle, on beginning her duties towards the end of 1668 inexperienced as she was, soon discovered that her mistress the Duchess of Orleans—usually called "Madame" in France—was deeply unhappy in her marriage. A disillusioning experience for a young girl to be transplanted from the Château de Keroualle to the court at Versailles where falsehood and dissimulation abounded.

Louise was horrified to discover that Monsieur, the Duchess of Orleans' husband, was dominated by his infatuation for a member of his household, the worthless and mischievous Chevalier de Lorraine, younger brother of Monsieur d'Armagnac, the Grand Écuyer.* Lorraine gradually acquired a complete ascendancy over the mind of Philippe ("Monsieur"), and with insufferable insolence attempted to rule him and his whole household. When the Chevalier seduced one of the Princess's maids of honour, Mademoiselle de Fiennes, Philippe was very jealous and insisted on the girl leaving Madame's household without telling his wife.

Most of Madame's contemporaries pay tribute to the fascination of her personality and to the beauty of her character. Her hair

---

* Equivalent to the Master of the Horse in the English Royal household.

was chestnut, and her eyes were brilliantly blue. A lady at the French court, Madame de Bregis, tells us that she danced with incomparable grace, that she sang like an angel, and played the spinet divinely. Yet during the early days of her marriage over seven years ago she was a natural flirt and had on occasions behaved indiscreetly.

Her friend, Daniel de Cosnac, Bishop of Valence, wrote of Princess Henrietta-Anne:

> Madame had a clear and strong intellect. She was full of good sense and was gifted with fine perception ... her whole conversation was filled with a sweetness which made her unlike all other royal personages ... The grace of her soul seemed to animate her whole being, down to the tips of her feet and made her dance better than any woman I ever saw.

She was twenty-four when Louise joined her household.

There is no doubt that Louise managed to insinuate herself into the good graces of her mistress. On her part, the Duchess of Orleans was attracted to Louise, and found her modesty, her discretion, and her piety most appealing. Perhaps she confided her marital troubles to her maid of honour, and Louise would have been highly indignant that her husband treated her so shockingly. When the Princess spoke of her brother Charles, since 1660 restored to his kingdom as Charles II, she always did so with great affection and emotion.

Louise and the other maids of honour, including Mademoiselle Marie-Simone du Bellay, Mademoiselle Hélène Fourré de Dampierre and "Madame" du Lude, were under the supervision of Mademoiselle Anne de Bourgogne; Mademoiselle Catherine d'Orville was *sous gouvernante*. In those early days Louise made no very marked impression at the French court. It is true that King Louis noticed her high breeding, but her beauty did not seem to attract him. He was fully occupied at the time with his sensual passion for Madame de Montespan. Louise at nineteen was still unmarried, and despite her pretty face no French suitor seemed anxious to seek the hand in marriage of this girl without a dower. We hear of Louise dancing at a *fête* given by the Duke and Duchess of Orleans to Morosini, the Doge of Venice, during January 1669.

In the course of this year Louise's only brother Sebastien took part in the expedition under the Duke of Beaufort, which Louis

XIV sent at the request of the Doge of Venice to give support to Candia against the Turks. Later, Mademoiselle de Keroualle heard the sad news that Sebastien had been seriously wounded whilst serving in this expedition.

Louise learnt valuable lessons in the household of Madame at the Palais-Royal, the necessity of dissembling her feelings, hard as that might be, that few people could be trusted at court, and, above all, to be discreet in conversation and circumspect in her actions. Watchful and silent the young Bretonne became aware early in 1669 that her mistress was involved in a political intrigue of great importance. It was a strangely exciting time. She knew that the Princess was frequently closeted in secret conference with King Louis. Although so young, Princess Henrietta possessed diplomatic ability and a lively intelligence, so that she was acting as an invaluable intermediary between the French king and her beloved brother in the long and intricate negotiations which preceded the Treaty of Dover.

Across the Channel King Charles II had now been restored to his uneasy kingdom for almost nine years.* He was at least six feet tall, and graceful in his movements, whether walking, dancing, riding or playing tennis. His swarthy, saturnine complexion betrayed his foreign blood, for he was half French through his mother, Queen Henrietta Maria, and his grandmother was Queen Marie de Medici, the Italian consort of King Henri IV of France. There were striking similarities of character between the young king and his maternal grandfather Henri IV. They were both political opportunists, and were secretive, knowing how to dissemble. Charles was as amiable as his grandfather in adversity, and both loved women. Charles's eyes were large, dark and very expressive, while his mouth was very sensual. Charles's reputation for indolence has been over-emphasised, for under an air of nonchalance he hid enormous ability, a real flair for kingship and a detailed knowledge of diplomacy and foreign affairs, acquired not so much from books but from intimate acquaintance with eminent statesmen during the early days of exile in Europe.† He was at times to prove himself a match for Louis XIV.

For instance, at the beginning of 1669 he was anxious for an

* He was born on 29th May 1630.

† The Lord Keeper, Guildford, declared that he thought King Charles II understood foreign affairs better than all his Councils and Counsellors put together.

alliance with France for family, dynastic and financial reasons, but he always insisted, because he was deeply interested in naval affairs, that Great Britain's naval supremacy must be safeguarded.[9] He informed the new French Ambassador in London, Charles Colbert, Marquis de Croissy (a brother of Louis XIV's minister) that a treaty of commerce in which England's maritime interests were clearly satisfied must precede the negotiations for an Anglo-French alliance. Earlier, Charles's foreign policy seems to have been directed against France, particularly when he agreed to join an offensive and defensive alliance on 23rd January 1668 with the Dutch, known as the Triple Alliance, because the treaty was later signed by Sweden. Both Charles and Louis, however, were unscrupulous enough not to allow any prior treaty to defeat their purpose now they wished to form an alliance.

Charles was well aware that the mass of Englishmen, who were Protestants, disliked the French, and that the negotiations should be conducted in secrecy. Englishmen were for the most part opposed to the conception of an absolute monarchy and a Catholic king. In his correspondence with his sister Henrietta, Charles showed how deeply he loved her, although they had been separated from one another for many years. His pet name for her was Minette, but he rarely used it. In an early letter he wrote her: "I assure you there is nothing I love so well as my dearest Minette, and if ever I faile you in the leaste way I am unworthy of having such a sister as you."[10]

His little sister, however, an ardent Roman Catholic, longed for England to revert to the ancient religion. She also used her influence with Charles to try and persuade him to become an open Roman Catholic. We know that King Charles held a secret conference on 25th January 1669 with his brother James, Duke of York, Lord Arundell, Henry Bennet, Lord Arlington and Sir Thomas Clifford in which he divulged his desire to become a Roman Catholic, and to obtain the help of France, so that he might make a public announcement of his religion. Charles may have been a secret Catholic at this period, but he dared not acknowledge it except to a few trusted people.

For almost seven years he had been married to a Portuguese princess, Catherine of Braganza, but she had borne him no children. It is probable that King Louis believed that King Charles II's mistresses, particularly the voluptuous and tempestuous Lady Castlemaine, possessed more influence than they in fact held. He wrote to his Ambassador in London, Colbert de Croissy: "I have heard read with great pleasure the curious details you have written to M. de Lionne [French Foreign Minister] about the intrigues of the English Court, and the broils of the ladies who are the chief personages there."[11] Colbert de Croissy, who on the whole was more successful in negotiating with men than ladies, assured His Majesty that he would continue to supply him with dainty morsels of information about the ladies. He had acquired the habit of bribing Lady Castlemaine with jewels and other presents, though it was clear that she was fast losing her hold over Charles II. He informed Louis: "The King often says that the only woman who has really a hold on him is his sister, the Duchess of Orleans."[12] He therefore advised that only unimportant gifts such as a pair of French gloves, ribbands or a Parisian undress gown should be given the favourite. Charles II, however, rather disliked Colbert de Croissy, though he at first found him congenial, and did not wish to admit him into the secrets of the Treaty of Dover.

It was considered far too dangerous for the secret negotiations to be told to Monsieur, for Louis XIV knew only too well that his brother was a babbler. Unfortunately the malicious, prying Chevalier de Lorraine, always keen to stir up trouble between the Duke and Duchess of Orleans discovered that a secret treaty was under discussion, and that Charles II was insisting as one of the conditions that the Princess must visit her brother in England. He repeated this information to Monsieur. Furiously resentful at being kept in the dark, and always jealous of his wife, Philippe complained to his brother the King.* Louis, however, although fond of his sister-in-law, did not sufficiently protect her interests.

Louis XIV surely misjudged Charles II's character in sending over to England the Abbé Pregnani, an Italian Theatine monk, as a kind of unofficial agent or spy. This amusing man had a real gift for casting horoscopes, as James Duke of Monmouth, Charles's bastard son had recently discovered on a visit to the French court. Pregnani was intructed to impress Charles II and the English courtiers by making astrological predictions emphasizing the many advantages of an alliance with France.[13] Charles was far too shrewd to be deceived. Though he was diverted by

* It is related that the old Marshal de Turenne had told Madame de Coetquen, one of Madame's ladies who had repeated it to the Chevalier de Lorraine with whom she was in love.

the Abbé's company and invited him to see the horse matches at Newmarket, he refused to take him seriously. He wrote Minette on 22nd March:

L'Abbé Pregnani was there most part of the time and I beleeve will give you some account of it, but not that he lost his money upon confidence that the stars could tell which horse would winn, for he had the ill luck to foretell three times wrong together, and James [Duke of Monmouth] beleeved him so much as he lost his money upon the same score.[14]

What impressed Louise most was the Duchess of Orleans's deep love of her brother Charles. When his letters arrived by special courier, she would eagerly open them and disappear into her salon to deal with her English correspondence. Charles gave her a lovely present—a barge lined with blue velvet and embroidered with gold, which she greatly cherished.

During the summer of 1669 Madame was in poor health, and Louise attended her when she left for her country residence at Saint-Cloud. Sometimes Monsieur visited his wife there, but it was a relief when he returned to court. Madame was *enceinte* and on 27th August she gave birth to a daughter,* much to the disappointment of her husband, who wanted a son. The late summer was saddened for the Princess by the death of her mother, Queen Henrietta-Maria, who died on 19th September at Colombes. Henrietta, her youngest child, was her favourite, and mother and daughter had always been very close to one another.

During those early autumn days, so beautiful and serene, Louise felt a new bond with her mistress, for she was also grieving for her brother Sebastien, who had recently died from wounds in Provence. Sometimes Madame would be visited by her devoted friend Madame de la Fayette, who wished to comfort the Princess in her great sorrow. Lying back on some cushions Henrietta, to relieve her mind, would dictate her memoirs to Madame de la Fayette.[15]

Meanwhile the Chevalier de Lorraine continued incessantly to intrigue against the Duchess of Orleans, and Louise, fearful for her sake, wondered how long she could endure his insolence. Lorraine openly boasted that it was owing to his influence that

* Her younger daughter, Anne Marie, Mademoiselle de Valois. In 1687 she married Victor Amadeus II, Duke of Savoy, afterwards King of Sardinia.

Madame de Saint-Chaumont, one of her intimate friends and governess to her children, had been disgraced and Daniel de Cosnac, Bishop of Valence, ruined. Once when she felt particularly depressed, Madame wrote that she was destined to bring trouble on the heads of all those who served her. Sometimes Louise could hardly restrain her indignation that her mistress should be treated in such a humiliating way. Madame complained to her brother, Charles II, and the French king promised that his brother's favourite would be punished. At last at the end of January 1670, King Louis ordered that the Chevalier should be arrested and conveyed to prison. It is related that Monsieur in despair threw himself at his brother's feet on hearing of his minion's arrest, and with tears streaming from his eyes begged for his release, but Louis would not relent.

The negotiations for a treaty were now far advanced. Charles, who longed to see his sister, wrote to the French king that a visit from Madame would be the best means to effect the final completion of the treaty. Monsieur was the difficulty. At first he was reluctant to give his consent, then he suggested that he should accompany his wife, so Charles had to find a suitable excuse for refusing Monsieur's request. Since his brother James Duke of York could not visit the French court at this time, it was not proper for the Duke of Orleans to come to England. At last Philippe was persuaded to give his grudging permission, but he stipulated that she should remain in England for only a few days, and that on no account would he allow his wife to go beyond Dover. This was exasperating for Charles II, because he would naturally have preferred to have received his sister in London.

Louise was aware that Madame was attached to her, and she was not wholly surprised to learn that she was among the persons chosen by Louis XIV to accompany her to England. She had managed to learn a little of the language but she hardly spoke it at all. The young Bretonne felt very elated at the thought of the journey, but embarrassed because she lacked new dresses. Madame behaved with her customary generosity and kindness. She gave her maid of honour a large present of money, so that she could spend it on herself.[16] Madame knew that some of Louise's companions were envious that she had been chosen to attend her. Louise occasionally played at *lansquenet*, a game much in vogue at Louis XIV's court, so she early acquired the taste for gambling which she always possessed. That the French king had deliberately selected Louise de Keroualle to attend his sister-in-law on her vital mission to England, thinking that her beauty, simplicity and innocence would appeal to Charles II, seems very unlikely, though Colbert de Croissy in England kept him well-informed as to Charles's taste for novelty and his indolent love of pleasure, and beautiful women. At this juncture Louis treated his sister-in-law with generosity, giving her 200,000 crowns towards her expenses.

NOTES

1. 15th May 1689.
2. Her pedigree can be found in Le Père Anselme, *Histoire Généalogique et Chronogique de la Maison Royale de France.*
3. Archives Nationales, J. 152.6; Forneron, *Louise de Keroualle.*
4. *Memoirs and Correspondence of John Evelyn*, V, p. 301.
5. Jeanine Delpech, *The Life and Times of the Duchess of Portsmouth.*
6. *Ecrits inédits de Saint-Simon*, E. 16, p. 485.
7. Philippe Erlanger, *Louis XIV*, translated edition, p. 126.
8. Julia Cartwright, *Madame, a Life of Henrietta Duchess of Orleans.*
9. Cyril Hughes Hartmann, *Charles II and Madame*, p. 223.
10. 8th September 1662.
11. Correspondance Angleterre, 20th January 1669; see also Forneron, *op. cit.*
12. 14th February 1669.
13. Correspondance Angleterre, XCIII, Lionne to Colbert, 23rd February 1669; Cyril Hughes Hartmann, *op. cit.*
14. Cyril Hughes Hartmann, *op. cit.*
15. Madame de la Fayette, *Vie de Madame Henriette.*
16. Jeanine Delpech, *op. cit.*

TWO

JOURNEY TO ENGLAND

The ostensible purpose of the French king's journey to Flanders on 28th April 1670 was to show his Queen Marie-Thérèse his new subjects, but it was necessary to conceal the real reason for the expedition, Madame's visit to England.

Voltaire in his great work *Le Siècle de Louis XIV* has written: "It is not merely the life of Louis XIV that we propose to write; we have a wider aim in view. We shall endeavour to depict for posterity, not the actions of a single man, but the spirit of men in the most enlightened age the world has ever seen." To some extent the writer succeeds. Voltaire describes the journey to Flanders as "a continuous triumphant procession, attended by the utmost magnificence". The triumph of Madame de Montespan (the new Mistress) was most apparent, wrote Voltaire; she accompanied the King in his gorgeous carriage . . . and when Madame de Montespan rode alone her carriage was escorted by four life-guardsmen. What Voltaire fails to mention was the appalling difficulty of travel by coach and carriage in the later part of the seventeenth century, particularly when torrential rains made the roads almost impassable, so that the carriage got stuck in the mud.

Anne-Marie Louise, Duchess de Montpensier, better known as La Grande Mademoiselle, the King's first cousin, wrote the best contemporary account of the journey to Flanders.[1] Madame rode in the great state coach with the King and Queen and Madame de Montespan. Following them was an enormous train of coaches and carriages containing members of the nobility, the important offices of state and other officials. Somewhere in the rear were the maids of honour, Louise de Keroualle among them. Before and behind the state coach marched an army of 30,000 soldiers[2] under the command of the Comte de Lauzun with whom La Grande Mademoiselle was in love.

Far from feeling jubilant Madame seemed very sad and spoke

very little. She probably resented Madame de Montespan's biting tongue and wit. "She never supped with us," wrote La Grande Mademoiselle, "sometimes she sipped some milk." She was, in fact, feeling tired and ill and often rested.

They had to traverse Senlis, Compiègne, Saint-Quentin, Arras, and travel from thence to Douay and Courtrai. Monsieur made himself as disagreeable as possible to his wife, telling her with gross lack of taste that an astrologer had recently predicted that he would have several wives. When he looked at her, especially noting her state of health, he could well believe that she would die soon.[3] It was a superstitious age, and Monsieur often consulted fortune tellers.

As the royal party approached the town of Landrecies night was falling. The weather was atrocious, rain fell in torrents and half a league from Landrecies the Sambre had overflowed its banks, sweeping away the only available bridge. Louis XIV decided that they would have to take refuge in a mean house (*une méchante maison*) in a field for the night. The King remained fairly cheerful, but his rather stupid Queen Marie-Thérèse, daughter of Philip IV of Spain, constantly complained. Mattresses were brought by some lackeys whereupon the Queen exclaimed in her peevish way: "How horrible! What? All of us sleep together?" The King merely remarked: "Where is the harm in lying on mattresses fully dressed? I see no harm. Ask my cousin what she thinks and let us follow her advice." La Grande Mademoiselle, who had a sense of the ridiculous, supported the King, saying surely there was no harm in ten or twelve ladies sleeping in the same room as the King and Monsieur.[4]

The chicken was so tough it was almost uneatable, and the soup so tasteless that the Queen, who was extremely greedy, refused to touch it. The others, however, including the King and Madame were famished and they gulped it down immediately.

We must hope that there was not too much snoring in that strange, primitive room that night. It was agonizing for the King's mistress, Louise de la Vallière, to be so near her successful rival Madame de Montespan. Louis XIV was inhuman and insensitive where his mistresses were concerned, much more so than Charles II. Perhaps to relieve the tension one of the ladies, Madame de Thianges, elder sister of Madame de Montespan, suddenly said that she heard cattle and donkeys in the adjoining stable, reminding her of the birth of Our Lord. This even made the Queen laugh, who could see nothing funny in the situation up to now. The next morning the royal party were able to move on to Landrecies.

When they arrived at Courtrai, Madame was much cheered to hear news that her brother Charles had already arrived at Dover. He begged her to embark as soon as possible in the English ships under the command of Edward Montagu, Earl of Sandwich, which were awaiting her at Dunkirk. Monsieur now made one last attempt to prevent his wife's departure, but was overruled by the King.

Who could predict that Madame's lovely maid of honour, Louise de Keroualle, would later acquire more influence at the court of Charles II than the arrogant Madam de Montespan at the height of her favour at the court of Louis XIV?

Voltaire wrote:

Madame took with her Mlle de Keroualle, who afterwards became the Duchess of Portsmouth, and whose beauty equalled that of Mme. de Montespan. She held later in England a position similar to that of Mme. de Montespan in France, but with greater honour [*plus de crédit*]. [5]

I take exception, however, to Voltaire's statement that Charles was ruled by her until the last moment of his life. Louise's ascendancy over Charles II was a gradual process. How far she dominated him is a controversial question.

Although Charles had requested his sister to come with a small suite, the Princess's entourage consisted of 237 persons, including the Maréchal du Plessis, the Comte and Comtesse de Gramont and the Bishop of Tournay. Madame, attended by her favourite maid of honour Louise de Keroualle, sailed from Dunkirk, and temporarily freed from the irksomeness of her husband's company, her health seemed to revive.

Louise, too, felt a sense of elation on the ship bearing her mistress and herself to England in the early hours of the May morning. The gusty wind and the shouts of the seamen reminded her of her childhood in Brittany. Then her mistress bade her come on deck to see the cliffs of Dover. Suddenly the Princess exclaimed: "There he is, my brother the King," and her eyes danced with pleasure. Louise had also descried him, a dark figure in a small boat, which was rapidly approaching their ship.

Charles now came on board, and Louise saw him clasp his sister in his arms. The affinity between brother and sister was very striking, yet even as he spoke Louise noticed that the King gave her a glance of admiration. The young Bretonne could hardly restrain her happiness that King Charles had noticed her. His companions in the boat now greeted the Duchess of Orleans, but Louise observed that her mistress embraced her brother James Duke of York in a very restrained way. He was followed by James Duke of Monmouth,* who adored his aunt, and by the King's cousin Prince Rupert.

The Duchess of Orleans was lodged as comfortably as possible in the ancient castle of Dover, but most of her suite were given accommodation in various cottages in Dover, at that time little more than a village.

What we do know for certain is that Louise was constantly in attendance on her mistress during the interviews between Charles and his sister, and the Breton girl made a deep impression on the King. She was now nearly twenty-one, of medium height, with an extremely pretty babyish face, dark hair falling over her shoulders and a lovely cream and rose complexion. There was a slight cast in one of her eyes, though they were black and beautiful. Her voice was sweet and low, and her manner pleasing and modest. Yet her air was noble and gave an impression of high breeding. Henri Gascar's painting of her at Lord Talbot's seat, Malahide Castle, near Dublin, a work which dates about 1671, is a true portrait of her at this period. It is not hard to understand why the King found himself greatly attracted to her, tired as he was of the violent temper of Lady Castlemaine and even, at times, of the vulgarity of Nell Gwyn, although he was certainly enchanted by her. If Louise was a designing minx there were as yet few signs to indicate it.

There was a great deal of business to discuss. Three days was clearly insufficient time, so Madame was overjoyed when King Louis wrote from Dunkirk towards the end of May that he had obtained his brother's consent to her staying in Dover ten or twelve days.[6]

On 1st June the secret Treaty of Dover was signed by Lords Arlington and Arundell, Sir Thomas Clifford and Sir Richard Bellings on behalf of England, and Colbert de Croissy, the French Ambassador, on behalf of France. Bellings and Arundell were

* Son of Lucy Walter by Charles II.

prominent Roman Catholics, while Arlington later became con-
verted to that Church. Sir Thomas Clifford (later Lord Clifford)
of Chudleigh, Devon, a member of the Cabal, had taken a vital
part in the negotiations, including the first draft of the secret
treaty itself.[7] Its main provisions have been admirably summarized
by Cyril Hughes Hartmann.[8]

A perpetual alliance was to be made between the Kings of
England and France. (A cynic would be inclined to be sceptical
about this sort of solemn pledge.)

Secondly, the King of England, being convinced of the truth
of the Catholic religion and determined to make a public declaration of it and to reconcile himself with the Roman Church as
soon as he was able, was to receive from Louis XIV the sum of
2,000,000 *livres tournois*, half to be paid three months after the
exchange of ratifications, and half three months later. The time
of Charles II's declaration was left entirely to his own discretion.
This was really a loophole for the King to evade honouring this
clause, if he saw fit, for he was aware of the anti-Catholic sentiment
among the mass of Englishmen.

It was decided that war was to be declared on the United Provinces (Holland) by both monarchs. They solemnly agreed that
neither would negotiate a peace or truce with the Dutch without
the permission of the other. This clause had no real difficulty for
Charles, for he considered that Holland was England's most
relentless rival, and always disliked the Dutch.

Now that the tiresome formalities were completed Madame
and her suite were free to enjoy themselves. We know that
Charles II seized every opportunity to show his ardent admiration
for Louise, but that the young Breton girl was troubled by "his
passionate wooing", as one of her biographers declared, is most
unlikely.[9] Louise was often in attendance on his sister, and even
Charles would have to be careful not to go too far.

How quickly those fugitive days of early summer passed!
Minette, happy in the companionship of Charles, went about with
a gentle flush on her face, determined to conceal from the
courtiers that she was sometimes in pain. She got on well with
her sister-in-law Queen Catherine of Braganza, who arrived in
Dover on 29th May. Afterwards she described her to La Grande
Mademoiselle as "a good woman, and so frank and amiable
[*complaisante*] that you could not help liking her."[10] However, the
Queen's stay was somewhat spoiled by her husband's open

admiration for Louise de Keroualle. Charles was always offering
the girl little attentions, and whenever the King addressed her,
Louise behaved most modestly. One day the King took his
sister to Canterbury, where a ballet and a play were acted in her
honour by members of the Duke's House. Afterwards there was
a splendid collation in the hall of St Augustine's Abbey. The
Queen felt uneasy when she noticed that her husband was gazing
too ardently at the pretty Bretonne, Louise de Keroualle as she
danced round an enormous maypole with others.[11] Perhaps
Catherine discussed her uneasiness with her friend, Frances
Stuart, Duchess of Richmond ("La Belle Stuart"), who had known
Minette well during the early days in France. She, too, seems to
have felt an instinctive and immediate dislike of Louise.

Madame possessed all the wit of her brother, and much of his
intelligence. During their brief reunion they went for many
expeditions on the sea, "where Madame is as bold as she is on
land, and walks as fearlessly along the edge of the ships as she
does on shore", wrote a member of her suite.

Soon, too soon! the time for departure drew close, and Charles
could hardly bear the thought of saying farewell to "his dearest
Minette". He was so smitten with Mademoiselle de Keroualle
that he was desperately trying to find a pretext so that she could
stay in England. Charles was generous to his sister, giving her
6,000 pistoles for her travel expenses, and 2,000 gold crowns to
build a chapel at Chaillot to commemorate their mother, Queen
Henrietta Maria.[12] The Duchess of Orleans, on her part, was
anxious to give a parting present to her brother. "Pray," she
said, "choose some jewels from my casket," and she called to
Louise, "Come, child. Fetch my jewel-case, so that His Majesty
may make a selection." When the girl returned Charles took her
by the hand, imploring his sister to leave her maid of honour
behind her in England. "She is the only jewel I covet," he said.
Minette felt slightly piqued, though she forced a laugh. She told
the King that she was responsible to Mademoiselle de Keroualle's
parents for their daughter, and had promised to bring her back
safely to France. Was Louise a sly hussy basking in the admiration
of the King? Any well-born girl would have been flattered with
Charles's spontaneous compliments, and Louise had been well
brought up by her parents. As she listened to Charles's ardent
pleading with downcast eyes, Louise felt a strange excitement.
To be singled out like this, among so many beautiful women,

pleased her greatly, for she was very proud. That she had schemed from the beginning to become Charles II's mistress, as Madame de Sévigné relates, is rather unlikely. She was attached to the Duchess of Orleans and knew that she had to return to France with her.

Charles II and the Duke of York accompanied the Duchess of Orleans on board the ship which was to bear her back to France, and sailed some way with her. Three times Charles bade his sister farewell, only to return to embrace her again, as if he had a premonition that he would never see her again. He was loath to part with her, but the mercurial King was also upset and found it painful to say farewell to Louise, for he was already enamoured of her. Henrietta was given an extremely cordial welcome by the French court, and Louis XIV treated her with the greatest honour.

From Paris Henrietta wrote on 24th June to her friend Sir Thomas Clifford, the only letter she ever attempted in her quaint English. She told him that she had begged her brother to confer a peerage on him and an earldom on Arlington. Here is the letter[13] in its original spelling.

When i have write to the King from Calais i praid him to tel Milard Arlington an you what he had promised me for bothe. His answer was that he gave me againe his word that he would performe the thing, but that he did not thing it fit to exequte it now.

I tel you this sooner than to Milard Arlington because I know you ar not so hard to satisfy as hee. I should be so myselfe, if I was not sure that the King would not promis mee a thing to faille in the performance of it.

This is the ferste letter I have ever write in Inglis. You will eselay see it bi the stile and ortograf. Prai see in the same time that I expose miself to be thought a foulle in looking to make you know how much I am your frind.

for Sir Thomas Clifort.
On June 24th.

On that day Madame went to her country home at Saint-Cloud with her husband and children. There she enjoyed beautiful summer weather, and on moonlit evenings she would sing and play the guitar to entertain her friends with all her old animation and charm. She walked in the beautiful gardens, and in the cool of the evenings would sit with Madame de la Fayette by the Grande Cascade, listening to the gentle murmur of the fountains. Rather unwisely, considering her delicate health, she bathed in the Seine on a very hot day and complained of sharp stabs in her side.

Madame suffered terrible pain after drinking a glass of chicory water, and many of her contemporaries suspected that she had been poisoned. She at first evidently thought so herself. Both Madame de la Fayette and another person, however, drank the remainder of the chicory water without ill effects, so it could not have been poisoned. Voltaire, writing many years later, relates that a servant of Madame's household told him the name of the alleged poisoner. According to this informant, the man was not wealthy but immediately returned to Normandy where he bought an estate. Such hearsay evidence is never satisfactory. Nor is it likely that her enemy, the Chevalier de Lorraine, actuated by motives of revenge because he blamed her for his banishment and imprisonment, bribed somebody to poison Madame. Lorraine was then in Rome. Voltaire writes: "It is more than a little difficult for a twenty-year old Knight of Malta in Rome to buy the death of a great Princess in Paris."[14] Monsieur Antoine Vallot, Louis's physician, mentioned that her state of health three or four years before her death was wretched, and that she lived, as it were, by a miracle. Today it is believed that she died from acute peritonitis, though the doctors maintained that it was owing to *Cholera morbus*. Yet the possibility of poisoning cannot be altogether ruled out. Monsieur's second wife, Elizabeth Charlotte Princess Palatine certainly believed that the first Madame had been poisoned by the Marquis d'Effiat at the instigation of the Chevalier de Lorraine, who was related to him. If this is true, it was done without Monsieur's knowledge; nobody would have dared to entrust Philippe with the secret.

La Grande Mademoiselle relates in her memoirs how she heard that Madame was dying: "Ah! *Quelle horreur!* that made me despair." So this gentle Stuart princess, who had a genius for friendship, died at three o'clock on the morning of 30th June 1670, surrounded by a mass of people including Louis XIV, her husband Monsieur and the ladies and gentlemen of the Court. To Ralph Montagu, the English Ambassador, she murmured tender messages which were to be conveyed to her brother Charles. "I have always loved him better than life itself, and now my only regret in dying is to be leaving him."[15]

For Louise de Keroualle, weeping for Madame who had been

such a generous mistress to her, her death seemed disastrous. She had lost her powerful protector. For a time she played with the idea of going into a convent, but she had no real vocation to be a nun. How well she knew the insincerity at the French court, the false compliments, the jealousies and intrigues and sly jokes. Did she now wistfully remember the King of England's ardent admiration, and wish she had stayed in England?

Since she was still unmarried her parents, bigoted Catholics, would have placed no obstacle to her entering a convent. Louise, however, remembering the refinement and luxury in Madame's household, soon recoiled in horror at the thought of the bare, disagreeable cloister. She was always a sincere Catholic, but she was not prepared to make the sacrifice.

Meanwhile, Charles II in London was stricken with grief when he heard of his sister's death. His resentment against Monsieur knew no bounds, and he was so bitter in his conversation with Colbert de Croissy that the Ambassador feared that the Anglo-French Alliance was in jeopardy. He wrote to the Foreign Minister, Lionne: "Must we abandon the great affair? It is to be feared that the grief of the King of England, which is deeper than can be imagined, and the malevolent talk and rumours of our enemies, will spoil everything."

Louis XIV's choice in sending over Maréchal de Bellefonds to present his official condolences was a sagacious one, for he was a fine courtly gentleman and very diplomatic.

Louis told the English Ambassador, Ralph Montagu, that he felt Madame's death as if she were his own wife. He was instructed to assure King Charles that "if there were the least imagination that her death had been caused by poison, no severity should be wanting either towards the discovering or the punishing of so horrid and infamous an act".

Among influential politicians now openly hostile to the French alliance was George Villiers, second Duke of Buckingham. This scheming and ambitious nobleman had fancied himself in love with the Duchess of Orleans. Although he was a boon companion of Charles II and amused him he had never been fully trusted by Charles with knowledge of the secret clauses of the Treaty of Dover. Buckingham had quarrelled with his cousin, Lady Castlemaine, and was anxious to find a rival mistress, who might be able to console the King in his deep unhappiness. He had noticed at Dover that Charles had been very much attracted to

Louise de Kerouaille. When the King saw Buckingham he very earnestly asked him to travel to France and offer Louise a position as maid of honour to Queen Catherine of Braganza. It cannot be supposed that the Queen willingly consented to this, for her intuitive mistrust of the young French girl had been aroused at Dover. However, she reluctantly agreed on the King's insistence. Charles had pleaded with tears in his eyes that Louise was the last link with Minette, and Catherine could not resist his entreaties. Had not her husband's sister during her last hours on earth implored him to protect her servants? So Buckingham, that dissolute rake, went over to France and was given a warm welcome at Louis XIV's court. He found Louise bewildered, still nursing her unhappiness at the death of the Princess. Buckingham, the subtle tempter, talked eloquently about the attractions of Charles II's court. She would be a maid of honour to the Queen, and thus be able to comfort the King in his distress. He even hinted rather darkly that Catherine of Braganza was sickly. Who knew what might happen? King Charles loved her and needed her. In such a way did this nobleman arouse Louise's ambitions. Even as he spoke she seemed to hear King Charles's sonorous voice pleading with her to stay in England. "She is the only jewel I covet," he had told the Duchess of Orleans. She remembered his strange ardent look after he had greeted his sister. Buckingham told her that by agreeing to his proposition she would be serving King Louis XIV and France. The proud young girl consented to go to England after obtaining her parents' permission.

It is true that Louis was eager for Louise de Kerouaille to go to Charles II's court, for Colbert de Croissy had kept him well apprised as to Charles's sentiments for the French girl. The French King wished to secure an influence over his brother sovereign in the interests of France. It was a golden opportunity for the Bretonne by her wiles to gain a complete hold over Charles II of England. Buckingham was bribed with a pension of 10,000 *livres* to regain his good-will, for the French Ambassador had warned Lionne that had it been possible, Buckingham would have picked a quarrel with France, if only to win popularity.[16] The mass of Englishmen detested the French.

Buckingham has been described by John Dryden as "everything by starts and nothing long".[17] He wrote of this brilliant clown with penetration:

Louise de Keroualle, Duchess of Portsmouth, painted in about
1670–71 by Henri Gascar (*by courtesy of Lord Talbot of Malahide and
the Courtauld Institute of Art*)

Henrietta-Anne, Duchess of Orleans (*by courtesy of the Mayor, Aldermen and Citizens of the City of Exeter*

> But in the course of one revolving moon,
> Was chymist, fiddler, statesman and buffoon.
> Then all for women, panting, rhyming, drinking,
> Besides ten thousand freaks that died in thinking.

His chief faults were his instability of character and his vanity, although he was a clever mimic, a playwright and occasionally possessed real brilliance as an orator. In his personal relations, however, he was capable of behaving with lamentable stupidity. He lent his travelling coach to Louise, so that she could proceed to Dieppe at the end of September, and some of his servants accompanied her. At the same time he assured the French girl that he would soon rejoin her, so as to escort her to the royal yacht, which Charles II had sent to bring her to England.

To her mortification, however, Louise soon discovered that Buckingham had forgotten his promise. She arrived in Dieppe in the second week of October. The weary days passed by and to her chagrin the Duke did not appear. Presumably from caprice or some other reason Buckingham had departed for Calais, where the yacht waited. In her pride she was deeply wounded. How dared he treat her, a nobleman's daughter, as if she were of no account?

Ralph Montagu, the English Ambassador in France, heard of Louise's plight and wrote home: "Mademoiselle Keroualle hath bin at Dieppe these ten days and hears nothing of the yacht that the Duke of Buckingham, Mr Godolphin tells me, was to send for her."[18] Louise never forgave Buckingham for his casual behaviour. He had made a powerful enemy for the future. Montagu was obliged to arrange for her to be transported in the King's yacht to Dover, and some of his servants accompanied her. Bishop Burnet relates: "So, the Duke of Buckingham lost the merit he might have pretended to and brought over a mistress whom his own strange conduct threw into the hands of his enemies."[19]

In London Louise was given a cordial welcome by Lord Arlington and his Dutch-born wife* who lived in a splendid mansion near Whitehall. Arlington, a politician of some ability who had taken an influential part in the negotiations leading up to the Treaty of Dover, was a pompous little man, a born intriguer, only too happy to listen to Louise's complaints against the Duke

* Isabella, daughter of Louis de Nassau, Lord of Beverweert and Count of Nassau, son of Prince Maurice.

3

of Buckingham, for he regarded him as a dangerous rival. If he curried favour with this French girl she might use her influence later on with Charles II against Buckingham. In his early days in exile in France, Arlington, when Henry Bennet, had been a favourite companion of the young King. He was proud of his black nose-plaster which he always wore to draw attention to a slight wound he had sustained during the Civil War in a skirmish at Andover.

NOTES

1. *Mémoires de Mademoiselle de Montpensier*, IV, p. 128.
2. Cyril Hughes Hartmann, *Charles II and Madame.*
3. *Mémoires de Mademoiselle de Montpensier*, IV.
4. V. Sackville-West, *Daughter of France.*
5. Voltaire, *Siècle de Louis XIV*, p. 339.
6. Correspondance Angleterre, XCVII.
7. One copy is now at the Dépôt de Traités at the Quai d'Orsay, the other is at Ugbrooke Park in Devonshire, home of the Cliffords of Chudleigh.
8. Cyril Hughes Hartmann, *op. cit.*, p. 310.
9. Jeanine Delpech, *The Life and Times of the Duchess of Portsmouth.*
10. *Mémoires de Mademoiselle de Montpensier*, IV, p. 157.
11. Hebe Elsner, *Catherine of Braganza.*
12. Julia Cartwright, *Madame.*
13. Clifford MSS. 27.
14. Voltaire, *Age of Louis XIV*, p. 284.
15. Cartwright, *op. cit.*
16. Forneron, *op. cit.*; Correspondance Angleterre, XCVIII, fol. 35.
17. "Absalom and Achitophel".
18. 19th October. State Papers France 130, 135.
19. Burnet, *History of His Owne Time.*

THREE

LOUISE'S SURRENDER

When Charles II saw Louise again, it is related that the hot tears welled in his eyes and poured down his cheeks, so keen was his distress at the loss of his sister. Yet he found himself greatly attracted to the young French girl, nineteen years younger than himself. It is true that Charles associated Louise in his mind with Minette, but he was also fascinated by her refinement of manner, her air of breeding, her gentle repulses and coyness. She tried to please him by relating how often her mistress had referred to him during the last weeks of her life, conjuring up any trick of phrase that would make the pain vanish in his eyes. She realized that he treasured anything that would remind him of his beloved sister. Charles, of course, wanted Louise as his mistress, for he was also physically in love with her. Her resistance only made him more eager in his pursuit.

From the first Louise was regarded by the English with dislike and mistrust as a foreign adventuress. Their instincts were to some extent correct. Politicians such as Lord Arlington made much of her, for he wished to pander to the King's sexual urges. If Louise were to become King Charles's mistress, he calculated, he could be influenced through her. John Dryden, too, hastened to welcome her to our shores, addressing a song to her named *The Fair Stranger*. There are four verses:

> Happy and free, securely blest,
> No beauty could disturb my rest;
> My am'rous Heart was in despair,
> To find a new Victorious Fair;
>
> Till you, descending on our plains,
> With foreign force renew my claims;
> Where now you rule without controal,
> The mighty sov'reign of my soul.

Your smiles have more of conq'ring charm,
Than all your native country's arms,
Their troops we can expel with ease,
Who vanquish only when we please.

But in your eyes, O! There's the spell!
Who can see them and not rebel?
You make us captives by your stay;
Yet kill us if you go away.

As maid of honour to Queen Catherine, Louise was modest
and respectful, but her duties were far from exacting. She was
given an apartment in the Palace of Whitehall. In those early
days it was easy for Charles to find pretexts so as to visit her in
the Queen's apartments. Colbert de Croissy reported to the
Foreign Minister, Lionne, during the autumn of 1670:
"The King is always finding opportunities to talk with this
beauty in the Queen's room. But he has not, contrary to what
is reported, gone yet to chat with her in her own room, contrary
to what has been said here."

John Evelyn was not impressed when he saw Louise for the
first time on 4th November. "I now also saw that famous beauty,"
he wrote, "but in my opinion of a childish, simple and baby-face,
Mademoiselle Querouaille, lately Maide of Honour to Madame
and now to be so to ye Queene."

Louise quickly became aware that she was hated by the rival
mistresses, particularly by Barbara Castlemaine, now Duchess of
Cleveland, and by Nell Gwyn, a witty, enchanting creature who
intrigued against her. Nell's character—she was shortly to leave
the stage—reminds one of Edward IV's celebrated mistress Jane
Shore with her rich golden hair, who that King once referred to
as the merriest of his concubines. Louise also knew that Frances
Stuart,* now Duchess of Richmond and Lennox, disliked her,
though she was forced to be polite. She took part in February
1671 in a lovely ballet at Whitehall together with Queen Catherine, the Duchess of Richmond and Lennox, and Anna Scott,
Duchess of Monmouth. Everybody was resplendently dressed,
and the music was very fine; so was the singing. Afterwards
there was dancing. A contemporary wrote that "the Duchess of

* La Belle Stuart, almost certainly never Charles's mistress though he had
ardently pursued her before her marriage.

Cleveland was very fine in a rich petticoat and halfe shirte and a short man's coat very richly laced, a periwig, cravate, and hat".[1]

Meanwhile Colbert de Croissy, who treated Louise as an inexperienced girl, was constantly urging her throughout the winter of 1670 to give herself to the King of England. Though she might listen to his advice Louise in her stubbornness would not follow it. There was a danger that King Charles would tire of her if she went on resisting him. It is true that Louise was delighted that the influence of the Duchess of Cleveland was on the wane. Although the Spanish Ambassador, the Conde Molina, had bribed the Duchess, the money had been largely wasted. The French Ambassador informed Louvois on 21st September 1671: "While she loses favour, the King of England's fancy for Mademoiselle de Keroualle grows stronger. The attacks of nausea she had yesterday, when dining with me makes me hope I shall find in her a useful ally as long as my embassy lasts." The cynicism of these worldly men is at times rather revolting. Colbert de Croissy, however, was mistaken as to Louise de Keroualle's indisposition, since it was owing to a slight chill. In his correspondence Colbert de Croissy always refers to Louis XIV as the King and Charles II as the King of England.

In France wagers were taken how long Mademoiselle de Keroualle would be able to hold out. Louis XIV and his ministers were anxious to be informed "of what may grow out of this situation, and of the terms on which she and the King have come to stand mutually".[2]

Louise had no more useful ally than Lord Arlington, who was at that period high in favour with King Charles. Though he was well versed in foreign affairs, "yet after all rather a subtle courtier, than an able statesman: too much regarding every inclination of his master, and too little considering his true interest and that of the nation".[3] Arlington had served abroad at the British Embassy in Spain, and with his rather fussy, pompous ways seemed unable to shake off a slight air of formality. Much to his fury he was ridiculed and mimicked for these traits by his enemy the Duke of Buckingham. Yet he entertained lavishly and was extremely hospitable to his friends. He had formerly been considered pro-Spanish, but he now favoured French interests.

He certainly got on well with Colbert de Croissy, and was often in conference with him. He told the Ambassador that he was much pleased at King Charles's new attachment with

Mademoiselle de Keroualle. Although the King never divulged
state affairs to ladies, for they could whenever they wished
render ill-service to statesmen and defeat their plans, it was of
advantage to the King's good servants that His Majesty should
have a fancy for Mademoiselle de Keroualle, who was not of an
evil disposition and was a lady. It was better to have dealings with
her than with lewd and bouncing orange-girls and actresses, of
whom no man of quality could take the measure. This was surely
a shrewd jibe by Arlington referring to Charles's fondness for
Nell Gwyn and other actresses. He hoped that Colbert de Croissy
would advise Louise de Keroualle to cultivate the King's good
graces and to ensure that His Majesty would find peace, enjoyment and contentment at her lodgings. He had suggested to Lady
Arlington that she should urge the new favourite either to give
herself unreservedly to the King, or to retire to a French convent.
Colbert added in his letter to Louvois: "I believe I can assure you
that she has so got round King Charles as to be the greatest service
to our sovereign and master, if she only does her duty."[4]

Louise's resistance certainly increased Charles's passion for her.
Her coyness and gentle repulses only made him more ardent. In
her temperament she was not a natural wanton, although many
influential ladies and gentlemen of the court were doing their
hardest to get her into the royal bed. She had been brought up
very strictly by her parents as a devout Catholic. Even now it was
not too late to enter a convent. Yet, she was tempted by Charles's
persistent declarations of his love for her to become his mistress.
He was so kind and generous, for he had recently given her a
finely furnished set of lodgings in Whitehall Palace. Every
morning at 9 o'clock the King came to visit her, often staying
for an hour and sometimes until 11 o'clock. He usually returned
after dinner, "and shares at her card-table in all her stakes and
losses, never letting her want for anything".[5] It was a wonderful
experience for Louise, after being neglected in France, to find
herself a person of consequence. All the ministers, knowing of
the King's attachment, seemed to seek her friendship. The luxury
of the court exceeded her most sanguine expectations. Yet when
Charles pleaded with her to yield herself to him, coaxing her
with his voice, she denied him this. She was flattered by his
ardent declarations, but her Bretonne pride held her back. Louise
was uneasily aware of the extent of anti-Catholic feeling in
England. In Parliament, too, there were ominous complaints

concerning the growth of popery. Rumours flew around that French subsidies and troops would be used to exterminate English liberties and religion. At this difficult juncture there stood at the King's side a fervent Catholic, Sir Thomas Clifford, a statesman described by John Evelyn, who was his friend, as "a bold young gentleman of a small fortune in Devon, but advanced by Lord Arlington, Secretary of State, to ye greate astonishment of the Courts".[6] Minette had confided in him her secret aims. He now urged the King to embark on bold measures, speaking with passion and a kind of rugged independence of an absolute monarchy and of the Catholic Church "at peace once more in an ancient land".[7]

It was probably a relief for Charles to try to forget state affairs in a visit to his fleet and arsenals at Portsmouth during July. He was passionately interested in all that concerned the navy, although Parliament was very niggardly in supplying him with sufficient funds to maintain its strength. Driven by a storm, Charles was compelled to land at Dartmouth in his yacht *Cleveland*, and was entertained by the Mayor, Emmanuel Wolley, in the Butter Walk. The beautiful panelled room where he was entertained can still be seen.

Among Louise's friends in London was the eccentric and distinguished philosopher and man of letters, Charles Marguetel, Seigneur de Saint-Evremond, who had been exiled by Louis XIV. Charles II liked and admired him so much that he had given him a small stipend and the picturesque post of Governor of the Isle of Ducks in St James's Park. We do not know whether or not Charles asked Saint-Evremond to plead his cause with Louise, but it is certain that Saint-Evremond addressed a curious letter to her in which he strongly advised her to yield to temptation. We do not really associate Saint-Evremond with Louise de Keroualle, for he was a much greater friend of her later rival in Charles's affections, Hortense Mancini, the Duchesse Mazarin. This letter is contained in Saint-Evremond's works—*Problème à l'invitation des Espagnols*[8]—addressed to Mademoiselle de Queroualle.

Happy the woman [Saint-Evremond wrote] who can discreetly manage her affairs without denying [*gêner*] her desires! for even if there is scandal in loving without reserve, it is a heavy hardship to go through life without love! Do not repulse temptations too severely—perhaps you are vain enough to be pleased only with yourself, but you will soon get tired of pleasing and loving yourself;

and whatever satisfaction you get from vanity, you will need another's love if your love is to be truly enjoyable. And so let yourself go into the sweets [*douceur*] of temptations instead of listening to your pride [*fierté*]. Your pride will soon make you return to France, and France will throw you, as has happened to so many others, into a convent; when you choose deliberately this gloomy retreat, you will still have to become worthy to enter it ... and how will a young girl do penance if she has done nothing? You will appear ridiculous to the other sisters, who have something to repent about, while you make your sham repentance.

The philosopher assured her of the miserable state she would be in, if she entered a convent.

For a life of celibacy in the cloister it was necessary to have a real vocation, and Louise, it must be confessed, lacked one. After all, Louise de Vallière only became a Carmelite nun in 1675 after Louis XIV had tired of her. How far Saint-Evremond's advice influenced Mademoiselle de Keroualle to yield to temptation is not possible to ascertain, though she may have been impressed by it. It has been too readily assumed that Louise was only holding out so as to obtain more advantageous terms from the King, who could load her with riches and honours. She had, however, genuine religious scruples, and that largely explains why it took almost a year for her to get into Charles's bed.

By the autumn of 1671 Colbert de Croissy hoped to tie King Charles with silken fetters to France, but he was increasingly concerned lest the King of England, surrounded as he was by many other court beauties, might tire of the new favourite. It was at this critical juncture that Lord and Lady Arlington together with the French Ambassador concocted a plot whereby Louise's complete surrender would be completed. The Arlingtons owned a magnificent country home named Euston near Newmarket and Thetford, and proposed to invite the King as their guest during Charles's autumnal visit to see the horse matches in October. Whilst entertaining Colbert de Croissy to dinner in London they also extended an invitation to him, artfully suggesting that he might bring with him Mademoiselle de Keroualle. It is amusing to think of Colbert as her chaperone, but he was no doubt delighted to accept the hospitality of Lord and Lady Arlington.

The French Ambassador hastened to inform Louis XIV: "I am going to the Arlington's place at Euston; and as the King's inclination for Mademoiselle Keroualle, who is to go there with me, is rising, I forsee that he will often run across from Newmarket to see her."[9] Louvois told Colbert de Croissy that Louis was vastly amused. He even made a joke on the subject, remarking "that there must be either small love for the mistress or great confidence placed in Colbert, to allow you to go to Euston in such jolly company".[10] In such a way did those cynical men jest about the proposed degradation of the French girl. As for Lady Arlington, she was only too happy to play her part in the scheme, for she knew that she would be suitably recompensed by the French king. After all, a procuress deserves her reward.

Among the Arlington's two hundred guests in this enormous mansion was John Evelyn, who gives an account of his stay in his diary.[11] It is a matter of regret that Samuel Pepys afflicted by blindness was no longer writing his, because the little man with his genius for gossip and scandal would have provided us with far more detail. Evelyn relates that Lord Arlington's guests passed the time hunting and hawking during the mornings, while they played at dice and cards until late at night, "I must say without noise, swearing, quarrel or confusion of any sort", he added, approvingly.

Euston was a lovely place. The staircase and some of the rooms of state were decorated with frescoes by the Italian artist, Verrio, being the first work he had done in England. They were beautifully furnished and in exquisite taste. Arlington was reputed to have more coaches in his stables than any nobleman in England. He had consulted Evelyn about extending his park, and was now advised to enlarge it so that it came up to the house. Evelyn had also urged him to plant firs, elms and limes on the estate. Lord Arlington was very kind to him.

The house was now filled with the lords and ladies of the court, including the Earl and the Countess of Sunderland and Sir Thomas Clifford. There, too, were Louise de Keroualle and Colbert de Croissy. King Charles was at Newmarket, delighting in the fresh air of the heath and enjoying the horse matches. During his stay of a fortnight, Charles often came over to Euston with his brother the Duke of York. He would dine and sleep at Lord Arlington's place, while the Duke returned to Newmarket. Euston was far more luxurious than the King's ancient palace at Newmarket. Charles eagerly showed his pleasure in Louise's company. Colbert de Croissy wrote to Louvois:[12]

The King comes here for his repasts; and after eating he passes several hours with Mlle Keroualle. He has already paid her three visits, and he invited us yesterday to Newmarket, to see the races. We went, and were charmingly entertained, and he seemed more than ever solicitous to please Mlle Keroualle. Those small attentions which denote a great passion were lavished on her; and as she showed by her expressions of gratitude that she was not insensible to the kindness of a great king, we hope she will so behave that the attachment will be durable and exclude every other.

The Ambassador was much too sanguine in expressing this latter wish. It is likely that Louise enjoyed the solicitous attentions of King Charles more than the sport at Newmarket, which never appealed to her very much. As for the King, the strong sweet air of Newmarket made him lusty.

Queen Catherine, who had recently been on a progress with her husband in East Anglia, certainly spent a few days with her husband at Euston, but she had already departed when a dramatic event occurred one night. We do not know exactly what happened, though it is certain that Louise became Charles's mistress. It has been suggested that the King and his favourite took part in a sort of mock-marriage ceremony, for Louise never regarded herself as an ordinary mistress. Perhaps the King and Louise took part in a country wedding, a mockery of real marriage. While Lord and Lady Arlington, Colbert de Croissy and Lady Sunderland stood around making sly jokes Louise was put to bed, almost deluding herself that she was a real bride and thoroughly confused in her mind. As she lay there for a few moments in her night-gown, Charles got into bed beside her, while the others tactfully withdrew from the room. He took her in his arms and caressed her. It was a night of passion. Nine months later Louise gave birth to an infant son.

John Evelyn was too much of a prude to be invited to the ceremony, though he alludes to it in his diary.

> It was universally reported that the faire lady—was bedded one of these nights, and the stocking flung, after the manner of a married bride; I acknowledge she was for the most part in her undresse (without stays and in negliges) all day, and that there was fondness and toying with that young wanton; nay t'was said I was at the former ceremony, but t'is utterly false; I neither saw nor heard of any such thing whilst I was there, tho' I had been in her chamber, and all over that appartment late enough, and was myself observing

all passages with much curiousity. However 'twas with confidence believed she was first made a *Misse*, as they call these unhappy creatures, with solemnity at this time.[13]

When robbed of her virginity Louise is alleged to have said in her broken English: "Me no bad woman. If me taut me was one bad woman, me would cut my own trote."

The devout Evelyn naturally disapproved of Charles II's court. After leaving Euston he lodged one night at Newmarket where he "found ye jolly blades raceing, dancing, feasting and revelling, more resembling a luxurious and abandoned rout than a Christian court". The dissolute rake, the Duke of Buckingham, was there with his mistress the Countess of Shrewsbury, and his band of musicians.

After his return to London Lord Arlington visited Colbert de Croissy to request him to transmit his thanks for a beautiful diamond necklace given to his wife by Louis XIV for services rendered.

Naturally Louis XIV was delighted to hear from his Ambassador of Louise de Keroualle's success. Colbert de Croissy wrote to Louvois at the beginning of November that the young lady was joyful when she heard of the pleasure with which His Majesty had learned of her brilliant conquest. Colbert thought that there was every prospect "that she would hold long what she had conquered". The news indeed created enormous interest, though some people were not surprised at it.

Bussy Rabutin, author of *Madame de Scudéry*, wrote from Paris: "Madame's death has been the cause of La Queroualle's good fortune. If it had not been for that, she would hardly have found so exalted a lover in France!"

Madame de Sévigné, too, alludes to her in a letter to her daughter on 30th March 1674: "La Querouaille whose fortune had been predicted before she left this kingdom, has fully verified it. The K... of England was passionately fond of her, and she on her side had no aversion to him: In short, she is now about eight months gone with child. Poor Castlemaine* is turned off: such is the fate of mistresses in that Kingdom."

Saint-Evremond wrote to Ninon de l'Enclos that the silk ribbon that girded the waist of Mademoiselle de Keroualle had united England to France.

* Lady Castlemaine had been created Duchess of Cleveland.

It was indeed a triumph for Louise, but she was soon made to realize that she would have to pay for it in a bitter struggle for supremacy with the other mistresses.

Although the Court of Charles II was immoral and ridden with vice, in the heart of England where men pursued a simple life, Puritanism was very strong, particularly in the eastern and south-western counties. After the Restoration, Puritanism was called "Fanaticism" by its Anglican opponents, and "Nonconformity" by the state.[14]

The mass of Englishmen dwelling in the quiet countryside were decent and law-abiding; they openly despised and derided the court. The total population of England did not much exceed 5,000,000.

When the Duchess of Portsmouth travelled westward later in her coach to take the waters at Bath, she went through empty villages, often scarcely seeing a soul on the road. England was still a very lovely country, unspoilt by commercial development. But for the traveller, the state of the roads presented appalling difficulties. The main roads often became impassable owing to heavy rains creating muddy ruts. It was a world of portly country squires, jovial, gregarious, fond of otter hunting and other sports, and of parsons and yeoman-farmers. In the serene countryside the old ways of life endured.

Even at Court there were virtuous ladies. Mary of Modena, who married the Duke of York as his second wife, was as enchanting as she was beautiful. Throughout her married life of twenty-eight years she was always loyal to her husband and never unfaithful to him. Then there was Charlotte Countess of Lichfield, natural daughter of Charles II by Lady Castlemaine. She was known for her upright character and goodness which is surprising considering how depraved her mother was. A shining example was Margaret Blagg, a maid of honour to the Queen and dear friend of John Evelyn's. He eulogizes her in his diary, referring to her "as a rare example of piety and virtue in so rare a witt, beauty, and perfection, in a licentious court and depraved age". She married a rising politician, Sidney Godolphin, at the Temple Church during May 1675. After her untimely death at the age of twenty-six in September 1678, Evelyn wrote of her: "Never was a more virtuous and inviolable friendship; never a more religious, discreet and admirable creature, beloved of all, admired of all, for all possible perfections of her sex."[15] She was buried at Godolphin in Cornwall, the family home of her husband, and a place which she much loved.

NOTES

1. Lady M. Bertie writing to Lady K. Noel.
2. Correspondance Angleterre, CII, fol. 283; Forneron, *Louise de Keroualle*.
3. *The Works of John Sheffield, Earl of Mulgrave, Marquis of Normanbury and Duke of Buckingham*, II, p. 61.
4. Correspondance Angleterre, CI, fol. 167, 8th October 1671; Forneron, *op. cit.*
5. Colbert de Croissy to Louvois, 8th October.
6. *Memoirs and Correspondence of John Evelyn*, II, p. 279.
7. Sir Arthur Bryant, *King Charles II*.
8. Saint-Evremond, *Oeuvres*, III.
9. 8th October 1671; Forneron, *op. cit.*
10. Correspondance Angleterre, CII, fol. 290.
11. *Memoirs and Correspondence of John Evelyn*, II, p. 350.
12. 22nd October 1671.
13. *Memoirs and Correspondence of John Evelyn*, II, p. 350.
14. Sir Arthur Bryant, *Restoration England*.
15. *Memoirs and Correspondence of John Evelyn*, II, p. 447.

FOUR

HER INCREASING INFLUENCE

George Savile, Marquis of Halifax, who knew Charles II intimately and possessed much of his cynical wit, made some
pregnant observations about Louise de Keroualle, Duchess of
Portsmouth. He wrote:

> His mistresses were as different in their humours, as they were in
> their looks ... The last [Louise] especially was quite out of the
> definition of an ordinary mistress; the causes and the manner of
> her being first introduced were very different. A very peculiar
> distinction was spoken of, some extraordinary solemnities that might
> dignify, though not sanctify, her function. Her chamber was the
> true Cabinet Council.[1]

Halifax, who was nicknamed The Trimmer, also maintained
that it was decided by others whom he should have in his arms
as well as whom he should have in his councils. However,
Charles was very strongly attracted to Louise from the beginning, and chose her for his mistress rather than have her thrust
upon him. Louise, it is evident, never regarded herself as an
ordinary mistress.

At the start of her career she was foolish enough to believe that
Queen Catherine, who was always delicate, had only a few
months to live. She entertained for a time the extravagant notion
that she might succeed her as Charles's Queen. In this view she
was encouraged by Charles's physician, Alexander Fraser, who
openly said that the little Portuguese Queen had only two or
three months to live, for she suffered from a dangerous consump-
tion. It is evident that doctors were just as inclined to make this
sort of false prediction in the Stuart Age as they are today. He
was proved utterly mistaken. Catherine survived for another
thirty-two years, dying in Portugal at the end of 1705.

It is possible that Alexander Fraser stated this opinion so as to curry favour with the King, because many people believed that Charles wanted to be rid of his childless consort, so as to be free to remarry. Despite his frequent infidelities he was, however, very fond of Catherine, and found her a sympathetic companion. Few people understood Charles's secretive and enigmatic character.

It was tactless and inexperienced of Louise de Keroualle to discuss the Queen's ailments from morning to night as if they were mortal.[2] By so doing she antagonized Frances Stuart, Duchess of Richmond, a close friend of the Queen as well as the King. Colbert de Croissy feared that by giving too free a rein to her tongue she might lose her position altogether. At first it was by no means too secure. The other mistresses, such as the Duchess of Cleveland and Nell Gwyn hated and attacked her, and the Queen instinctively disliked her.

No greater contrast could be found between Barbara Duchess of Cleveland and Charles's new favourite. Barbara was a nymphomaniac, tempestuous and unfaithful. Her appeal was frankly sensual and physical. She knew how to give pleasure. Only in their insatiable ambition to acquire riches and honours did the two mistresses bear a certain resemblance. The Duchess of Cleveland had given Charles II four children, and this was now her main hold over him. Louise, on the other hand, was gentle, tender, languishing, easily prone to tears, sly, and a born political intriguer, an interest she had acquired whilst in the service of the Duchess of Orleans. While she was usually respectful enough in the presence of Queen Catherine, Louise's arrogance soon became apparent. She had a sense of mission that it was for her to continue the work of the Duchess of Orleans.

Above all, Louise as a young woman of twenty-two took infinite pains with all the subtlety of her nature to understand Charles's peculiar temperament. She had taken to heart Lord Arlington's advice that she must give the King peace and contentment at her lodgings. Louise possessed many qualities, such as considerable intelligence, refinement in taste, a love of the beautiful, artistic sensibility and a fondness for music, which appealed strongly to Charles II. If she was grossly extravagant and greedy to acquire wealth and possessions, and that cannot be disputed, she at least showed considerable taste in her manner of using her riches. With a French woman's instinctive cleverness she was a good listener, and she quickly learned to sense her lover's moods, so that she knew when to discuss politics with him and when to offer herself to him. Her mental qualities appealed as much to the King as her physical charms. It must not be forgotten that Charles possessed artistic tastes. He was fond of poetry and music, and his favourite instrument was the violin. He was wont to carry a copy of Samuel Butler's poem *Hudibras* in his pocket, which exposes the hypocrisy of the Puritans. Above all Charles was passionately interested in drama, and certainly exercised a strong influence on contemporary dramatists. For instance, Charles suggested the plot for John Dryden's *Secret Love*, in which Nell Gwyn enjoyed enormous success.

Whilst an exiled prince at the French court he had acquired a taste for the plays of Molière, and he also took a lively pleasure in the performances of Signor Scaramuccio and his Italian players. Louise could never really share Charles's interest in the theatre, partly because of her poor knowledge of English and partly because she was revolted by the indelicacy and coarseness of the language used on the stage. Charles showed his inclinations for France in other ways. He obtained his clothes from a Paris tailor named Claude Sourceau, and he persuaded him to settle in London.[3] Le Nôtre suggested to Charles II improvements in St James's Park, while Queen Catherine of Braganza's dress-maker, Desborde, was a Paris milliner. Charles's wines were selected by Monsieur de Pontac, a Gascon. Evelyn wrote that too much learning had made him mad.

At the end of 1671 there died Monsieur de Lionne, French Minister of Foreign Affairs. He was succeeded by Arnauld de Pomponne, a very able man, noted for his good judgment though too prone to allow complex situations to work out their own solutions rather than to grapple with them as they rose.[4]

During January 1672, we find Louise "infinitely in favour" with her royal lover, according to a letter from Charles Lyttleton to Charles Hatton. "She is wondrous handsome," he wrote, "and she has, they say, as much witte and addresse as ever anybody had."[5]

A year later we hear of Charles walking by Louise's coach, on "a delicate, clear frosty day" the whole way from Whitehall to Hampton Court.[6]

Nearly all Louise's contemporaries, except Evelyn, pay tribute to her beauty, so there is no need to take too seriously the biased statements of historians who wish to denigrate her.

Charles II by Sir Peter Lely (*from Goodwood House by courtesy of the Trustees*)

Henry Bennet, Earl of Arlington, after Sir Peter Lely (*by courtesy of the National Portrait Gallery*)

Anthony Ashley-Cooper, Earl of Shaftesbury, painted about 1672, after Greenhill (*by courtesy of the National Portrait Gallery*)

As the French King's agent at Charles's court, Louise showed political acumen, and was both adroit and cunning. She soon realized that it was mistaken policy for King Charles to declare himself a Roman Catholic, since such an influential part of the nation was anti-popish. She therefore persuaded Colbert de Croissy to write to Louis XIV warning him that if Charles should profess himself to be a Roman Catholic, he would certainly be ruined. The wisest policy was to gradually accustom the English to a revival of Roman Catholic rites and ceremonies. Louise's attitude was certainly calculated, for her secret aspirations that she might yet be Queen of England had not yet been extinguished.

On 15th March 1672 a Declaration of Indulgence was published by Charles II, a measure which was on the whole unpopular among many of his subjects. They suspected that it was only a cloak to conceal the intended reintroduction of Roman Catholicism and arbitrary government. It was enacted that the penal laws should be suspended, and places of public worship promised to Protestant Nonconformists. Catholics were to be allowed freedom of worship in their own houses.

Two days later Charles officially declared war against Holland, in accordance with his promises in the Treaty of Dover. James Duke of York, commanded the English fleet and during the course of the third Dutch war showed considerable gallantry. He fought his flagship *The Prince* until her main topmast was shot by the board, her fore topsail, her starboard mains shrouds and all the rest of her rigging and fighting sails shot and torn to pieces, and above two hundred of her men killed and wounded.[7]

Evelyn describes the fleet on 14th May 1672: "Such a gallant and formidable navy never, I think, spreade saile upon ye seas. It was a goodly yet terrible sight to behold them as I did passing eastwards by the Straits twixt Dover and Calais on a glorious day."

Five days earlier Colbert de Croissy informed the King of France that King Charles had returned from visiting his fleet at Portsmouth.

James's first wife, Anne Hyde Duchess of York, had died at the end of March 1671, "a very good Catholic" according to the French Ambassador.

Among the mass of English people, Louise de Keroualle was more hated than any of Charles's mistresses, partly because she was French and it was suspected, not without reason, that she was a spy in the service of Louis XIV. She was nicknamed Madame Carwell, for the English found it difficult to pronounce her name. In comparison, her rival Nell Gwyn was popular. Much as Charles doted on Louise, he was incapable of fidelity to one woman. The French favourite complained to her lover with tears in her eyes that the King was humiliating her by his visits to such a vulgar creature as Nelly. The latter took her revenge by openly mocking at and defying her rival, calling her "Squintabella", because of the slight cast in one of her eyes. Nell Gwyn frankly appealed to the sensual Bohemian aspects of Charles's complex character, and Louise seemed powerless to oust Nell. Louise at least had the satisfaction of knowing that she was the *Maitresse en Titre*, and that Charles treated her as a great lady.

All sorts of wild, ridiculous rumours flew around. Henry Ball, an official in Whitehall, wrote to a Secretary of State, Sir Joseph Williamson (a protégé of Lord Arlington) whilst he was abroad at the Congress of Cologne. Ball was Williamson's chief clerk. It was related that the King had given Nell Gwyn £20,000, which had so angered the Duchess of Cleveland and "Mademoiselle Carwell" that they had invited Nelly to supper with them at Berkshire House. While they were drinking the Cockney mistress was almost smothered with a napkin. Henry Ball ends his account to Williamson: "this idle thing runs so hotte that Mr Philipps asks me the truth of it, believing it". Ball, however, was able to assure his friend that he had seen Nell yesterday evening in the park.[8] Anyway, Nell Gwyn was quite capable of holding her own with Louise de Keroualle and the Duchess of Cleveland. Henry Ball informed Sir Joseph of Louise's luxurious tastes and that she possessed a resplendent sedan chair, far more splendid than those of the King and Queen. He was shrewd enough to cultivate the friendship of Mademoiselle de Keroualle.

It is interesting to study the correspondence of Sir Joseph Williamson, because Louise's increasing influence is very apparent. In late July 1673 she was hostess at a dance and supper "when the King, Duke and all the young Lords and Ladies went up to Barn Elms, and there intended to have spent the evening in a ball and supper amongst those shades, the trees to have been enlightened with torches, but the report of it brought such a traine of spectators that they were faine to go dance in a barne and sup upon the water". Ball told Sir Joseph that the treat was at the cost of "Mademoiselle Carwell". It must have been a lovely sight on this July night, with the beautiful dresses of the ladies of the court, the animation and the music, with the soft lapping of the water against the boats as the courtiers ate and drank.

I studied a curious document in the British Museum, which shows that Louise soon learnt to spend money. It is a bill for dresses and clothes made for "Madame Carwell", now Duchess of Portsmouth. Louise wore the dress at a masque or ballet in which she took part:

For making dress, coloured and figured brocade coat, Ringraw breeches and cannour,* ye coat lined with lutestring, and interlined with call: ye breeches lined with lutestring, and lutestring drawers, shomard all over with a scarlet and silver'd lace sleeves and cannour whipt and laced with a scarlet and gild'd lace, and a point lace trimmed with a scarlet figured and plain sattine Ribb, and scarlet and silver twine £02.00.00

Canvas, Buckram, silk threed, Gallon and Shamey pockets	£00.11.06
For fine call, to interline ye coat	£00.06.00
For silver threed for buttonholes	£00.03.00
For 6 doz. of scarlet and silver vellam buttons	£01.00.00
For ½ doz. of brest buttons	£00.00.06
For 10 yds. of Rich Brocade at 28 shgs. ye yard	£14.00.00
For 8 yds. of Lutestring to line ye coat and ye drawers at 8 shgs. ye yard	£03.04.00
For a pair of silk stockings	£00.12.00
For an Imbroidered Belt and Garters	£03.15.00
For 36 yds. of scarlet and 4 yds. figured Ribb, at 18d. ye yard	£02.14.00
For 36 yds. of 2d. Sattine at 5d. ye yard	£00.15.00
For 75 yds. of scarlet and silver twist	£
For 22 yds. of scarlet and silver vellam	£00.15.00
Lace for coat and cannour at 18 shgs. ye yard	£19.16.00
For four yards of narrow lace for button holes	£00.12.00
For one piece of scaret	8d
To hair	£01.12.00
For a black Beaver hatt	£02.10.00
For a scarlet and silver'd edging to ye hatt	£01.10.00
For 36 yards of scarlet 4d. Taffety Ribb	£00.18.00
Tottall is	£59.15.09[9]

Madame Embor supplied this dress. It is related that another of

* Cannours were the frills worn at the knees.

Charles's mistresses, Mrs Knight, wore cherry-coloured taffeta, green satin, silver and gold tabby at this ballet.

On 29th July 1672, nine months after the festivities at Euston, Louise de Keroualle gave birth to an infant son, who was named Charles Lennox. For the time being he was not publicly acknowledged by Charles II. Louise was a devoted and ambitious mother, and later eagerly sought his advancement.

Evelyn relates in his diary[10] that on 1st August he was present at the marriage of Lord Arlington's only daughter, Isabella, at the tender age of five, to the Duke of Grafton, the King's natural son by the Duchess of Cleveland. Evelyn thought her a very sweet child.

Since Louise was greedy for honours she petitioned the King of France at the end of 1672, for permission to become an English subject, and "so benefit by the gifts and honours which King Charles wanted to lavish on her". About now she petitioned her royal lover that she might be endowed with leases in Ireland, then almost expired, in the districts around Dublin, Donegal, Fermanagh and elsewhere. The King assigned her a pension of £10,000 from the revenue of Irish lands. There was indeed some confusion concerning the title deeds, for it was thought that some of these lands had already been granted to the Duchess of Cleveland. Seven months later, John Richards wrote Sir Joseph Williamson, Louise's friend, that she had been created Duchess of Portsmouth and Countess of Fareham. The first title chosen for her was Duchess of Pendennis, but it was almost immediately changed to that of Duchess of Portsmouth. Lord Arlington, who had certainly helped Louise attain this honour, wrote to his officials to ascertain whether the titles of Petersfield, Alresford (Anresford) or Alton had been hitherto granted. Louise was then also created Baroness Petersfield. Sir Joseph Williamson, on hearing of Louise's elevation to the rank of Duchess of Portsmouth, immediately wrote to congratulate her. In reply Louise sent him a letter written in her native French, saying how grateful she was to him for his help in this affair.[11] A few months later Louise seems to have quarrelled with Lord Arlington, who accused her of ingratitude in not appreciating how much he had done for her. Arlington also succeeded in influencing Colbert de Croissy against her.

Yet Girolamo Alberti, a Venetian diplomat in London, wrote the Doge and Senate on 18th August that Arlington was becoming

more and more pro-French every day. "He has formed a close
intimacy with the new favourite, Mademoiselle Karwel, and he
helped her obtain the title of Duchess of Portsmouth." What is
interesting is Alberti's opinion of the increasing antipathy of the
English nation for the French. He wrote: "They cherish the
suspicion that by her means [the Duchess of Portsmouth's] the
ministers of the most Christian nation [France] can insinuate and
persuade the King here to do all that they wish. The more politi-
cally minded dwell upon the quantity of gold which the King has
given and which he lavishes daily upon his most favoured lady,
who is a French woman."[12] William Dugdale in his *Baronage of
England* speaks of Louise Duchess of Portsmouth as "of such
honourable women whom His Majesty hath deservedly raised to
high titles of honour". Anthony à Wood, who was invariably
hostile to Charles II's mistresses, wondered what was in her that
deserved this honour.

It is evident that the favours heaped on the Duchess of Portsmouth were deeply resented by the people. They indignantly
murmured among themselves that their favourite, Nell Gwyn,
had complained "that she has no house yet",[13] although they
were under the impression that the King had promised to create
her Countess of Plymouth. Nell never received any title from
Charles II, but shortly before his death he considered creating her
Countess of Greenwich.

It was a relief to the King to confide to Louise concerning his
troubles with his parliaments. He told her, on 8th March 1673
that there was no other course (*parti à prendre*) but to dissolve
Parliament, and to establish peace with the least possible dis-
advantage to himself.[14] Louise repeated the gist of the conversation to Colbert de Croissy, who added when writing to his
Foreign Minister that the King of England had not confided this
matter to Lord Arlington.

When Charles demanded supplies for the fleet, Parliament
opposed him by insisting that financial supplies for the Dutch
war would not be allowed, unless the policy of toleration was
abandoned. On their insistence Charles was compelled to withdraw the Declaration of Indulgence. When Charles II is criticized
and abused for becoming a pensioner of Louis XIV let us be
mindful that Parliament assigned him a totally inadequate
revenue, both in peace and war.

Before agreeing to pass the Bill of Subsidies, so that the fleet

could be maintained, Parliament wished to pass a Test Act.* It
was a cruel and arbitrary measure, for it enacted that all persons
who refused to take the Anglican sacrament and an oath against
the Catholic doctrine of transubstantiation were to be prevented
from holding public office. Much to his chagrin the King was
compelled to consent to this Act, which effectively prevented his
brother the Duke of York, an avowed Roman Catholic, from
continuing to command the fleet and to take part in the naval
campaign of 1673.

Although James was not yet a professed Catholic, his conscience
would not permit him to take the Anglican sacrament. It was a
personal tragedy for the Duke of York, for he was compelled to
lay down his offices of Lord High Admiral, Governor of Portsmouth and Warden of the Cinque Ports—to which he had given
devoted service.

Much of Colbert de Croissy's correspondence during the first
part of 1673 is concerned with lively news about the Duke of
York's matrimonial intentions, for he was considering remarriage.
The choice of a new bride was indeed of vital importance. There
was now no possibility whatsoever of Queen Catherine giving
the King an heir, and James's only surviving children by his first
marriage were Mary and Anne. It was imperative that he should
have a male heir.

James in his solemn way insisted that he must marry a beautiful
wife, though he preferred his mistresses to be ugly. Various
candidates were proposed, a German, various French women and
an Italian. On learning that one of the proposed princesses had
red hair, the Duke of York turned her down because he hated red
hair. He considered marrying the Princess of Wurtemburg, but
the project lapsed when he discovered that she had a harridan of a
mother. Protracted negotiations were begun for the hand of
Claudia Felicitas, Archduchess of Innsbruck, but they finally
came to nothing. Charles, irritated at his brother's insistence on
beauty, told him: "The more or less of beauty that a wife has,
contributes nothing to, and takes nothing from, the happiness of
marriage, and in a week one gets so accustomed to her face that
it neither pleases nor displeases one."[15]

Since Louise Duchess of Portsmouth is usually considered a
spy of Louis XIV's it is interesting to see that she could oppose
him on certain occasions. Louis XIV and Louvois strongly

* Which was not repealed until 1828.

favoured the widow of the Duke de Guise as their candidate to marry the Duke of York, but James thought her ugly. Louise, on her part, intrigued incessantly in favour of Françoise Marie, daughter of her friend the Duchess d'Elboeuf, who had been attached to Minette in France. She took a great deal of trouble to obtain portraits of Françoise Marie to show to James. Colbert de Croissy was so angered by Louise's interference in this affair that he could hardly conceal his enmity. He wrote to Arnauld de Pomponne that the Duchess of Portsmouth was contriving in every possible way to push this marriage as much to show what power she exercised as to give proofs of friendship for the House of Lorraine. His own instructions were to work for a marriage with the Duchess de Guise. On 24th July, Louise de Keroualle drew aside the French Ambassador in the Queen's bedchamber to discuss the Duke of York's matrimonial intentions.[16]

In the end Louis XIV, with the approval of Charles II, chose Maria Beatrice D'Este, sister of Francesco Duke of Modena, as James's prospective bride. She was only fifteen, a beautiful and devout girl who would have preferred to have entered the Convent of the Visitation in Modena rather than marry a husband about twenty-five years older than herself.

Colbert de Croissy, smarting at his diplomatic defeat in the affair of the brides, wrote to Pomponne: "Lord Arlington neither likes nor esteems Mlle. de Keroualle, and reproaches her with having as soon forgotten the obligations he conferred on her, as any of the good dinners she had eaten."[17]

Louise was consumed by ambition not only in England, but in France. In her native country "La Petite Keroualle' had been despised and considered of little account. She now longed to patronize some of the noblest families in France, and to show them the extent of her power and influence. Her ultimate ambition was a stool, or *tabouret*, of Duchess in the presence-chamber at the Court of Versailles. To achieve this desire Louise was prepared to scheme with ruthless efficiency, for the *tabouret* was more coveted by Frenchwomen than any other honour in the seventeenth century. Before Marie d'Arquien became the Queen of John Sobieski, King of Poland, she strove unavailingly to obtain the ultimate reward of a *tabouret* at the Court of the Louvre. The King of Poland thought it highly ridiculous, particularly as he had a sense of humour. He told her in a letter: "How you long for that miserable stool on which nobody can sit at ease!"[18]

The first step was to persuade Louis XIV to assign her ducal lands in France. She had her eyes on Aubigny, which had been made a Duchy by Charles VII and had been inherited by the Duke of Richmond, husband of La Belle Stuart. He had recently died in Denmark where he was Charles's ambassador. The estates had, therefore, reverted to the French Crown.

Sometime during the summer of 1673 Louise spoke to Charles II of her desire of being granted the estate of Aubigny-sur-Nièvre in Berri. It lay in a flat and fertile countryside between Gien, Sancerre and Bourges. Charles took the opportunity in a talk with Colbert de Croissy to raise the matter, telling him that he desired that Louise de Keroualle should be assigned the fief of Aubigny, not only for her life, but that she should be able to bequeath it to her son, Charles Lennox.

The French Ambassador was highly indignant at Louise's effrontery in asking for a French Crown Land, particularly as he had keenly resented the favourite's opposition to the Duchesse de Guise as a prospective bride for the Duke of York. Though it was a disagreeable task, for he now constantly complained of Louise's interference, he sat down to write to the Foreign Minister, Arnauld de Pomponne, what the English King had discussed with him. He wrote on 17th July:

> I own I find her on all occasions so ill-disposed for the service of the King, and showing such ill-humour against France (whether because she feels herself despised there, or whether from an effect of caprice), that I really think she deserves no favour of His Majesty. But as the King of England shows her much love, and so visibly likes to please her, His Majesty can judge whether it is best not to treat her according to her merits ... I have, however, told him upon what conditions alone the fief could be granted, and what he asks is just the contrary.

This letter is of curious interest, revealing as it does that Louise occasionally opposed Louis XIV's wishes, if they conflicted with her own ambitions.

It is evident that the French King was convinced that Louise was a valued intermediary between himself and Charles II, and could give him enormous service in the future. There were difficulties in assigning the Aubigny estates to Louise and her bastard son, but means must be found to do so. It was Colbert de Croissy who suggested the drawing up of a deed of gift in favour of the

Duchess of Portsmouth so that, after her death, it would revert to such of her children by the King as it would please him to nominate.[19] Colbert's suggestion was adopted. At the end of the year Louise was delighted to receive ducal lands in France, and she now determined to scheme in her tortuous way to become a French Duchess.

In Parliament that November a member, Sir Thomas Clerges, made a complaint that as much as four hundred thousand pounds had been squandered since the last session, and that the Duchess of Cleveland and Duchess of Portsmouth had been given the greatest share. The Duke of York's proposed marriage with Princess Maria D'Este of Modena was very unpopular both in Parliament and among the mass of people, particularly as she was a papist.

Thomas Player wrote to Sir Joseph Williamson that there was seditious talk in the coffee-houses which abounded in Restoration London:

> But the common people talke anything, for every carman and porter is now a stateman; and indeed the coffee-houses are good for nothing else. It was not thus when wee dranke nothing but sack and clarett, or English beere and ale. These sober clubbs produce nothing but scandalous and censorious discourses, and at these nobody is spared.[20]

The coffee-houses were certainly a grave embarrassment for the government.

It was rumoured, which was true, that the Duchess of Modena was coming with her daughter. People said, however, that she was the Pope's niece—an absurd distortion of the truth. A courtier, Sir Gilbert Talbot, wrote to Williamson that on gunpowder day* the Pope had been burnt with great solemnity at several places in London, and that several people including Sir John Packington and Sir Anthony Cope had taken part in these lugubrious ceremonies. Very barbaric, he thought, and no nation except the Dutch could also have been guilty of such behaviour.

Princess Maria of Modena was described as an Italianate beauty: "She is tall and slender, of a pale complexion and browne hair ... Some cry her up for a very fine woman, and generally all say she will be a fine woman when she is somewhat more spread;

* 5th November 1673.

and in the meantime praise her witt."²¹ She was never really on
friendly terms with the Duchess of Portsmouth.

Meanwhile, the hatred of the French became even more acute.
When a French ship was forced to anchor in Falmouth the towns-
men picked a quarrel with the seamen, and taunted them as
cowards.

Charles II was fond of visiting his confidential page of the back
stairs, Will Chiffinch, at his country home known as Filberds at
Witley in Oxfordshire. They would talk over various plans to
make a deer-park, so as to make the place more beautiful. The
gossips said that whilst at Filberds Charles was visited by Nell
Gwyn, who was also on friendly terms with Will and often
supped with him below stairs.

What worried many people was that the King's health was
affected by his over-indulgence in sex. It was said that Charles
had lately suffered three apoplectic fits, the first whilst in the company of the Duchess of Portsmouth. Even Louise felt obliged to
beg her royal lover for the time being to refrain from visiting her
at night.

NOTES

1. George Savile, *A Character of Charles II, and Political, Moral and Miscellaneous Thoughts and Reflections.*
2. Colbert de Croissy to Louvois, 24th December 1671.
3. Jeanine Delpech, *The Life and Times of the Duchess of Portsmouth.*
4. Forneron, *Louise de Keroualle.*
5. *Hatton Correspondence* I, 77.
6. Sir Arthur Bryant, *King Charles II.*
7. F. C. Turner, *James II*, p. 103.
8. *Letters addressed to Sir Joseph Williamson*, I.
9. This bill can also be seen in *Catherine of Braganza*, by Lillias Campbell Davidson.
10. *Memoirs and Correspondence of John Evelyn*, II, p. 372.
11. *Letters addressed to Sir Joseph Williamson*, I, p. 18.
12. Venetian State Papers 1671–1675.
13. Henry Ball to Sir Joseph Williamson.
14. Correspondance Angleterre, CVI, fol. 129.
15. F. C. Turner, *op. cit.*
16. Correspondance Angleterre, CVII, fol. 111.
17. Forneron, *op. cit.*

18. *Ibid.*
19. The Patent of Grant, dated December 1673, is in the Archives des Affaires Etrangères, Angleterre, CVIII, fol. 234.
20. *Letters addressed to Sir Joseph Williamson* II, p. 68.
21. Robert Yard to Sir Joseph Williamson.

FIVE

LOUISE'S RELATIONS WITH LORD DANBY

In midsummer 1673 Lord Clifford of Chudleigh—a Roman Catholic—was forced to resign from his high position as Lord Treasurer because of the Test Act. Much to the disappointment of Lord Arlington,* whose influence by now was somewhat diminished, Clifford was succeeded as Lord Treasurer by Sir Thomas Osborne, a talented member of the old Cavalier party. Osborne was created Viscount Latimer and Earl of Danby by Charles II. The King was a shrewd judge of character. Although he never really much liked Danby, he recognized his ability. It is said that the Duke of York had a great deal to do with the appointment of Osborne, but he later fell out with him.[1] Danby was a Yorkshire man, hard, efficient, passionate, with a touch of ruthlessness. He had no patience with fools. He was a capable financial administrator, and realized that it was essential to end the Dutch war. Although his own sympathies were reputed to be anti-French, he was wise enough to cultivate the friendship of the Duchess of Portsmouth, and she became a close ally of his.

J. H. Jesse,[2] who is always biased when referring to Louise de Kéroualle, wrote that "her affection for Charles seems to have been no bar to her conferring her favour on others". He thought that Lord Danby, who possessed considerable advantages of person and fortune, shared her favours with the King. It is possible that Danby attempted to seduce her, but it is extremely unlikely that Louise would risk losing the King's love by an occasional infidelity with the new Lord Treasurer. She was far too ambitious and too circumspect in her behaviour to make such a gross error. Besides these considerations she really loved Charles. Though incapable of being faithful to one woman, he was more constant to Louise than to any other of his mistresses. That she enchanted

* Arlington became Lord Chamberlain to Charles II and subsequently to James II. He died in 1685.

the King to the end is true, but she never really duped Charles, as Jesse surmises.

Louise's relations with Danby were in fact rather complex. She undoubtedly, like many women, coveted jewellery, and she was greedy and acquisitive. During March 1674 she wanted to possess a pearl necklace costing £8,000 which belonged to a merchant. She had also heard that Lady Northumberland was offering for sale a pair of earrings costing 3,000 guineas. At a propitious moment when she was relaxing with the King she told her lover how much she desired these beautiful things. Charles, pleading lack of money in the royal coffers, resourcefully sent her to Danby. The Lord Treasurer, eager to win Louise's friendship, listened sympathetically to her, and granted her request by allowing her the money to buy the jewels. In such a way did rumours begin that the hated French favourite was my Lord Treasurer's mistress. Through her influence Lord Latimer, Danby's eldest son was admitted to the royal bedchamber.

Bishop Gilbert Burnet—a contemporary—wrote of Danby: "He was a positive and undertaking man. So he gave the King great ease by assuring him all things would go according to his mind in the next session of parliament."[3]

Andrew Marvell in his bitter attacks on Charles II and his court refers to Louise's friendship with Osborne (Lord Danby). The poem "Britannia and Ralegh" is satirical and full of venom.

> But his fair soul, transformed by that French dame,
> Had lost all sense of honour, justice, fame.
> Like a tame spinster in's seraigle he sits,
> Besieged by whores, buffoons and bastard chits;
> Lulled in security, rolling in lust,
> Resigns his crown to Angel Carwell's* trust;
> Her creature Osborne the revenue steals.

These vicious criticisms of Charles II by opponents of the court were, in fact, extremely unfair. To provide a balance they took no account of his constant interest in and visits to the fleet, of his vigilance during the eternal Council meetings (even if he fondled a spaniel while discussing business), and of his interest in the foundation of a mathematical school at Christ's Hospital, where merchant officers could be trained.[5] If he loved to take his ease at gay parties on the river at Chelsea, he worked hard for it.

* Louise de Keroualle.

Lord Danby proved an extremely able administrator, and during 1674 and 1675 England enjoyed a fair measure of commercial prosperity. Louise watched his career with interest.

Among those who cultivated the friendship of the new Lord Treasurer was Robert Spencer, second Earl of Sunderland, a rising young politician. Some years later, on 28th August 1679, Danby referred to the intimate relations between Louise and Sunderland in a letter. At this period Danby was in disgrace, having eventually incurred the displeasure of the Duchess of Portsmouth. The politicians were well aware of the French lady's influence with the King. He wrote: "As I have always found your lordship knew her better than any, so I found also that nobody knew so well how to manage her . . . I cannot but impute so much of my sufferings to her ill-usage of mee with the King. I dare not trust what I may do if I shall be hard pressed by the Parliament to speak things which may not please Her Grace."[6]

If Danby succeeded at first in forming a close partnership with Louise, he failed altogether to cope with his wife Lady Bridget (Bertie), who, according to Burnet, was half mad and compelled her husband to pursue all her quarrels as well as his own.

Louise's rival, Nell Gwyn, disliked Danby, particularly as the Bretonne enjoyed such close relations with him. Later when Danby refused to support her claims to be created a Countess, "Mrs Nelly" as she was known to her friends was "at perfect defiance with him".[7] Much to Charles II's rich amusement, Nell together with her friend the Duke of Buckingham would give clever imitations of the Earl and Countess of Danby at her home in Pall Mall. Lord Danby's daughter Bridget Osborne married Charles II's bastard son, Charles Fitz-Charles by Catherine Pegge, now Lady Greene. He was created Earl of Plymouth and often came to court. Nell was furious because she had coveted the title for herself.

On 11th January 1674 Colbert de Croissy was succeeded as French Ambassador in London by Henri de Massue, Marquis de Ruvigny, an elderly aristocrat and distinguished soldier, now almost seventy. Ruvigny was leader of the French Protestants, a man of considerable integrity, and he possessed many qualities such as shrewdness, resourcefulness and tact which were useful to him in London. Louis XIV was well served by his ambassadors, and chose them very carefully for their qualities.

It was to Ruvigny that Charles II constantly complained of the obstinacy and intransigence of his brother the Duke of York. It is only fair to admire James for his principles, but he caused the King great embarrassment and certainly exasperated him. Daily throughout the kingdom he was becoming more and more unpopular, mainly because he could hardly be restrained from making a public declaration of his change of faith.[8] Formerly almost "the darling of the nation" for his bravery during the Dutch wars, he was now deeply mistrusted by many Englishmen. Charles confided in Ruvigny, whom he liked: "You know my brother long ago, that he is as stiff as a mule. If it were not for my brother's folly [*la sottise de mon frère*] I could get out of all my difficulties."[9] On the same day that Ruvigny was appointed Ambassador, Charles received the payment of eight million *livres* from Louis XIV.

At the end of 1673 Anthony Ashley-Cooper, Earl of Shaftesbury, a member of the Cabal, was dismissed from the Lord Chancellorship. He was to become Charles II's most dangerous opponent and the Duke of York's vindictive enemy, for he detested the papists.

Ruvigny was too honourable a man not to feel distaste, even disgust, for the methods of his master, Louis XIV, in bribing Charles II and members of Parliament through the Duke of Buckingham. The Ambassador would refer to these transactions as "filthy traffic" (*sale traffique*). Yet he showed indelicacy and a gross lack of taste when jesting about the English King's sexual adventures. He wrote to the French Foreign Minister, Pomponne, on 14th May 1674:

I have a thing to tell you, Monsieur, for the King's information which should remain secret as long as it pleases His Majesty to keep it so, because if it gets out it might be a source of unseemly raillery. While the King was winning provinces, the King of England was catching a malady which he has been at the trouble of communicating to the Duchess of Portsmouth. That prince is nearly cured, but to all appearance the lady will not so soon be rid of the virus. She has, however, in a degree been consoled for such a troublesome present by one more suitable to her charms—a pearl necklace worth four thousand jacobus, and a diamond worth six thousand, which have so rejoiced her that I should not wonder if for the price, she were not willing to risk another attack of the disease.[10]

It is quite obvious that Charles had caught the pox (as syphilis was then known) from one of his minor mistresses. To joke in this cynical, insensitive fashion about such a matter at least reveals that Ruvigny had little understanding of Louise's nature. Far from being compensated by Charles's generous presents, she was deeply hurt. Her Breton pride made her resentful, for she could not bear the sly sniggers of the courtiers. She constantly reproached the King with tears in her eyes for his infidelity. It is unlikely that Louise ever fully forgave her royal lover for the injury and disgrace he had inflicted on her. She had a woman's long memory for grievances. Two years later she openly attacked Charles in the presence of another French Ambassador, Honoré de Courtin, for his infidelities. She told the diplomat how much she had suffered from the King's misconduct with trulls. Courtin wrote Louvois that the English King had given him details how his doctor had prescribed for the Duchess of Portsmouth.

Louise was no longer the naïve young girl who had attended the Duchess of Orleans on her journey to England. After three and a half years in London she felt disillusioned, saddened by the insincerity of the courtiers and sickened by the prevailing falsehood. Her recent distressing experience served to harden her. Aware that she was surrounded by enemies, many of whom were eager to ruin her, she tried to outwit them as much as possible. Who can condemn her altogether for profiting from the King's infatuation? However, for the present she suffered from a demoralizing sense of insecurity, knowing that her rivals rejoiced at her setback and were trying to supersede her in the King's affections. How hard it was to dissimulate, to pretend that she did not care when her pride was so deeply hurt.

When her doctors advised her to visit Tunbridge to take the waters, so that she might be cured, Louise received a rebuff. She rented a house there, but she arrived in Tunbridge only to discover that an aristocratic English lady, the Marchioness of Worcester, had already installed herself there. The Duchess of Portsmouth was furious, and arrogantly reminded her that as a duchess she claimed precedence over a marchioness or countess. Lady Worcester told Louise in no uncertain terms that as titles acquired by prostitution conferred no such privilege she suggested that the Duchess of Portsmouth should seek accommodation elsewhere. Louise, of course, complained to the King, who, to soothe her pride, sent a detachment of the Household Guards to escort her with some ceremony to Windsor, where she became a patient of one of Charles's physicians named Crimp. It was quite a long time before she was completely cured.

Despite these temporary setbacks Louise's influence with Charles II increased rather than diminished. She often sought favours for her relations from Louis XIV. Charles II told Ruvigny that it would please him immensely if the French King would agree to bestow the first abbey vacant on her aunt, Dame Suzanne de Timeur, a nun in the Abbey of Lajois at Hennebon, in the Bishopric of Vannes.[11] Occasionally the Duchess of Portsmouth received a snub from Louis XIV, although he was careful not to offend her. When she recommended her relation Monsieur Calloet for the post of syndic of the States of Brittany, a form of nepotism she was very partial to, Louis did not bother to refer to the matter. He rather naturally resented any interference in internal matters of this sort. However, he sent her a present of pendant diamond earrings, which gave her enormous pleasure. She assured the French King of her passionate zeal for his service.

It was a consolation for Louise to confide her troubles to her younger sister Henriette, who arrived in London from Brittany during May 1674 in a yacht, escorted by one gentleman. Henriette lacked most of Louise's attractions, although she possessed her sister's rapaciousness and fondness for acquiring all sorts of beautiful things. Sir Peter Lely painted her portrait, which is at Wilton House. Charles, with his customary generosity gave her a pension of six hundred pounds a year. She married Philip Herbert, seventh Earl of Pembroke and Montgomery, as her first husband. A drunkard and a rake who neglected her, his behaviour was very wild and eccentric, even for that age.

He fought a duel with a man named Vaughan, related by marriage to John, ninth Earl of Rutland, and wounded him so severely that it was thought he would not recover.[12] On another occasion Pembroke was on a balcony in the Haymarket with some other gentlemen when "some blades passed by and fixed at him, but mist him and killd another".[13] Henriette de Keroualle's marriage with Philip Herbert was to prove unhappy.

Violence sometimes occurred in the streets of Restoration London near the Palace of Whitehall where the Duchess of Portsmouth basked in such splendour in her apartments. Even a great nobleman, James, first Duke of Ormonde, had an alarming experience during the winter of 1670—the very year Louise de Keroualle first came to London. One dark evening His Grace

5

was travelling in his coach by way of Pall Mall to St James's Street when some robbers threatened his coachman with a pistol. The man was dragged from the coach and robbed of some money.*

Sometimes coachmen were not satisfied with their fares. A former page of Lady Shrewsbury, a Mr Doughty, on one occasion[14] took a coach from the New Exchange to Westminster on a very rainy day. On paying the coachman a shilling the man swore that it was not enough. "Mr Douty thereupon struck at him with his hand, ye coach[man] thereupon whip'd him, and Mr Douty drew out his sword and ran him through. But the coachman, it was thought, was cured, went abroad, got drunke, fell into a fever and dyed." Eventually Douty was tried for wilful murder.

Young bloods frequently resorted to quarrels about the players (actresses). Mr Scrope sitting by Sir Thomas Armstrong at the Duke's playhouse in Lincoln's Inn Fields struck him over the shins twice because both men wished to gain the favour of Mrs Susanna Uphill, who came into the theatre masked. Armstrong challenged Scrope to a duel, and killed him at the first pass.[15]

When Louise's infant son Charles was aged three, she persuaded the King on 9th August 1675 to create him Duke of Richmond. The title was now vacant since the death of La Belle Stuart's husband in Denmark in 1672. At the same time he was created Baron of Setrington, Yorkshire, and Earl of March. On one early occasion when the King was visiting his mistress and their son intending to confer the order of the garter on him, he spontaneously took the noble badge from his own neck and deftly slipped the left arm of the infant duke through the ribbon. Hitherto the custom was that the order of the garter was worn round the neck. Henceforward it was always put on from left shoulder to right side. Charles Lennox grew up a handsome little boy, beloved and rather pampered by both his parents. He resembled Charles II in appearance, although the King regarded himself as an ugly fellow. A Scots lady of high character, the Countess Mareschal, was appointed governess to the little Duke of Richmond, and granted a salary of two hundred pounds a year. When he was about eight and a half Richmond was appointed Master of the Horse and he succeeded another bastard of Charles II, the Duke of Monmouth, in this office. The duties were exercised during his minority by three commissioners.

* The notorious Colonel Thomas Blood instigated this affair.

The Duke of Richmond—her descendant—still bears the motto chosen by Louise de Keroualle for her own use: *"En la rose je fleuris."*

The rivalry between the Duchesses of Portsmouth and Cleveland caused much amusement at court. Barbara was determined that her second son, Henry Fitzroy, Duke of Grafton, should have precedence over Louise's son, but her rival proved too cunning and adroit for her. Precedence depended on the patent that was first signed. Louise now made good use of her friendship with Lord Danby by secretly contacting him and persuading him to receive her lawyer at midnight just as he was about to start for Bath in his coach to take the waters. Much to her fury Barbara discovered that she had been outwitted by Her Grace of Portsmouth. When her lawyer waited on the Lord Treasurer, Danby had already departed for Bath. Consequently Grafton's patent was delayed. So today the present Duke of Richmond outranks the Duke of Grafton by a narrow margin.

That summer of 1675 was passed by Charles II partly at Windsor, a place for which he showed increasing affection. It is customary to think of Queen Catherine as continually unhappy and neglected, but it is pleasing to know that she, too, experienced tranquillity and joy during the warm summer days, especially delighting in al fresco picnics in Windsor Forest. Lady Chaworth's letter of 7th September gives us an enchanting picture of such a picnic:

All the Queen's servants treated her by everyone bringing their dish, who then attended her into the forest, and she ate under a tree. Lady Bath's dish was a chine of beef, Mrs Windham's a venison pasty, but Mr Hall brought two dozen of ruffs and reeves and delicate baskets of fruit, Mr Chiffinch, for his daughter's behalf, twelve dozen of choice wine. The Queen wonderfully pleased and merry, and none but herself and servants.[16]

So, in these sylvan woodlands they found diversion. By this time Charles's little Portuguese Queen had been forced to accept her husband's need for his sultana ladies, although Louise continued to cause her anxiety and uneasiness.

That summer Louise's parents, the Comte and Comtesse de Keroualle, visited England, but their pride prevented them from profiting from the great favour which their eldest daughter enjoyed with the King. They stayed quietly in the country with

Sir Richard Browne,* Evelyn's father-in-law who was now able
to return the hospitality he had received many years ago in
Brittany. John Evelyn met Louise's father and thought him "a
soulderly person and a good fellow, as the Bretons generally
are".[17] While talking to him in his garden he was interested to
discover that several words of the Breton language were the
same as Welsh. Presumably the Keroualles still disapproved of
their daughter's liaison with Charles II, for we do not hear of
their attending any court functions.

It was in the murky air of the coffee-houses of Restoration
London, nurseries of sedition, that the Duchess of Portsmouth
was mercilessly attacked and criticized. All sorts of wild stories
about her had their origin here, for instance that she was secretly
married to the King, or that she was with child by another man.
During 1675 the Government attempted to suppress coffee-
houses by proclamation, but it was later withdrawn. Sir George
Sitwell in his absorbing book *The First Whig* remarks that all the
great calamities of Charles II's reign came about owing to their
existence. They were frequented by infamous men and corrupt
politicians, breeding hotbeds of disaffection and sedition. A
typical ballad runs:

> But besides these there is another sort,
> infects the coffee-house as these haunt the Court,
> a sort of raskels in whose tainted veins
> the blood of their rebellious fathers reigns;
> Villains that Faction daily do forment,
> and practise to defame the Government,
> assembling their cabal, at whose discretion
> the royal line must prostrate the succession.

Seditious newsheets and newspapers attacking Charles II and
the Government were sold or distributed in coffee-houses, a
serious embarrassment to the anxious King.

A man named Stysted was imprisoned in the Tower for alleg-
ing that Charles II had sold Tangiers and that "Madame Carwell"
was to be given the proceeds of the sale. He was interrogated by
Sir Joseph Williamson, Louise's friend.

The Government tried to enforce a law forbidding coffee-house
keepers to allow newspapers or newsheets on their premises. In

---

* After the Restoration, Clerk of the Council to Charles II.

September 1677 twenty of their number were summoned before the Privy Council for permitting this type of literature to be read in their coffee-houses. Their licenses were not renewed.

It was in 1675 that the famous Green Ribbon Club,[18] first known as The King's Head Club, was founded. It later became the headquarters of the opposition or country party, whose leader was the sinister Lord Shaftesbury, perhaps the most able politician in England. The Green Ribbon Club bore its name from 1679 onwards because of the green ribbons its members wore in their hats. They met at the King's Head tavern at Chancery Lane End, an inn formerly supposed to be a private house belonging to Sir John Oldcastle, who is usually considered to be the model of Shakespeare's Sir John Falstaff. This was the favourite haunt of the Whig peers. They met in a long oak-panelled room, its tables laden with sack and claret, pewter candlesticks and snuffers. It reeked of tobacco smoke as they puffed at their clay pipes. The atmosphere was sinister, and an aura of mystery pervaded everywhere—not least because of the presence of the little crippled Earl of Shaftesbury with his piercing eagle-eye. Witty and brilliant, he presided over the activities of the club with diabolical efficiency. Other Whig peers who frequented it were the Earls of Essex and Bedford, Lord Mulgrave, and the sinister Lord Grey of Werke, boon companion of the impressionable Duke of Monmouth.

Most of the coffee-houses had their political affiliations. Kid's coffee-house, known as the Amsterdam, was later frequented by the Whigs—it was a favourite haunt of Titus Oates. He once had a dish of coffee flung in his face. Jonathan's in Exchange Alley and Gray's Inn coffee-houses were chiefly patronized by the Tories. Will's—a very celebrated coffee-house—was much frequented by poets and people interested in literature. It was situated between Covent Garden and Bow Street, then a fashionable part of London. Most people went to Will's to see John Dryden the poet laureate, who in winter sat in a chair by the fire discoursing about the latest tragedy of Racine or Otway's *Venice Preserved*. If a young student managed to get a sniff from Dryden's snuff box, he deemed it a great honour. On stuffy summer days Dryden's chair was moved to the balcony. Garraway's was usually thronged with surgeons and apothecaries. There were puritan coffee-houses where no oaths were ever heard. There lean men discussed the immorality at Charles II's court. There were popish coffee-houses where, it was believed, that the Papists were again plotting to set fire to the City of London.

NOTES

1. F. C. Turner, *James II*, p. 121.
2. J. H. Jesse, *Memoirs of the Court during the Reign of the Stuarts.*
3. Burnet, *History of the Reign of Charles II.*
4. Andrew Marvell, "Britannia and Ralegh".
5. Sir Arthur Bryant, *King Charles II.*
6. Add. MSS. 28049, fol. 70. B.M.
7. Sir Robert Southwell in a letter to James, first Duke of Ormonde.
8. F. C. Turner, *op. cit.*
9. *Ibid.*
10. Correspondance Angleterre, CX, fol. 201; Forneron, *Louise de Keroualle.*
11. Forneron, *op. cit.*
12. 27th November; *Hatton Correspondence.*
13. *Verney Family Memoirs*, II.
14. 15th July 1680; *Hatton Correspondence.* Letter from Charles Hatton.
15. *Verney Family Memoirs.*
16. H.M.C. Rutland II, 27; Sir Arthur Bryant, *op. cit.*, p. 244.
17. *Memoirs and Correspondence of John Evelyn*, II, p. 406, 15th June 1675.
18. Sir George Sitwell gives a fascinating account of the Green Ribbon Club in *The First Whig*.

SIX

WHITEHALL PALACE

The ancient Palace of Whitehall lay for almost half a mile beside the river, a warren of galleries, apartments and gardens. Both Charles II's apartments and the Queen's faced the Thames, being built round three sides of a small court or garden.[1] Foreigners, when they visited England after the Restoration, often expressed bewilderment and surprise that the King and Queen should manage to exist in such cramped and inadequate surroundings.

Some favoured politicians and courtiers were provided with separate houses of their own on the west side of the imposing stone gallery. Laurence Hyde, a younger son of Lord Clarendon, and Lord Lauderdale,* who managed Charles II's Scottish business, both lived here.

The Stone Gallery was where the King sometimes transacted business, and it was customary for him to walk at a rapid pace, so that his ministers and members of Parliament found it hard to attract his attention. "He walked by his watch", as Lord Halifax phrased it. On the walls of the Stone Gallery Charles II had hung many of the valuable pictures acquired by his father.

The Duchess of Portsmouth's apartments lay near the celebrated Stone Gallery, at the south end of the Privy Gardens, and overlooked the sundial lawn.[2] The dial is supposed to have been a tribute from an old faithful servant of Charles II's, Tobias Rustat, Keeper of Hampton Court and Yeoman of the Robes. Louise's apartments were furnished and decorated with exquisite taste, although she was justly criticized and envied by many people for her ostentatious extravagance and love of splendour. They were far more luxurious than those of the Queen, who from 1675 onwards lived much at Somerset House. There we can imagine Louise in the heyday of her glory receiving the homage of the King and the flattery of the obsequious courtiers.

* Second Earl and first Duke of Lauderdale (1616–1682).

After her leisurely rising in the morning, she was wont to sit in front of her toilet mirror in her dressing-room while her maids combed her lovely dark hair, so characteristic of her Breton ancestry. There she would queen it, giving audiences to politicians and French Ambassadors, and intrigue incessantly in her own interests, and sometimes in those of her native country. We can picture her with her pouting, spoilt mouth, with a sulky expression on her pretty face, taking special care of her lovely fair skin and complexion, and talking English, which she never really mastered, in her soft voice.

There have been many more brilliant mistresses, but none made it their business to understand the kings they subjected more skilfully than she did in her subtle and intuitive understanding of Charles's character. If, on occasions, she failed to gain her way with Charles, she had the intelligence never to storm at him, but to resort to tears. Nell Gwyn called her "the weeping willow". Sometimes she feigned illness. She learnt from experience that few men can indeed resist the tears of their loved ones. Yet Charles was very rarely deceived. On one occasion many years later when Anna Scott, Duchess of Monmouth was reminiscing about her days at the Court of Charles II, she told a story about the King and Louise, which throws a curious light upon their relations.[3] The King was standing carelessly by the window of his apartments when a courtier came and told him that the doctors were of the opinion that the Duchess of Portsmouth could not live half an hour. Charles replied in his sceptical way: "Odds Fish! I don't believe a word of all this. She's better than you or I are. She wants something; that makes her play her pranks over this. She has served me so often in this way, that I am sure of what I say as if I was part of her."

Louise was never allowed to forget that by becoming Charles's mistress she had forfeited the respect of many people, even if she played the part of a great lady. To her fury, she once found a paper stuck in her chamber door with the verse:

> Within this place a bed's appointed
> For a French bitch and God's annointed.

John Evelyn, one of the finest minds of his age, naturally disapproved of Louise. On one later occasion he followed the King and a few of his attendants through the Whitehall galleries to the Duchess of Portsmouth's apartments. He was unfavourably

impressed by "the rich splendid furniture of this woman's apartments, now twice or thrice pulled down and rebuilt to satisfy her
prodigal and expensive pleasures".⁴ Well might Evelyn moralize
"What contentment can there be in riches and splendour of this
world, purchas'd with vice and dishonour!" There were exquisite
Gobelin tapestries, and priceless pictures from the Palaces of
Versailles and Saint-Germain. Some of these were landscapes,
hunting scenes, and paintings of "exotic fouls and all to the life,
rarely don". People marvelled at the beautiful Japanese cabinets,
screens and pendulum clocks. The windows of her apartments
were of the finest crystal glass. If Louise was avaricious, she
certainly possessed superb artistic taste.

For Charles the Palace of Whitehall held bitter memories as
well as happy associations. It was from Whitehall some years
earlier that Frances Stuart, who he had loved passionately, yet in
vain, had eloped to marry the Duke of Richmond. Now that
time of anguish had grown dim, but the soft lapping of water
against Whitehall steps occasionally stirred his memory.

Above the King's apartments lay those occupied by Lady
Castlemaine, now Duchess of Cleveland. From 1676 onwards
they were sometimes the lodgings of her elder daughter by the
King, the Countess of Sussex. How often had Charles been compelled to endure the violent tempers of Lady Castlemaine. Now
to visit Louise in her apartments and to listen to her gentle conversation while she lay languishing in his arms, seemed peace
indeed. She was jealous and scornful of his other mistresses,
particularly of Nell Gwyn, but the King was amused rather than
troubled by it. Some verses, which have been attributed to John
Sheffield, Earl of Mulgrave, refer to Cleveland and Portsmouth,
the rival mistresses.

> In loyal libels we have often told him
> How one has jilted him, the other sold him,
> How that affects to laugh, How this to weep,
> But who can rail so long as he can keep?
> Was ever Prince by two at once misled,
> False, foolish, old, ill-natured and ill-bred?

Mulgrave was banished from court some years later for having
the effrontery to show excessive admiration for the Princess Anne
of York.

One of Charles's faithful servants was Will Chiffinch, the

celebrated page of His Majesty's bedchamber and keeper of his private closet since 1668. Chiffinch was more trusted with confidential secrets than most of the politicians. He possessed a duplicate of a private key of the King's closet, which was reached by a tiny, narrow flight of stairs from Charles's bedroom. Charles was very proud of the clocks and watches he had collected in this closet, and would show them on occasion to appreciative visitors.

Will Chiffinch, however, was far more than a confidential agent, for his more serious duties consisted of acting as treasurer for the enormous payments made by Louis XIV to Charles II.[5] Ralph Montagu, the English Ambassador in France referred to Chiffinch in a letter to Lord Danby during November 1677. He is pleased to hear that Mr Chiffinch is to be the French treasurer, "and in this, and everything else that can concern your Lordship, you shall find me as careful and faithful as any servant you have".

On one earlier occasion a French Ambassador in London, Honoré de Courtin, negotiated an enormous payment in great secrecy in Chiffinch's lodgings. It was for two million livres.*

Will had other uses for a master such as Charles. At his gay supper parties he was in the habit of encouraging his guests to drink. When in their cups he would report to the King whether they were rogues or honest men.

We do not hear of Louise at Will Chiffinch's supper-parties— she probably thought herself too great a lady to attend them, but Nell Gwyn was a good friend of Chiffinch's and was sometimes present at them.

Woe betide the courtier who was unfortunate enough to incur the rancour of the Duchess of Portsmouth, for she was not easy to appease. During the summer of 1675 she was increasingly upset and annoyed by the filthy lampoons which were sold in the coffee-houses. All sorts of wild rumours were being circulated, for instance that she had sent large sums of money into France, that she was taking the King to France to live with her, and that she had told Queen Catherine that she (the Duchess) was married to the King.

Amongst the brilliant rakes at Charles II's court was John Wilmot, second Earl of Rochester, a satirical poet with a touch of genius. A favourite companion of Charles II, who delighted in his wit, he sometimes had the misfortune to incur the King's

* £150,000.

displeasure, and was banished to the country. Rochester had travelled in France as a very young man where he had known the King's youngest sister, the Duchess of Orleans. On one occasion she entrusted him with a letter to King Charles, which he delivered on his return to the court in London on Christmas Day, 1664. Among his more daring adventures was the abduction of the heiress, Elizabeth Mallett, during the year of the Great Plague, 1665. For this offence he was sent to the Tower for almost a month. In 1667 he married his heiress, and took her to his home, Adderbury, near Banbury in Oxfordshire.

Rochester's most intimate friend at court was Henry Savile, a younger brother of Sir George Savile (later Marquis of Halifax). In appearance Savile was a complete contrast to his friend, for his complexion was ruddy. He was a round-cheeked, moist-lipped, plump-bottomed man, while Rochester was lean and handsome.[6] When his friend was in the country, Savile was in the habit of writing him the court gossip.

During late August 1675, Rochester was riding in the woods near his home when he was thrown from his horse. He was badly bruised and had to be put to bed. At this unfortunate juncture he received a letter from Harry Savile telling him that he had incurred the deep displeasure of the Duchess of Portsmouth. Rochester complained in a long letter to his friend that he had no idea of the reason for Her Grace's displeasure.

It seems very likely, however, that Rochester had offended both Louise and the King in one of his verse libels. He had criticized them in *A Satyr on Charles II*:[7]

> Restless he rolls about from whore to whore
> A merry monarch, scandalous and poor;
> To Carwell, the most dear of all his dears,
> The best relief of his declining years,
> Oft he bewails his fortune, and her fate:
> To love so well, and he beloved so late.
> For though in her he settles well his tarse,
> Yet his dull, graceless ballocks hang an arse.
> This you'd believe, had I but time to tell ye
> The pains it costs to poor, laborious Nelly,
> Whilst she employs hands, fingers, mouth and thighs,
> Ere she can raise the member she enjoys.

For a talented poet with a touch of genius, Rochester was capable of coarseness and gross lack of taste.

Rochester puts into the mouth of the King in *Dialogue*:

> KING: When on Portmouth's lap I lay my head,
> And Knight does sing her bawdy song,
> I envy not George Porter's bed,
> Nor the delights of Madam Long.

Mary Knight was a singer with a lovely voice, and was, in fact, one of Charles's minor mistresses. George Porter was a Groom of the Bedchamber to Charles II, and one of Rochester's disreputable cronies,[8] while Jane Long was one of the original actresses of the Duke's House, and George Porter's mistress.

Rochester's letter to Harry Savile is worth quoting, and is interesting at least in illustrating how the courtiers dreaded the animosity of the powerful French mistress. He may have met her in France, and certainly knew her fairly intimately at the English court. He wrote:

> That night I receiv'd by yours the surprising account of my Lady Dutchess's more than ordinary indignation against me, I was nearly brought in dead of a fall from my horse, of which I still remain bruis'd and Bedrid, and can now scarce think it a happiness that I sav'd my neck. What ill star reigns over me, that I'm still marked out for ingratitude, and only us'd barbarously to those I am obliged to! Had I been troublesome to her in pinning the Dependence of my Fortune upon her Solicitations to the King, or her unmerited Recommendations of me to some great man, it would not have mov'd my wonder much, if she had sought any occasion to be rid of a useless trouble: But a creature, who had already receiv'd of her all the obligations he ever could pretend to, except the continuance of her good opinion, for the which he resolv'd and did direct every step of his life in duty and service to her; . . . By that God that made me, I have no more offended her in thought, word or deed, no more imagin'd or utter'd the least thought to her contempt or prejudice, than I have plotted Treason, conceal'd Arms, train'd Regiments for a Rebellion . . . I thought the D. of Portsmouth more an angel than I find her a woman; and as this is the first, it shall be the most malicious thing I will ever say of her. For her generous Resolution of not hurting me to the King, I thank her; but she must think a man much oblig'd, after the calling of him knave, to say she will do him no further prejudice . . .[9]

He begged Savile to have one further talk with Louise and desire her to give him the fair hearing she would grant any footman of hers, who had been complained of.

It is usually supposed that Rochester hated the Duchess of Portsmouth, but in April 1676, when she was temporarily out of favour with Charles II, who at this time was enamoured of the Duchess Mazarin, Rochester wrote to Savile:

I am sorry for the declining D. [Louise] and would have you generous to her at this time, for that is true Pride, and I delight in it.

All the same this poet-earl, who was capable of writing exquisite lyrics, refers to Louise with bitterness in his verses, particularly in "The Royal Buss". He attributed to her most of the ills of the nation, which might have been cured by Parliament in 1673, except that:

> Portsmouth, the incestuous Punk
> Made our most gracious sov'raign drunk.
> And drunk she made him give that Buss
> That all the kingdom's bound to curse,
> And so red hot with wine and whore,
> He kickt the Commons out of door!

In "Portsmouth's Looking Glass" (1679) he makes fun of her, and attacks her in merciless satire for finding it necessary to "varnish and smooth o'er those graces", which had rubbed off during those nights of hot embraces with Charles.

It is a solace to turn from Rochester's ribald verses to the exquisite lyrics so characteristic of his best work. For instance, the first verse "My Dear Mistress has a Heart":

> My dear Mistress has a Heart
>   Soft as those kind looks she gave me,
> When with Love's resistless art,
>   And her Eyes, she did enslave me.
> But her Constancy's so weak,
>   She's so wild and apt to wander;
> That my jealous Heart would break,
>   Should we live one Day asunder.

If he disliked Louise he certainly had no reason to like the Duchess of Cleveland. On one occasion she threw him on his back when he attempted to kiss her as she stepped from her chariot at Whitehall-Gate. Rochester brilliantly conceived these lines as he lay on the ground before getting up.

By Heavens! 'twas bravely done,
First to attempt the Chariot of the Sun,
And then to fall like Phaeton.

Once when staying at Althorp in Northamptonshire, Harry
Savile, Rochester's great friend, had an amusing adventure typical
of the restoration rakes. Late at night he came to the chamber of
the beautiful and widowed Lady Northumberland, crying gently
"Madam! Madam!" when the startled lady awoke, he said that
he had come to acquaint her of the passion he had for her, which
he durst not own to her in the light. Lady Northumberland rang
a bell by her bedside, but Savile begged her not to discover him.
If he had done more and said less, it is possible that he would
have been more successful. Harry Savile always contrived to give
the impression that he was a mere dilettante or idler, but in reality
he was an extremely talented writer of letters which are still a
delight to read. He later also revealed diplomatic ability when he
was appointed Ambassador to France.

The Duke of Buckingham on several occasions fell foul of
the King, mainly owing to the influence of the Duchess of
Portsmouth. Sir John Reresby,* a Yorkshire squire, refers to the
Duke's disgrace in his *Memoirs*, and to Louise as "a very fine
woman, and as most thought sent over on purpose to ensnare
the King, who was easily taken with that sort of trap".[10] When
Reresby's son, Tamworth, was aged twelve, he asked Louise to
put in a word for his son with the King, for he wanted him to
become a page of honour. Certainly Louise was very kind to
Sir John Reresby and his wife, asking them to dinner with her
at Windsor, and telling them that whenever they were to come
there "to make her table their own".

It is related that the notorious Judge Jeffreys, when a handsome
and rising young lawyer, owed his advancement to the Duchess
of Portsmouth, who mentioned him to Charles II as a young man
who deserved well of the court party.[11] After becoming Common
Sergeant, Jeffreys was knighted in 1677. On a summer day during
the following year Sir George Jeffreys entertained the King and
the Duchess of Portsmouth to dinner at his country home,
Bulstrode House and Park in Buckinghamshire. Charles II was
so delighted by Jeffreys' lavish hospitality that he drank to him
"full seven times".

* Born April 1634.

A contemporary lampoon refers to Louise's influence on Jeffreys' career:

> Monmouth's tamer, Jeff's advance,
> Foe to England, spy to France.

The Duchess of Portsmouth also used her influence with her royal lover on behalf of Ralph Bridoake, Dean of Sarum to be appointed Bishop of Chester[12] during February 1675.

Much as been written about the rivalry between Louise and Nell Gwyn, though the latter never seriously challenged the Duchess of Portsmouth's position in Whitehall as *Maitresse en Titre*. There was room enough in Charles's capacious heart for both of them. Nell seldom interfered in politics, for she understood little about them. Nell's witty tongue and vulgarity, however, caused Louise considerable annoyance and uneasiness. Nell often got the better of her, as is illustrated by the following story. One day Nell appeared at Whitehall dressed in an extremely rich suit of clothes. Louise remarked with slight venom in her voice: "Nelly, you are grown rich, I believe, by your dress; why, woman, you are fine enough to be a queen."

"You are entirely right, Madam," answered Nell, "and I am whore enough to be a duchess."[13]

Across the Channel Madame de Sévigné mischievously took a perverse delight in the rivalry between the two mistresses. She wrote her daughter on 11th September 1675:

> With regard to England, Mademoiselle de K—has not been disappointed in anything she proposed; she desired to be a mistress to the King, and she is so. He lodges with her almost every night in the face of all the whole Court. She has had a son, who has been acknowledged, and presented with two dutchies. She amasses treasure and makes herself feared and respected by as many as she can. But she did not foresee that she should find a young actress in her way, whom the King dotes on; and she has it not in her power to withdraw him from her. He divides his care, his time and his health between these two. The actress is as haughty as Mademoiselle; she insults her, she makes grimaces at her, she attacks her, she frequently steals the King from her, and boasts whenever he gives her the preference ... She has a son* by the King, and hopes to have him acknowledged. As to Mademoiselle, she reasons thus: This dutchess, says she, pretends to be a person of quality; she says she

---

* Charles Beauclerk, Lord Burford, first Duke of St. Albans.

is related to the best families in France; whenever any person of distinction dies, she puts herself in mourning. If she be a lady of such quality, why does she demean herself to be a courtezan? She ought to die for shame. As for me, it is my profession; I do not pretend to anything better ... This creature gets the upper hand, and discountenances and embarrasses the dutchess extremely. I like these original characters.[14]

It is easy to poke fun at Louise de Keroualle; she was indeed related to several aristocratic families in France, and was a distant cousin of the King. All the same, she made rather a fool of herself during 1682 by dressing herself in deep mourning for the Chevalier de Rohan, a distinguished French aristocrat, although she found it hard to establish a relationship. To Louise's fury, Nell, the former orange wench for whom she could scarcely conceal her disdain, at once went into mourning. On being asked by a courtier why she was wearing black, the mistress retorted: "Why! Have you not heard of my loss in the death of the Cham of Tartary?" She insisted, to everybody's intense amusement, except the Duchess of Portsmouth, that she had as much right to call herself a relation of the Cham of Tartary as Louise had by her pretensions to be related to de Rohan. When Louise commissioned Gascar to paint her in an elegant lace smock, with one breast bare, against a background of resplendent draperies, Nell had herself painted on a bed of flowers, with the identical background of draperies.

There is a portrait of Louise, Duchess of Portsmouth, painted by Sir Peter Lely about 1670, and the style of her hair created a fashion in England. This picture is undoubtedly of strong sensual appeal, and Mr C. H. Collins Baker[15] included it in his work. It was formerly owned by the Earls of Craven at Coombe Abbey, but it was later sold at Sotheby's. Lely also painted Nell Gwyn leaning on a bed with one of her children. Charles was present on one occasion when Lely painted Nell naked.

A curious document[16] in the British Museum reveals that Louise received from 27th March 1676 to 14th March 1679 the enormous sum of £55,198.07.11 while Nell Gwyn was paid the much smaller amount of £16,041.15.00. On 21st July 1677, for instance, the Duchess of Portsmouth was given £11,000.

On 27th October 1676 Letters Patent of Charles II granted "Our Right entirely beloved Cousin Louise Duchess of Portsmouth an annuity of £8,600 payable out of excise duties".[17]

Thomas Osborne, Earl of Danby, from the studio of Sir Peter Lely, painted about 1680 (*by courtesy of the National Portrait Gallery*)

James Duke of Monmouth as Master of the Horse, attributed to Jan Wyck (*by courtesy of the Duke of Buccleuch and the National Galleries of Scotland*)

The great seal is broken on red and white cords and is signed "By writt of Privy Seal. Pigott".

Even the Duke of York's graceful and enchanting young wife, Mary of Modena, was obliged to call on the French favourite, though she disliked and disapproved of her. This only occurred after Hortense, the Duchesse Mazarin, arrived in England at the end of 1675. The Duchess of York made much of Hortense, a cousin of hers, and Louise out of pique complained to her royal lover that his brother's wife was showing her no attention. The Duke of York, well aware of Louise's power over the mind of his brother, and in order to appease her, made his Italian-born wife accompany him when he visited her in her apartments in Whitehall. There Louise received them with her long black hair puffed into a mass of small ringlets. The King later joined them, and showed his pleasure at his sister-in-law's compliance by paying her many compliments.

By pleasing Louise, however, the Duchess of York deeply offended Queen Catherine. That very evening at a ball Maria of Modena gave the Queen a profound curtsey, as was the custom, but instead of acknowledging it, Catherine showed her resentment by turning her back on her, a humiliating experience for the young bride.

Charles's court was full of malicious people only too ready to sow mischief between the royal ladies. Louise, although she had friends among the politicians, including Lord Sunderland and Sir Joseph Williamson, had three implacable enemies, Ralph Montagu, the Duke of Buckingham, and the Earl of Arlington, who had once been her mentor. Ralph Montagu, the English Ambassador in France, hated Louise, partly because she was the ally of the powerful Lord Treasurer Danby. The former enemies, Buckingham and Arlington, plotted during the winter of 1675–1676 the best means of ruining Danby and of getting rid of the French favourite. At this juncture Ralph Montagu, a sly, subtle intriguer who had known the beautiful and unconventional Hortense, Duchesse Mazarin, at Chambery in Savoy, gave her an invitation to visit England. It was his object that Hortense should supplant the Duchess of Portsmouth in the King's affections.[18] Hortense's great friend, the Seigneur de Saint-Evremond, the exiled philosopher, used his influence with her so as to persuade her to accept the invitation.

For the first time since coming to England Louise became aware that her position as *Maitresse en Titre* was gravely threatened. She had noticed of late a coolness on the part of the King. She was now *enceinte*, and the capricious temperament of her royal lover caused her deep distress. Despite the weak state of her health, Louise determined to make a stubborn fight against her adversaries.

NOTES

1. Arthur Irwin Dasent, *Nell Gwyn*.
2. J. E. Sheppard, *Old Royal Palace of Whitehall*.
3. *Diary of Mary Countess Cowper*, p. 95.
4. *Memoirs and Correspondence of John Evelyn*, III, p. 100, 4th October 1683.
5. *Copies of extracts of some letters written to and from the Earl of Danby*.
6. Charles Norman, *Rake Rochester*.
7. *The Complete Poems of John Wilmot, Earl of Rochester*.
8. *Ibid*.
9. *The Rochester-Savile Letters*.
10. *Memoirs of Sir John Reresby*, p. 93.
11. Seymour Schofield, *Jeffreys of the Bloody Assizes*.
12. Anthony à Wood, *Life and Times*, II, p. 309.
13. J. H. Wilson, *Nell Gwyn, Royal Mistress*.
14. *Letters of the Marchioness de Sévigné*, IV.
15. C. H. Collins Baker, *Lely and the Stuart Portrait Painters*, I, p. 172.
16. Add. MSS. 28094, fol. 54.
17. Goodwood MSS. 1.
18. Cyril Hughes Hartmann, *The Vagabond Duchess*.

SEVEN

HER TEMPORARY ECLIPSE

Hortense, who was to cause such a sensation at Charles II's court, was the youngest and favourite niece of Cardinal Mazarin. She was the fourth daughter of Mazarin's sister, Jeronima and her husband Lorenzo Mancini, an Italian gentleman from Rome, who dabbled in astrology.

Although Italian by birth, Hortense was brought up at the French court. To complete her education she was sent to the Convent of the Visitation in the Faubourg Saint Jacques in Paris, where her uncle sent her presents of fans and other baubles.

It is curious that a project for a marriage between the exiled Charles and Hortense Mancini was first broached towards the end of 1659 when the Cardinal was still alive. Mazarin had formed an alliance with Cromwell, and wrongly believed that Charles would never regain his throne. Consequently, he refused to consider the match. She was eventually married to Armand de la Porte, Marquis de la Meilleraye, who received from the Cardinal the title of Duc Mazarin and a dowry of twenty-eight million francs.

The Duc Mazarin was an eccentric, who unfortunately possessed an excess of religious zeal. He acquired the habit of mutilating the finest statues, and forbade the wenches on his estate to milk cows, since he feared that might suggest evil thoughts.[1] He had a passion for litigation, and during his lifetime engaged in almost three hundred lawsuits, nearly all of which he lost. The Duc Mazarin was unbalanced rather than actually insane, but for a woman of Hortense's pleasure-loving, rather frivolous temperament he was an unsuitable husband. He was insanely jealous of her, not without solid reason. Eventually she escaped from him, and lived for some time as an adventuress in various parts of Europe, having many lovers.

Despite her frivolous temperament, Hortense was extremely

clever and intelligent. She spoke several languages fluently. She had a rare gift for forming intimate relationships, and her incomparable charm and beauty made her irresistible. She was about twenty-nine when she first came to England, a dark southern lady with jet black hair which curled naturally. She possessed an exquisitely shaped mouth, but her most striking feature were her lovely eyes "neither blue nor grey, nor altogether black, but a mixture of all three".[2] A panegyrist describes her as "one of those lofty Roman Beauties, noway like our Baby-visaged, and Puppet-like Faces of France".[3] A sly dig at the Duchess of Portsmouth. Such a woman seemed likely to prove a dangerous rival for Louise.

On Christmas Day 1675, Madame de Sévigné wrote to her daughter that she thought the Duchesse Mazarin was in England, "where, as you know, there is neither faith, nor law, nor priest, but I believe that she would not desire as the song has it that they should have expelled the King".

Actually Hortense, after a stormy voyage, landed at Tor Bay. Dressed as a Cavalier and attended by seven servants she made for London.

The Marquis of Ruvigny, the elderly French Ambassador in London, followed Hortense's progress with keen interest, frequently mentioning her in his reports to his Foreign Minister. Hortense was related to the Duchess of York through her Martinozzi cousins, and it was with the King's brother and sister-in-law that she first had lodgings in St James's Palace. The Duke of York later allowed her the use of a house in St James's Park.[4]

Ruvigny wrote: "The Duke of York is taking a particular care of the Duchess Mazarin. The Duchess of York has affection for her. She is always with her."[5] The King had a splendid excuse to visit his sister-in-law, for she was *enceinte*. He thus found an opportunity to converse with Hortense Mazarin, and his sister-in-law arranged meetings between the two.

Later, suspecting that a liaison had already started, the Ambassador wrote to Louis XIV: "Sire, I have just learnt that there is a certain and very secret *intelligence* [understanding] between the King of England and Madame Mazarin. She carries on her intrigue with him very quietly."[6]

On 16th March we find him writing: "It seems that the King takes the interests of this lady more at heart than he did at the beginning, and that with time he could well have a passion for her."

Meanwhile, Hortense, who only lived for pleasure, enjoyed herself in her own way in London being escorted during September by the Duchess of Portsmouth's enemy the Duke of Buckingham to Bartholomew Fair, where they delighted in the mummery. Her great friend in England was the Seigneur de Saint-Evremond, who had once advised Louise de Keroualle to yield to temptation. Saint-Evremond was an eccentric: tall, distinguished and very courtly. Instead of wearing a periwig, he wore a cap over his white hair. He seemed a grotesque character, for an enormous wen which had grown up between his eyes disfigured his whole face.[7]

The Duchess of Portsmouth could not conceal her jealousy at the success of her rival, and felt deeply mortified. The first part of 1676 was an unfortunate period in her life. Everything seemed to go awry. Louise felt ill and jaded, for she was with child and her pregnancy ended with a premature birth. Ruvigny wrote to his Foreign Minister that during the annual visit of the court to Newmarket, the King did not offer her any lodging. She was obliged to hire a house in a neighbouring village. She bitterly complained to Ruvigny, and the Ambassador was able to offer her nothing but cold comfort, for he was convinced that Madame Mazarin's star was in the ascendant.

Many exulted at Louise's supposed downfall. Nell Gwyn, in her customary malicious way, went into mourning. To recover her health and to nurse her grief, Louise left for Bath to take the water. She was there from 25th May till 4th July. Bath was then becoming very fashionable. Most people of quality stayed at the White Hart. Access to the largest, the King's Bath, was limited to people of the highest rank. It was the custom for the gentlemen to sit on a circular seat with a stone cross, while the ladies faced them under the arched vaults submerged to the neck in warm water. For this occasion they wore yellow gowns with huge sleeves. The Baths were situated in a hollow, so it was possible to saunter to and fro and stare down at the recumbent ladies and gentlemen. It was really very agreeable because an orchestra played most of the time. The Sergeant of Baths, an important official, had the congenial duty of making suitable compliments to distinguished visitors. Whilst in Bath a lady advised Louise to put into the waters she drank coral, crab's eyes and pearls, but she preferred to drink the waters "pure and simple". Bath delighted Louise, for it was then a little town of jumbled houses and narrow streets. Eight years before, during June 1668, Samuel Pepys had visited Bath, and on the way to that town dined well at a tavern at Norton St Philips (called by Pepys Philips Norton). Somersetshire greatly pleased him and Mrs Pepys. On entering the gateway to the town the visitor would be greeted by the ringing of the church bells for which he would be charged £1. Henry Chapman, Mayor of Bath in 1664 and again in 1676—the year when the Duchess of Portsmouth took the waters—had sumptuous lodgings at the West Gate.[8] Bath was celebrated also for its fine hostelries and taverns, such as The Three Tuns, The Catherine Wheel, The Cross Bow and The Cross Dagger.

While Louise was in Bath her friend Sir Joseph Williamson, a Secretary of State, sent her a consignment of her favourite Rhenish wines from the Windsor cellars. She also sent for six dozen bottles of white wine from the Duke of York's cellars in St James's Palace.[9]

On 5th July, the day after her return to London, the Duchess went in her coach to dine with the King at Windsor Castle, but much to her disappointment he did not invite her to stay the night.[10] Honoré de Courtin, the dapper little diplomat from Normandy, who was soon to supersede Ruvigny as ambassador in London, reported to his master, Louis XIV, that the Duchess of Portsmouth's visit to Bath had greatly improved her health, "but she is still a little thin. She hopes that by resting to become plump again".

Naturally Nell Gwyn took every opportunity of ridiculing Louise. Courtin wrote delightfully to his Foreign Minister "that the actress, who is known as Mistris Nesle, affected to be greatly alarmed at the Duchess of Portsmouth's return, and declared that she would have to arm herself to the teeth to protect herself against the resentment which would be bound to fall on her owing to the frequent visits Charles had paid her during the absence of the official mistress".[11]

Louis XIV's appointment of Honoré Courtin, Seigneur de Chanteroine, as French Ambassador in London in May 1676 was an extremely sagacious one, for the former Councillor of the Parliament of Rouen* had a genius for petticoat diplomacy. He was a diplomat with a ripe wit, a good judgment and was very

* At the age of 14.

subtle and clever. His letters to his old friends Pomponne and Louvois are more entertaining than those of any of the other ambassadors at the court of Charles II. Though he seemed frivolous and pleasure-loving in temperament Courtin, in fact, served his country with devotion and remarkable ability. King Louis thought so highly of Courtin that he invited him to Marli, an honour which he did not give to any other member of his profession. He remained a great favourite of the King's until his death in 1703. Louis allowed him the privilege of appearing before him without a court mantle, with a cane and Councillor's ruffles.

Courtin enjoyed himself enormously in London, but grumbled at the climate. It is related that King Charles advised him to wear flannel underclothing to protect himself against the English climate, "a plain sort of woollen stuff woven in the cottages of Wales".

Before undertaking his embassy Courtin was given careful instructions on 1st April as to how he was to conduct himself. He was commanded to treat the Duchess of Portsmouth with the deepest respect. It was suspected, however, that she had formed too close an alliance with Lord Danby, who was considered to be anti-French. Consequently it was necessary to be wary of her. He was told that the influence that the ladies always have on Charles II renders their good or bad offices of considerable importance. A passage in Courtin's instructions reads: "The arrival of the Duchesse Mazarin has caused a great stir in that court. The King of England appears to have been attracted by her beauty, and though the affair has so far been conducted with some secrecy, it is likely that this growing passion will take the first place in the heart of that prince."[12] Courtin's delicate duty was to ascertain what the sentiments and intentions of the Duchesse Mazarin were towards King Louis. There was reason for believing that Hortense was annoyed with the King of France because he was not applying pressure on her husband, the Duc Mazarin, to have her pension increased from eight thousand crowns to twenty thousand crowns.

Courtin certainly handled both Louise and Hortense extremely adroitly. He took infinite pains to study their characters.

The summer of 1676 was warm, and London's riverside had almost a southern air. Courtin reported to Pomponne on 2nd July that the King of England bathed every evening. "He goes

out on the river in four or five little boats with three or four persons," he wrote. There were gay parties on the Thames. Hortense
did not accompany Charles when he bathed in the river. "The
ladies do not go with the men," wrote Courtin to Louis XIV.
"It is the only decency which they observe in this country."[13]

On 8th July the Duchess of Portsmouth gave a magnificent
dinner party in honour of the Ruvignys, who were about to
return to France. After dinner three musicians of the King of
France named La Forest, Gandomeche and Gilet performed at a
concert. When Charles came in for at least an hour after dinner,
Louise was unable to conceal her jealousy. She observed him as he
obviously enjoyed the beauty of the music, beating time with his
hands. Then she turned to the conductor: "Play for His Majesty
a Spanish song, 'Mate me con non mirar mas no mate me con
celos'."* Her guests did not trouble to refrain from laughing,
while Charles's saturnine face looked richly amused. He was
especially attentive to Louise on this evening, but Courtin, who
was present, suspected that Charles's purpose was to find opportunities to deceive her.

Louise was certain that Hortense was already Charles's mistress,
and that he visited her in the apartments of the Countess of
Sussex,† his illegitimate daughter by the Duchess of Cleveland,
which lay above his own apartments in Whitehall. These were
formerly lived in by Barbara when Countess of Castlemaine.
She was now in France, where she shrilly warned Louis XIV of
the dangers which encompassed him if "Madame de Portsmouth"
were to fall from power. Louise on her part keenly resented that
Charles was making assignations with her rival in the apartments
of Lady Sussex. This lady who was *enceinte* and passionately fond
of her friend Hortense Mazarin, had made a powerful enemy in
antagonising Louise. Some of the courtiers openly asserted that
Anne Fitzroy Lady Sussex was really the daughter of Lord
Chesterfield, the Duchess of Cleveland's earliest lover. At this
period she was scarcely more than a child.

The rivalry between the three mistresses, Louise de Keroualle,
Hortense Mazarin and Nell Gwyn inspired Edmund Waller to
write a poem "The Triple Combat":

---

* 'Kill me by not looking at me, but do not kill me with jealousy.'
† She married in August 1674 Thomas Lennard, Lord Dacre, who became
later Earl of Sussex.

When thro' the world fair Mazarine had run
Bright as her fellow-traveller the sun;
Hither at length the ROMAN eagle flies,
As the last triumph of her conq'ring eyes.
As heir to JULIUS she may pretend
A second time to make this island bend.
But PORTSMOUTH,* springing from the antient race
Of BRITONS, which the Saxons here did chase,
As they great CAESAR did oppose, makes head,
And does against this new invader lead.
That goodly nymph, the taller of the two,
Careless and fearless to the field does go.
Becoming blushes on the other wait,
And her young look excuses want of height.
Beauty gives courage, for she knows the day
Must not be won the AMAZONIAN way.

Nell is "the lovely Chloris" of the poem.

Meanwhile Courtin chaffed Pomponne in his amusing letters: "Since you wish to know how I am in England, I may tell you that up to now the air has not done me any harm. Were I younger and less wise than I have become through your example I should find plenty to occupy my time very agreeably. Madame Mazarin is coming to dine with me today with the Countess of Sussex, eldest daughter of the Duchess of Cleveland. Near me dwells Madam de Middleton, who is the most beautiful woman in England. Poor Saint-Evremond has fallen passionately in love with her in his dotage [*sur la fin de ses jours*]." He told Pomponne that Montagu, who had a mind to conduct an intrigue for the King with her, had himself fallen in love with her. The gossips asserted that Montagu was being unfaithful to the beautiful Jane Middleton.[14] It is unlikely, however, that Montagu's interest in Hortense was other than political. It was in the house of his intriguing sister, Lady Harvey, that the King often met Hortense.

Yet Charles still contrived to visit Louise every day, though the courtiers stayed with the King in her apartments and did not bother to withdraw, which they would have formerly done.

Courtin reported to Pomponne that when poor Louise gave herself a black eye, Bab May, an obsequious courtier, remarked to the King that she would probably like to black the other one also to make herself look more like Madame Mazarin.[15] It was

* Louise de Keroualle.

just the sort of malicious remark one would expect this man to make, and Charles should have reproved him for it.

Courtin was well aware that the English nation hated France. Even Lord Danby, the Lord Treasurer, with whom Louise had been intimate, had not the courtesy of calling on the French Ambassador. Courtin lived in a house, 8 St James's Square, which was just becoming fashionable. Apple Tree Yard off St James's Square indicates that it once lay in the countryside. He found it very convenient for nocturnal walks in St James's Park on summer nights, particularly in the moonlight. Sometimes he stealthily left Whitehall in a hired carriage, so as not to be recognized. He met his agents in dimly lit taverns and other places in London. He wrote to the Foreign Minister: "You cannot imagine how five or six bottles of wine sent at the right moment smooth the temper, because when a session of Parliament ends, people go to dine at each other's homes, and this is the moment when factions are formed."

Courtin was the ideal representative of his country in London in the summer of 1676. By temperament he was pleasure-loving and knew that it was either necessary to be *un homme de plaisir* in England, or never get anywhere at all. We get delightful glimpses of him watching with pleasure Hortense Mazarin as she danced the *furlana* to the guitar, like a Neapolitan gipsy. He formed a sincere friendship with Louise, and he was more charitable than his friend Louvois in France in showing sympathy for the favourite in her misfortunes. Louise made this charming little sprightly diplomat her chief confidant. On 2nd August he visited her in Whitehall, to be greeted by Louise, her face swollen with tears. He told Pomponne:

Yesterday evening I saw something which aroused all my pity and which would perhaps have touched you, wise and serious as you are. I went to see Madame de Portsmouth. She opened her heart to me in the presence of two of her maids, of whom perchance you know one named Ballex, who formerly was in the service of the Comtesse de Plessis. Madame de Portsmouth explained to me what grief the frequent visits of the King of England to Madame de Sussex cause her every day. The two girls remained propped against the wall with downcast eyes; their mistress let loose a torrent of tears. Sobs and sighs interrupted her speech. Indeed, I have never beheld a sadder or more touching sight.[16]

Courtin advised her in her own interest to conceal her grief, if possible; remaining with her until midnight. No wonder he was so popular with the ladies, for he knew just how to handle them.

Although he personally found her attractive, Courtin was becoming apprehensive as to the increasing ascendancy of the Duchesse Mazarin. In St James's Square he pondered that at all costs Louise and Hortense must not be allowed to form two opposing parties. If this should happen, there was acute danger that Louise's enemies would support Hortense. He now saw the urgent necessity of trying to persuade the two ladies to make friends with each other, a far more difficult task than negotiating peace between two countries. That he ultimately succeeded to some extent proves his ability as a diplomat.

Meanwhile, Courtin gave lively parties for Hortense and her friend Lady Sussex at the Embassy. He wrote the Marquis de Louvois that among his guests were Madame Hamilton's sister, and Mademoiselle Trevor, the prettiest of the Duchess of York's maids of honour who was not displeasing to the Duke. Also a Secretary of State who he had known in Cologne. This was Sir Joseph Williamson, an excellent musician, and capable of dancing country dances for six hours on end without stopping. Williamson was the son of a poor clergyman in Cumberland, who had served under Lord Arlington, although he later showed him no gratitude for his advancement.[17] Courtin wrote Louvois: "I shall play at ombre with Madame Mazarin, and we shall let the young people dance as much as they like ... I shall never degrade myself like all the other foreign ambassadors, who all keep mistresses—beginning with Monsier Vanbeunengen [the Dutch Ambassador], who is as much in love as you were at the time when you so often went to Chelles."[18] This is a delightful touch, just the sort of chaff one would expect between two old friends.

Louvois replied: "The description of the party you were going to give made me long to be there. I should not have joined the Secretary of State who was prepared to dance for six hours on end, and I don't know the first card in ombre, so that all I could have done would have been to fasten my eyes on Madame Mazarin."

Fortunately Courtin was present on one occasion when the three mistresses, Louise de Keroualle, Hortense Mazarin and Nell Gwyn all made their appearance. Courtin reported to Pomponne: "Everything passed off quite gaily and with many civilities from one to the other, but I do not suppose that in all England it would be possible to get together three people more obnoxious to one another."[19]

After Louise had departed Nell Gwyn in her vulgar way boasted shamelessly to the Ambassador about her relations with Charles II, telling him that she did much better service to the King than the Duchess of Portsmouth. Courtin did not take "the frisking comedian" very seriously, but he could hardly restrain his delight when she lifted up her petticoats for his inspection, to reveal extremely elegant undergarments and her shapely legs.

One day Courtin by chance met Lady Harvey and Jane Middleton, whom he greatly admired at the theatre. He now suggested that they should both come to supper with him one evening. If they cared to bring Louise and Hortense with them he would be delighted. So the intriguing party was held, and the rival ladies sat opposite each other at the French Ambassador's table. Lady Sophie Bulkeley, a friend of Louise's, accompanied her. She was a younger sister of La Belle Stuart, and ten years later was among the Jacobites who attended Queen Mary of Modena* in her exile at Saint-Germain. So excellent were the wines and food provided by the Ambassador that his diplomacy had the desired effect. The brilliant idea of locking the Duchess of Portsmouth and the Duchesse Mazarin together in a closet suddenly occurred to him. To everybody's surprise when the door was unlocked, Louise and Hortense came forth skipping and laughing. Henceforward, although the friendship was hardly sincere, Louise and Hortense could occasionally be seen in a coach together. Perhaps Louise had the intelligence to realize by this time that Hortense, owing to her mercurial and amorous temperament was unlikely to remain Charles's mistress for long. Hortense, however, assured Courtin that she would always be loyal to France. Anthony à Wood related that about Christmas the Duchess of Portsmouth went to the King's Chapel twice to attend the Protestant service. He alleged that Louise pretended to turn Protestant, though this is unlikely to be true.

It was a bitterly cold winter, so that the Thames was frozen over. People went over in their coaches and carts to buy brandy and wine from vendors, who had erected huts "made of snow"; some went on foot, lighting their way with the help of torches.

Throughout the spring of 1677 Hortense's ascendancy seemed assured. At the opening of Parliament it was clear to everybody

* Duchess of York until 1685.

that she was Charles's mistress, for she was in a very prominent position, raised above all the other ladies behind the throne.[20] About this time Hortense was even more extravagant than her wont, and people gossiped that she was receiving a generous pension from the King.★

Like her friend Buckingham, Hortense was a brilliant mimic. When Valenciennes was captured by Louis XIV's armies commanded by himself, Hortense amused the French Ambassador by crying in a hoarse voice, like a news-hawker: "Capture of Valenciennes by the King's army commanded by His Majesty!" "Several times I felt inclined to curse the hawker", admitted the diplomat, ruefully to Louvois.[21]

It is sad to relate that the little Countess of Sussex, who was later almost as wanton as her mother, the Duchess of Cleveland, was now separated from the Duchesse Mazarin. Barbara wrote from France exasperating letters to Charles II arguing that Lady Sussex should return to her husband in the country. On his part Lord Sussex resented his wife's passionate friendship with the fascinating Hortense. In this bitter quarrel between mother and daughter, Charles supported Lady Sussex. Not only was he obliged to endure the abuse of the Duchess of Cleveland, but Louise nagged him about Lady Sussex, saying she was the intermediary in his liaison with Hortense. Hortense and Lady Sussex were fond of practising fencing in St James's Park. After they had caused a sensation one night by appearing in the park with drawn swords under their night-gowns, Lord Sussex insisted on taking his wife to his country estate, Hurstmonceaux Castle in Sussex.

Hortense's inconstant temperament made it certain that she was incapable of remaining faithful to one lover for long. During the winter of 1676-7 the elegant young Prince of Monaco visited London. Soon he was passionately in love with her, but Courtin informed Louvois that the prince's deep melancholy made it doubtful whether his ardent pleading with the lady would be successful. In the summer of 1677, however, the Prince, perhaps tiring of Hortense's feigned resistance, announced his imminent departure for Monaco. His pretext was that the London climate did not agree with him. It was then that the Duchesse Mazarin became the prince's mistress, which so angered Charles II for a time that he revoked his handsome pension. He soon, however,

---

★ It was actually £4,000.

restored it. Although Hortense occasionally gave Charles II her favours in the future, her ascendancy was over.

Meanwhile, Louise had again been taking the waters at Bath. After her return to London, Courtin wrote to Pomponne: "Her skin has grown again so fair and fresh that I cannot imagine how Charles, palled as he is with beauty, will be long in her company without becoming once more her slave."

The Duchess of Portsmouth returned in triumph to court, and her ascendancy was never again seriously threatened for the rest of the King's life. Attempts were made at times to supplant her, and she was as much disliked as ever.

NOTES

1. Forneron, *Louise de Keroualle*.
2. Cyril Hughes Hartmann, *The Vagabond Duchess*.
3. "The Picture and Character of the Duchess Mazarin", a letter written by Saint Real.
4. Cyril Hughes Hartmann, *op. cit.*
5. Correspondance Angleterre, CXVII, fol. 149.
6. March 1676.
7. Cyril Hughes Hartmann, *op. cit.*
8. Charles E. Davis, *The Bathes of Bathe's Ayde in the Reign of Charles II as illustrated by the drawings of the Kings and Queens Bath.*
9. Jeanine Delpech, *The Life and Times of the Duchess of Portsmouth.*
10. Honoré de Courtin to Pomponne, 6th July.
11. Correspondance Angleterre, CXIX, fol. 1.
12. Correspondance Angleterre, CXXa, fol. 17.
13. Correspondance Angleterre, CXIX, fol. 1.
14. Correspondance Angleterre, CXIX, fol. 15.
15. Correspondance Angleterre, CXIX, fol. 87.
16. Cyril Hughes Hartmann, *op. cit.*
17. A Secretary of State since July 1674. *Memoirs and Correspondence of John Evelyn*, II.
18. Cyril Hughes Hartmann, *op. cit.*
19. Correspondance Angleterre, CXXII, fol. 52.
20. Cyril Hughes Hartmann, *op. cit.*
21. Correspondance Angleterre, CXXIIIc, fol. 118.

EIGHT

STRUGGLES AND INTRIGUES

Honoré de Courtin was succeeded by Paul Barrillon d'Amoncourt, Marquis de Branges as French Ambassador. Courtin was on the whole an honourable man, but too scrupulous to suit the policy of Louis XIV in 1677. For some time Courtin had been complaining that the foggy air of London was harming his health. At the beginning of May Barrillon arrived in England, ultimately to re-place him. Before leaving London Courtin introduced Barrillon to the Duchess of Portsmouth. He told his master, Louis XIV, that it was essential for a French Ambassador to call on the Duchess of Portsmouth every day, and at no matter what hour.

I studied many of the letters of Barrillon in the Quai d'Orsay and felt a reluctant admiration for the astuteness and industry of the diplomat. Yet he lacked the sparkling wit of his predecessor. Pomponne prompted Barrillon as to the important role of the Duchess of Portsmouth at the English court. The new French Am-bassador was cynical and worldly, and knew how to ingratiate him-self with the ladies of Charles II's Court. He came of a legal family and his training was invaluable in his dealings with unscrupulous politicians. Barrillon had no illusions about human nature. He has been described as a master in the art of corrupting men, and accused of a cold ruthlessness in concealing his contempt,[1] for those whom he corrupted. His account books reveal that many prominent people were on his pay-roll. Lord Berkshire, a member of the Court Party and of the Government received a bribe of £1,000, while Edward Coleman, who was for a time secretary of the Duchess of York, was paid £360.[2] He was later arrested as a traitor and charged with giving information to the French. The Republican, Algernon Sydney, a brother of the diplomat, Henry Sydney, received a bribe of £500 from the French King every parliamentary session.[3]

The time is now ripe to discuss the political parties in 1677. The

Court Party, ultimately to be known as the Tory Party, was led by Lord Danby who had a real talent for organization. Opposed to it was the Country Party, later known as the Whigs, originally founded by Sir Anthony Ashley-Cooper about 1667 in order to sustain the Protestant religion and the liberties of England. It can be maintained that some of its members were at first inspired by noble ideals, but were later corrupted.

The origin of the terms "Tory" and "Whig" is very curious. They were applied as abusive nicknames, a tory being an Irish Catholic outlaw, and a whig a Scottish Covenanting fanatic.

Anthony Ashley-Cooper, later Earl of Shaftesbury, was one of the most able and unscrupulous politicians of his time. He was born at Wimborne St Giles in the county of Dorset on 22nd July 1621. At first he supported Charles I, then he deserted to the Commonwealth. Having no fixed principles he later abandoned the Commonwealth, because his political instinct told him that the Restoration of Charles II was inevitable.[4] Ambition, controversy, the love of conflict and the pursuit of power were the dominant impulses of his chequered life.[5] Ashley-Cooper was a member of the Cabal Government, and later became Lord Chancellor in 1672. A year later he quarrelled with the King and the Duke of York and, as already mentioned, was dismissed from office. When he was deprived of the Great Seal he exclaimed with a dangerous glint in his eyes: "It is only laying down my gown and putting on my sword."[6] Henceforward he was to become Charles II's vindictive and implacable enemy, and the history of the years 1676-1682 is really the struggle between the King and Shaftesbury in Parliament and the country.

Shaftesbury possessed a fiery eloquence in the House of Lords, and he was a master in the art of propaganda and in inflaming the minds of the rabble against the Court Party. He organized the vast anti-Catholic processions through the London streets on the birthday of Queen Elizabeth I, 17th November, from 1677 onwards when an effigy of the Pope was burnt. London today with its demonstrations and periodical waves of violence was not unlike the great city in the latter part of Charles II's reign. In this age of protest Shaftesbury would feel curiously at home. From 1674 onwards he was the avowed enemy of the Catholics, who were about twelve thousand in number in a population of over five million people. The minds of the rabble were riddled with a kind of confused fear and hatred of the Catholics. Although the Papists were

Louise de Keroualle, Duchess of Portsmouth, by Sir Peter Lely (*by courtesy of the Earl Spencer and the Courtauld Institute of Art*)

Palatium Regis prope Londinum, *vulgo* White-hall.

A print of Whitehall in about 1648 by Wenceslas Hollar (*by courtesy of the British Museum*)

comparatively few in number they were extremely vociferous and influential. They were regarded as the spear-head of a mighty propagandist power overseas, France, whose intention was the subversion of the existing policy of the country.[7]

A year before, James Duke of York had made the firm decision to cease to attend the services of the Church of England. It was freely acknowledged that he now took the Sacrament in accordance with Roman rites. Shaftesbury became his most bitter enemy, for he argued that James, as the King's heir presumptive, should be altogether excluded from the throne.

The Hatton Correspondence has an interesting, though macabre, account of the Pope-burning ceremonies in London on Saturday 17th November 1677 when "a most costly pope was caryed by four persons in divers habits and ye effigies of two divells whispering in his eares, his belly filled full of live cats who squawked most hideously as soone as they felt the fire; the common saying all ye while it was ye language of ye pope and ye Divel in a dialogue between them. A tierce of claret set out before ye Temple Gate for ye common people." It seems to us a cruel and barbaric ceremony, and it was said to cost £40. It was clever of the Whigs to be so generous with the claret so as to gain the goodwill of the people.

The Earl with "his pigmy body"[8] was in constant pain owing to an accident in his youth, when the pole of his coach pierced his side. It is therefore charitable to think that his rancour against his opponents was aggravated by his physical troubles.

He certainly had a poor opinion of the Duchess of Portsmouth, but it was extremely biased. He described her as "a creature of France, a Frenchwoman by birth of the lowest of the gentry there, of no fortune, of worse fame, her being mistress to a great person preferred her to a court service, a very indifferent beauty, and of wit hardly enough for a woman (her cunning and French mode supplying that defect)."[9] That she was of humble birth is absolutely false, for she sprang from an aristocratic family. It is obvious that she possessed considerable beauty when we look at her portraits.

In the autumn of 1677 Prince William of Orange, Louis XIV's most relentless enemy, visited England with the object of detaching his uncle, Charles II, from the French alliance. He decided to ask for the hand of the Princess Mary, elder daughter of the Duke of York in marriage, though negotiations had been in progress for some time. William was twenty-seven at this time, a thin, rather

7

austere young man, who seemed churlish and abrupt. He wore his own hair instead of the fashionable periwig.[10]

Whilst staying with his uncles at Newmarket William made his formal request for the hand of the princess, an attractive girl of only fifteen. Two influential people, who strongly favoured the match, were Lord Danby and the diplomat Sir William Temple. After much haggling and evasive behaviour Charles II agreed to it, although the Duke of York was very reluctant to give his consent and was finally forced to do so by the King.

After the Court returned to Whitehall, William had the intelligence to make frequent visits to the Duchess of Portsmouth in her apartments, and succeeded in ingratiating himself with her. The new French Ambassador, Barrillon, occasionally found William of Orange with Louise. He knew that his master the King of France was strongly opposed to the marriage, but by 22nd October the negotiations were so far advanced that it seemed futile to oppose it. He wrote to Pomponne on 1st November asking for instructions and suggesting to the Foreign Minister that it might be the wisest policy to accept the inevitable and compliment the Prince of Orange on the success of his suit. The mass of Englishmen on the whole rejoiced that Princess Mary was about to marry the Protestant Prince William, the enemy of the hated King of France.

The Duchess of Portsmouth with her subtle political instinct realized that William of Orange would get what he wanted, and that it was useless to oppose him. Was she also actuated by animosity against the Duke of York, whom she disliked? She was well aware that York only gave way out of deference to the King's wishes. She attended the festivities held in honour of the Prince of Orange.

The marriage was celebrated on the evening of 4th November, the Princess's birthday, in Mary's bedchamber in St James's Palace. As King Charles drew the curtains of the marriage bed, he exclaimed lustily: "Now nephew to your work! Hey St George for England!"

After the Prince of Orange and his bride had sailed for Holland, the Duchess of Portsmouth became ill and was obliged to take to her bed from about 11th December till 20th January 1678. It was at her bedside that Charles received the French Ambassador, Barrillon, who told him of King Louis's anger and mortification at the wedding. It would have required all Louise's tact to reduce the tension between the two, though Barrillon assured King Charles that he could still count on the King of France. We know that Barrillon found Charles II very secretive on occasions. It was very difficult to delve into the hidden recesses of his Machiavellian mind and to discover his true intentions. Louis XIV, too, felt a strong sense of injury and blamed Lord Danby for his part in forwarding the match.

Harry Savile refers to her illness in a letter to Lord Rochester on 17th December 1677. He wrote: "My Lady Portsmouth has been ill to the greatest degree. The King imputes her cure to his dropps, but her confessor to the Virgin Mary, to whom hee is said to have promised in her name that in case of recovery she should have no more commerce with that known enemy to virginity and chastity the monarke of Great Britain, but that she should return to a cloyster in little Brittany and there end her dayes . . ." Savile told his friend that a lovely young French actress, aged fifteen, among a company of comedians now playing at Whitehall had more beauty and sweetness since "a friend of ours" left the stage. He is referring to Nell Gwyn. Savile added in his humorous way: "It were a shame to the nation shee [the French comedienne] should carry away a maydenhead shee pretends to have brought and that noe body heer has either witt or addresse or money enough to goe to the price of."[11] The King heaved a mighty sigh, and said in his cynical way that nobody but Sir George Downing or Lord Ranelagh could possibly afford to purchase her.

When Louise believed herself to be dying, she took her crucifix in her hand and warned her royal lover of the danger he ran, unless he forsook his mistresses and lived a virtuous life.[12] While she was ill she was only too well aware that Mrs Fraser, daughter of the King's Chief Physician, and others were trying to supplant her. The lot of a royal mistress is not an easy one. Hardly recovered from her illness, Louise made an effort to get up to go to a French play in her sedan chair. She took her place by Charles II, who was with the Duchesse Mazarin.

In France the voluptuous, sensual Madame de Montespan still reigned as Louis XIV's mistress, but her days were numbered. Madame de Sévigné described her in the summer of 1676 after she had visited Bourbon to take the waters: "Her beauty and her shape are really surprising." She was dressed in French point, her hair fell in a thousand curls very low upon her cheeks, she wore on her head black ribbons, and her hair was braided with the pearls which

had once belonged to the Maréchale de l'Hôpital. She was as fond
of jewels as Louise de Keroualle, and possessed pendants of
diamonds of a great value. Yet her position was in reality much
less secure than Louise's, partly because of her temperament.
Despite her faults, her malevolence, and her cruelty, Montespan
was magnificent.

During the summer of 1678 the Duchess of Cleveland and her
daughter, Lady Sussex, were both in Paris, and there was much
discord between the two ladies. According to Harry Savile, now
the English Ambassador in France, Ralph Montagu had taken the
opportunity of seducing Lady Sussex while her mother was in
England. As Montagu had been a former lover of the Duchess of
Cleveland's he certainly had a way with the ladies. Barbara now
hated Montagu, and in a letter to Charles II written in Paris she
abused the ambassador and at the same time complained of her
daughter's behaviour.[13] She told the King that Montagu had tried
to induce her to enter into a plot whereby the Lord Treasurer,
Danby, and the Duchess of Portsmouth might be ruined. Barbara
assured King Charles that she wished no harm to "my Lady
Portsmouth", nor the Lord Treasurer, but that she had told
Montagu that the devil was not more designing than he was.
She wrote:

> I was never so surprised in my holle life time, as I was at my coming
> hither to find my Lady Sussex gone from my house ... she has
> every day gone out with the Embassadour, and has often layen four
> dayes together at my house and sent for her meate to the Embas-
> sadour ... this has made so great a noise at Paris, that she is now
> the holle discours. I am so much afflicted that I can hardly write
> this for crying to see that a child that I doated on, as I did on her,
> should make me so ill a return to join with the worst of men to
> ruin me.

It would hardly endear Montagu to the King to be told by
Barbara that the Ambassador despised Charles in his heart, and
also the Duke of York. For his part he fervently hoped "that
Parliament would send you both to travell, for you were a dull
governable fool, and the Duke a wilful fool, so that it was yett
better to have you than him."

It was true that Ralph Montagu was now Danby's vindictive
enemy, and was determined to ruin him, probably because he
himself aspired to the position of Lord Treasurer. Louis XIV also
had not forgiven Lord Danby for promoting the wedding of the

Princess Mary to Prince William of Orange. He was at this period intent on stirring up as much trouble as possible for the King of England. At the instigation of the King of France, Montagu revealed to the House of Commons a very confidential letter written by Danby during March 1678 regarding a payment of six million livres which King Charles was to receive as the price of withdrawal from the treaty with Holland, for the postponement of the session of Parliament.[14] The many enemies of the Lord Treasurer were jubilant at his downfall. Although the King attempted to save his minister by proroguing Parliament, and later dissolving it, the new parliament which came into being during March 1679, in a mood of vengeance pressed for Danby's impeachment. He was later sent to the Tower, where he was incarcerated for five years.

It was now necessary for the Duchess of Portsmouth to look for another political associate.

NOTES

1. Forneron, *Louise de Keroualle.*
2. Correspondance Angleterre, CXXX, fol. 68.
3. Correspondance Angleterre, CXXX, fol. 148.
4. Hesketh Pearson, *Charles II, his life and likeness.*
5. Christie, *Life of Lord Shaftesbury.*
6. John, Lord Campbell, *Lives of the Lord Chancellors*, III.
7. F. C. Turner, *James II.*
8. John Dryden, "Absalom and Achitophel".
9. Shaftesbury's Paper, written by him at the opening of the New Parliament, 9th March 1679.
10. Nesca A. Robb, *William of Orange*, II.
11. *The Rochester-Savile Letters.*
12. Madame de Scudéry writing to Bussy Rabutin.
13. Harleian MSS. 7006, fol. 171. B.M.
14. F. C. Turner, *op. cit.*

NINE

THE POPISH TERROR

Never has there been an epoch in our history when men were more blinded by hatred, intolerance, fear and fanaticism than 1678–81. It was a period when the people of England went mad, deluded by false propaganda and by the powers of suggestion of evil and depraved men. London was a city of terror by day and by night, seething with tensions and with violence. A wave of spiritual darkness engulfed our country. To understand what transpired during the autumn of 1678 and the following years, it is necessary to fathom the depths of the natural hatred and mistrust of the Papists. A difficult task for us living in a more enlightened age, at least as far as religious tolerance is concerned. Men have long memories and they recalled with horror the Marian persecutions and blood-bath, now over 120 years ago. The minds of the rabble were inflamed with primitive passions, and obsessed with hatred of the Papist minority, particularly of Charles II's Portuguese-born Queen Catherine of Braganza and of his most important mistress, the Duchess of Portsmouth, a foreigner and a Papist. The Duke of York, now an openly acknowledged Roman Catholic, was extremely unpopular.

John Dryden in his great satirical poem "Absalom and Achitophel" wrote of the Popish plot with insight:

> Some truth there was, but dash'd and brewed with lyes;
> To please the Fools, and puzzle all the Wise:
> SUCCEEDING times did equal folly call,
> Believing nothing, or believing all . . .
> This plot, which fail'd for want of common sense,
> Had yet a deep and dangerous consequence;
> For as, when raging fevers boyle the blood,
> The standing lake soon floats into a flood,
> And every hostile humour, which before
> Slept quiet in its channels, bubbles o'er;

So, several factions from this first ferment
Work up to foam and threat the Government.[1]

When published on 21st November 1681 this poem had a larger
sale than any publication down to the end of Queen Anne's reign,
with the exception of the sermon for which Dr Sacheverel was
impeached.[2]

One day in the high summer of 1678—13th August—Charles II
was walking in St James's Park at a rapid pace, well ahead of his
attendants when he was accosted by a man called Christopher
Kirkby, who warned the King that he had personal knowledge of
a plot to assassinate him. Charles, who read men's faces like books,
thought Kirkby's expression vaguely familiar, and it suddenly
flashed on him that he had once been employed as an assistant in
his laboratory. Charles told the fellow to refer the matter to
Chiffinch, and resumed his walk. Next day he left for Windsor
after ordering Lord Danby, then Lord Treasurer, to probe into the
affair.

The investigations proved extremely alarming. This monstrous
plot, so eagerly fastened on by the over-credulous, was said to be
the discovery of a meddling clergyman named Israel Tonge, a
former Rector of Aston in Hertfordshire, and the notorious Titus
Oates, a renegade Jesuit novice and son of an Anabaptist preacher.
It is indeed uncertain who invented the Popish Plot. According to
a contemporary, the Honourable Roger North, Lord Shaftesbury
was the contriver and inventor, but North was too biased to be
reliable. On the other hand, Lord Campbell[3] maintained that
Shaftesbury was not the originator of the plot, but that he made
great mischief out of it. He told Alderman Sir Thomas Player that
unless precautions were taken for the defence of the City of London
"all the Protestant citizens might rise next morning with their
throats cut". Although he was far too intelligent to believe in it,
he used his great gifts in making propaganda and creating panic
among the people.

The story of the original informer, Titus Oates, as told to the
Council was that the Pope, King Louis XIV and the General of the
Jesuits had all united in a dastardly plot to assassinate the King, set
up the Duke of York, plunge Ireland in civil war, impose Catholicism by sword and destroy English commerce.[4] Roger North
described Oates: "He is a low man, of an ill-cut, very short neck;
and his visage and features are most particular. His mouth is the

centre of his face . . . he has an enormous chin, little shifty eyes and a grave, prophetic utterance." His voice was loud and harsh and he affected an aristocratic drawl. Maybe Oates's grotesque ugliness was the psychological cause of his depravity, for the man had always been despised and hated since boyhood. That Shaftesbury, for his own ambitious ends, provided financial support for this rogue and backed him when he gave false evidence, cannot be denied.

Charles II was far too shrewd ever to believe in the reality of the plot. He told Barrillon at Newmarket on 31st October that he was convinced that it was an imposture.[5]

Again, Sir John Reresby was present one evening in the Duchess of Portsmouth's apartments when the King and Danby were also present. "The King told me," relates Reresby, "that he took Titus Oates's story to be some artifice, and that he did not believe one word of the plot."[6] Many of the Council, however, believed in its machinations and that it was inspired by the Papists.

The King caught Oates lying on at least two occasions. When he declared in his vehement way before the Council that Don John of Austria had promised to provide finance for the murder of the King, Charles asked Oates to describe Don John. He replied: "Oh, he is lean, tall and black." Charles smiled and remained silent, for he knew that Don John was short, fat and red-haired. Oates then stated that the plot was at first hatched in the house of the Jesuit fathers near the Louvre in Paris. Charles could not refrain from saying: "Man, the Jesuits have no house within a mile of the Louvre." Oates made a sworn deposition of his evidence before Sir Edmund Berry Godfrey, a popular London magistrate, who owned a thriving business as merchant of wood and coal in Hartshorn Lane near Charing Cross. He was the sixth son of Sir Thomas Godfrey, a knight who hailed from Kent, and was educated at Westminster School.[7]

The murder of this magistrate is a fascinating unsolved mystery. Godfrey was an exceptionally tall man, who walked with a characteristic stoop and wore a black periwig. He usually wore a broad-brimmed hat with a gold band. On 12th October he left his house, and was never seen alive again. Five days later his body was found in a ditch in the fields at the foot of Primrose Hill. Barrillon, the French Ambassador, informed Louis XIV that "the marks on his throat suggest that he has been strangled".[8] It is probable that his body had been carried to the place of discovery and transfixed with a sword. Godfrey was a steadfast Protestant and a zealous and conscientious magistrate, but he was known to be on friendly terms with prominent Papists such as Edward Coleman. For some time before his death Godfrey had been depressed. He feared for his own safety for he had warned Coleman to burn incriminating papers.

One authority, Sir James Fitzjames Stephen, believed that Oates was the murderer, while Roger North maintained that the patrons of Oates killed Godfrey in order to give credence to the plot. Another ingenious theory put forward by Mr J. G. Muddiman was that Godfrey was murdered for reasons of revenge by that drunken rake the Earl of Pembroke, the Duchess of Portsmouth's brother-in-law.[9] Others alleged that Godfrey committed suicide. My first opinion was that the magistrate was murdered by a notorious criminal whom he had apprehended stealing valuables from corpses in the pest-houses during the plague year (1665). It may have been an act of revenge, but if so the thief certainly bided his time. However, that cannot be the truth, because this depraved criminal was later transported to the colonies. It is more likely that the magistrate was murdered by the friends of Oates because he knew too much.

Whatever the truth, Shaftesbury with diabolical zest made use of Godfrey's murder to give reality to the plot. At every street corner, in the taverns and in the coffee-houses the cry arose: "The Papists have murdered Sir Edmund Berry Godfrey."[10] With his instinctive feeling for propaganda, and talent for organization, Shaftesbury incited the Whig party to attempt to derange the legitimate succession to the throne, and he was nearly successful in his objective.[11] Godfrey's corpse became an important figure in the dramatic annual ceremonies of Pope Burnings, organized by the Green Ribbon Club.

During Charles II's reign an enterprising London citizen named William Dockray organized a penny post which delivered letters and parcels six or eight times a day in the district surrounding the Exchange.[12] Such was the fever aroused by Godfrey's murder, that Titus Oates publicized false rumours that the penny post was a Popish contrivance, and that the bags contained treasonable material.

Excitement and alarm among the population was intense. People feared to sleep at night, lest they were assassinated by the Papists. As the autumn days gradually merged into winter London was gripped by blind, unreasoning terror. It was a tragic city, pervaded by hatred. Night after night the trained bands stood to arms and paraded the streets as if an insurrection were expected before morning.[13] Fashionable ladies, like Lady Shaftesbury, never walked abroad without loaded pistols in their muffs. It was the fashion for them to have scenes from the plot painted on their fans.

Oates made wild charges against the Catholics which he was seldom able to substantiate. On Sunday, 24th November, he insolently accused Queen Catherine of high treason. He maintained that she had been aware of a project of her physician, Sir George Wakeman, to poison the King, her husband, although everybody knew she adored him. Forneron[14] criticized Charles II in very harsh terms for his alleged cowardice at this juncture without any real justification, but he was at least manly enough to champion his wife and to protect her from her enemies. He said: "They think I have a mind to a new wife; but for all that I will not see an innocent woman abused."

Louise de Keroualle, Duchess of Portsmouth, observed events from her apartments in Whitehall with increasing apprehension. She was well aware that she had many enemies in Parliament, and that she was detested in the country. Once in a scornful mood she called Parliament the "Five Hundred Clowns",[15] but she now realized what a menace they were. She certainly seriously considered leaving England and retiring to France. Louise was constantly an opportunist in her political opinions, and it cannot be maintained that she possessed lofty courage. Yet it is essential to be mindful of the passions aroused at this time. Louise had very real fears that she might become a victim because of the popular clamour against the Papists. She had a Catholic chaplain in her household, and dreaded lest she would have to give him up. Barrillon wrote to King Louis on 1st December 1678: "She is not sure that she can stay in England. There are many persons who are minded to name her in Parliament as conspiring against the Protestant religion or for the King of France. She thinks that it would not be a great misfortune to be obliged to retire to France, especially since Your Majesty has assured her through Lord Sunderland of your kind protection." Robert Spencer, second Earl of Sunderland, was now Ambassador in France, and a close friend and political associate of Louise's. There was, however, a period of nine or ten months during 1680 when Sunderland was estranged from her.[16] It is curious that the Duchess of Portsmouth seems to have known about the fate of a mistress of Edward III in his dotage, for she told Barrillon that she could not help remembering how three hundred years earlier Alice Perrers, a rapacious woman, was forced to appear before Parliament and swear that she would never see that King. Louise was tormented by the fear that Parliament might oblige her to take the same oath. It is unlikely that it gave Louise much satisfaction to hear that Titus Oates had accused her pleasure-loving rival, the Duchesse Mazarin, of complicity in the plot, for he could charge her with the same crime. However, she was somewhat reassured to be told by Charles that Parliament had permitted her to stay in England.[17]

Among those arrested was Edward Coleman, a former Secretary of the Duchess of York who was employed unofficially in her service in the autumn of 1678. There was some damning evidence to prove that this man had been corresponding for some time with French Ambassadors in London. Barrillon wrote to the Foreign Minister on 13th October: "Coleman has sent me word to be in no wise uneasy, because nobody can find in his papers a scrap of paper to testify to his transactions with me."[18] It is true that Titus Oates and another perjured wretch named Bedloe accused Coleman of being privy to a plot to assassinate the King, but no evidence of this was found among his letters. There are some interesting allusions to Coleman in Barrillon's correspondence. Whilst at Newmarket Charles II spoke of Coleman as a man who would not escape death if justice was to be done.[19] Yet Charles told Barrillon that he was convinced the Popish Plot was an imposture. Although Coleman expected to be reprieved, he was executed.

We obtain an interesting impression of the macabre horror of those times in the pages of Narcissus Luttrell,[20] a contemporary writer. It was a Sunday in the middle of February 1679, "about eleven in the morning" when a prodigious darkness overshadowed the sky, "the like never known, and continued about half an hour". The darkness was so great that candles had to be lit in churches. During Mass at Somerset House it was spread abroad that the ghost of Sir Edmund Berry Godfrey had appeared in the Queen's Chapel. It was now sometimes known as Godfrey Hall. Whether there is any substance in this story or not, it at least reveals how superstitious people were in this era.

It is nauseating to read that Charles II was compelled to give Oates lodgings in Whitehall and a pension of £1,200 per annum.

Roger North relates that he strutted about with the guards, who had been assigned to him for fear of the Papists murdering him. He referred to himself as "the saviour of the nation". This un-principled scoundrel donned episcopal robes, and wore a silk gown and cassock. On his ugly head was an enormous hat with a satin hat-band. The inflammatory atmosphere is easy to perceive when wild rumours were raised that the Lord Chief Justice Scroggs had issued a warrant for the apprehension of Madame Carwell (Louise) for being privy to the conspiracy to murder the King in Somerset House.[21] Out of zeal for her religion she was reported to have spat on Godfrey's face, a ridiculous rumour because Louise was incapable of such coarseness and brutality.

Sir William Scroggs, who was created Lord Chief Justice in 1678, was alleged to be the son of a butcher, and his mother a big fat woman with a red face like an ale-wife. Actually, he was the son of an Oxfordshire squire.

Lord Shaftesbury plotted with considerable success that James Duke of York, the heir-presumptive and an acknowledged Roman Catholic, should be altogether excluded from the Throne. His own candidate to succeed Charles II was the King's bastard son James Duke of Monmouth, a Protestant, son of his Welsh mistress Lucy Walter. He was a handsome, vain nobleman, weak and unstable, interested in astrology and very superstitious, though capable of great bravery in warfare. Shaftesbury used him as a puppet, and encouraged him to claim his right to the Crown. It was rumoured that Lucy Walter had been privately married to the King during his exile, and that proof of this marriage existed in a mysterious Black Box.[22]

Shaftesbury lived in Thanet House in Aldersgate Street in the City, and under his superintendence pamphlets were published, emphasizing the horrors of a Popish succession and recommending the Protestant Duke of Monmouth, who was popular in the coun-try, in preference to his uncle the Duke of York. When we con-demn Shaftesbury for his brazen effrontery in championing Monmouth's claims, we must be mindful of the fact that he was responsible for the Habeas Corpus Act, a great piece of legislation, which guaranteed the personal liberty of the subject.

Throughout that terrible winter 1678–79 innocent men were condemned to death for crimes which they did not commit. When the death warrants were laid before Charles II, he said sadly to Lord Thomas Bruce, later Lord Ailesbury: "Let the blood lie on those who condemn them, for God knows I sign with tears in my eyes."[23] Among innocent men unjustly convicted of the murder of Sir Edmund Berry Godfrey were three servants of the Queen, Robert Green, Henry Berry and Laurence Hill. The indictment against Robert Green in the State Trials[24] is very curious. It reads:

> And that thou Robert Green a certain linnen handkerchief of the value of six pence about the neck of the said Sir Edmund Berry Godfrey, then and there feloniously, wilfully and of thy malice a forethought didst fold and fasten; and that thou the said Robert Green, with the handkerchief aforesaid, by thee the said Robert Green in and about the neck of the said Sir Edmund Berry Godfrey folded and fastened then and there him the said Edmund Berry Godfrey, didst choak and strangle, of which said choaking and strangling of him the said Sir Edmund Berry Godfrey then and there instantly died.

The trials took place before Lord Chief Justice William Scroggs on Monday, 10th February 1679, and they were sentenced to death.

The King took infinite pains in cross-examining the Crown witnesses during sessions of the Privy Council, and managed to shake their evidence. Had he insisted on exercising his right of pardon, the mood of the nation was so treacherous and dangerous that it is almost certain that an armed insurrection and civil war would have ensued. To "let the laws take their course" may seem cowardly and ignoble, but the alternative would surely have been worse. In the new year (1679) the King's predicament was so grave, that he admitted to Barrillon that he would have to withdraw his ambassador from the Continent.

It is certain that Louise de Keroualle favoured the exclusion from the throne of the Duke of York and used her influence with Charles II among others to persuade him to send his brother into temporary exile during March 1679. Although she feared Shaftesbury, she was a realist in politics, and had a healthy respect for his Machiavellian duplicity. Moreover, her ambitions for her son the Duke of Richmond were very great. Once she had even dreamt of herself as Queen of England, if Catherine of Braganza was to die. Now she was tempted by Shaftesbury's evil suggestions, who told her that were the Duke of York to be excluded from the throne, Charles would then be in a position to choose his own successor. Might not the King designate the Duke of Richmond, a promising boy who had been reared as a Protestant? Louise's ambition was again aroused for her son, and her eyes shone with a new light. Shaftesbury's real purpose, however, was to make her use her influence with the King to convince him that the English would never tolerate a Catholic on the throne. He was making use of her for his own ends.

It is to Charles's credit that he held fast to the conception of the legitimate succession, though exasperated by his brother's intransigence. Nevertheless, he was forced to send him into temporary exile to Brussels on 3rd March 1679. Despite the outward amity between Charles and James, the French Ambassador, Barrillon, was aware of their cool relations. When he was slightly intoxicated Charles would refer in disparaging terms to the stupidity of his brother. Barrillon reported to Louis XIV that the King of England, "when he talks freely in wine, shows much bitterness, and even aversion from his brother". Yet Charles was fond of James, and even respected him.

In July the Lord Chief Justice Scroggs showed courage in openly stating his doubts as to the truth of the evidence of Oates, who appeared at the trial of Sir George Wakeman, the Queen's physician. Oates implied that Catherine of Braganza knew of the plot to poison her husband. On the 18th Wakeman was acquitted, after a tedious trial, a verdict which was greeted with violent abuse by the rabble. Scroggs was a convenient scapegoat, and they flung a half-hanged dog into his coach. Evelyn was present at the Old Bailey, and wrote that the result of the trial was an extraordinary triumph for the Papists.

That August Charles fell seriously ill after playing a game of tennis at Windsor, and unwisely taking a walk along the river banks in the cool of the evening. The King was in a high fever, and on 23rd August his life was actually despaired of. So alarmed were Charles's chief Counsellors, Sunderland, Essex and Halifax that they actually sent a secret message to the Duke of York in Brussels (the Spanish Netherlands) to return home as speedily as possible. The King's recovery owed much to the calmness of his temperament, though he benefited from a dose of Jesuits' bark, later to be called quinine. The Duke of York wished to remain in England, but returned to Brussels after obtaining his brother's sanction that Monmouth should be deprived of his military command and also go into exile. Charles's illness was a great shock for the nation, though the republicans rejoiced. Many of the courtiers were greatly alarmed. Harry Savile alluding to the King's possible death wrote on 11th September: "Good God! What a change would such an accident make! The very thought of it frightened me out of my wits."[25] The alarm aroused by the King's illness, however, at least had one beneficial result that it diverted men's minds from the Popish terror.

As he grew older, Charles became more and more dependent on his favourite mistress Louise de Keroualle, and he certainly listened to her counsel, but did not always heed it. Indeed, he opposed her on one vital political issue, that of the Exclusion Question. It was owing to her influence that Robert Spencer, Earl of Sunderland, a powerful minister from 1679 onwards, favoured the Exclusionists. Yet Charles confided in Louise concerning most of his affairs, and she remained the indispensable intermediary between himself and the King of France. It was in her apartments that Charles interviewed Barrillon, discussing with him the desperate state of the country, and his strained relations with Parliament. Unless Louis XIV was prepared to allow him substantial further subsidies, England would no longer remain a monarchy, but become a republic.

The persecution of the Papists continued, but the judges and juries were less ready to convict accused persons on perjured evidence. Among the informers who bore false testimony against them was a rogue named Thomas Dangerfield, the contriver of the so-called Meal Tub Plot during October 1679. He was a handsome man, known for his gallantries to the ladies. When a packet of forged letters were discovered in a tub of meal, there was great excitement. In reality Dangerfield's part in the affair had been to persuade some Roman Catholic ladies that a Presbyterian plot existed to kill the King. He now turned King's evidence, and received a substantial pension for his treachery.

With the tumult of the mob ringing in her ears, Louise implored the King not to rush headlong to destruction. If he were to give way to the demands of the Country Party concerning the question of a Catholic Successor, all might yet be well. Charles might at times be tempted to yield to their exhortations, but his honour forbade him to desert his brother, his legitimate successor, if he, the King, were to die.

NOTES

1. *Poems of John Dryden*, I.
2. John, Lord Campbell, *Life of Lord Shaftesbury*, I.

3. John, Lord Campbell, *Lives of the Lord Chancellors.*
4. Sir Arthur Bryant, *King Charles II.*
5. Correspondance Angleterre, CXXXI, fol. 113.
6. *Memoirs of Sir John Reresby*, p. 146.
7. Richard Tuke, *Memoirs of the Life and Death of Sir Edmundbury Godfrey.*
8. Correspondance Angleterre, CXXXI, 31st October.
9. Jane Lane, *Titus Oates.*
10. *Ibid.*
11. Sir George Sitwell, *The First Whig.*
12. Macaulay, *History of England*, I, p. 385.
13. Sir John Pollock, *The Popish Plot.*
14. Forneron, *Louise de Keroualle.*
15. *Verney Family Memoirs*, IV, p. 264.
16. J. P. Kenyon, *Robert Spenser, Earl of Sunderland.*
17. Correspondance Angleterre, CXXXI, fol. 331; 19th December 1678, Barrillon to Louis XIV.
18. Correspondance Angleterre, CXXXI, fol. 3.
19. Correspondance Angleterre, CXXXI, fol. 113.
20. Luttrell, *Brief Relation of State Affairs.*
21. Calendar of State Papers Charles II, January 1679.
22. Lord George Scott discusses Lucy Walter's alleged marriage with Charles II in *Lucy Walter, Wife and Mistress.*
23. *Memoirs of Thomas Bruce, Earl of Ailesbury.*
24. *Oates Plot Trials Collection.*
25. Blencowe (ed.), *Diary of the Times of Charles II* by Henry Sydney.

TEN

LOUISE AND LORD SUNDERLAND

Among Louise's intimate political friends was Robert Spencer, second Earl of Sunderland, appointed a Secretary of State to succeed Sir Joseph Williamson.* He is said to have paid Williamson over £6,000 for the seals.

Lord Macaulay had a low opinion of Sunderland. He wrote of him: "In this man the political immorality of his age was personified in the most lively manner. Nature had given him a keen understanding, a restless and mischievous temper, a cold heart and an abject spirit. His mind had undergone a training by which all his vices had been nursed up to the rankest maturity."¹ Yet Sunderland was an accomplished diplomat, possessed a deep knowledge of foreign affairs and also considerable administrative abilities. Charles II and the Duchess of Portsmouth both favoured the appointment in 1679, since they were well aware that it would receive the support of Louis XIV. Madame de la Fayette mentioned Sunderland in a letter to her friend Madame de Sévigné on 30th December 1672 when he was Ambassador in France. She sent that lady a packet of letters from Lord Sunderland, which were to be delivered to the beautiful Lady Northumberland, a great friend of the nobleman.

His portrait when aged twenty, painted in 1661 by Sir Peter Lely, shows that he was handsome with long fair hair, dark slanting eyes, and sensitive, artistic hands. Sunderland inherited his feminine beauty from his mother, Lady Dorothy Sydney, called by the poet Edmund Waller "Sacharissa". He married in 1663 Lady Anne Digby, younger daughter of the Earl of Bristol. Sunderland and his wife had been present at Euston at the strange pagan ceremony when Louise de Keroualle first became Charles II's mistress. Lady Sunderland was jealous of her husband's close partnership and friendship with the Duchess of Portsmouth, and

* 11th February 1679.

referred to her as "that abominable jade".[2] Lady Sunderland wrote
to her intimate friend Henry Sydney, who had succeeded Sir
William Temple as British Ambassador in Holland: "The Duchess
of Portsmouth is so damned a jade . . . she will certainly sell us
whenever she can for £500." She implored Sydney to engage her
husband "in what may be irreconciliable with that Jade, that
would sell us all, and does daily grow so odious, that being in any
of her affairs were enough to ruin one."[3] Sunderland usually
spoke with an aristocratic drawl.

It was during 1673 that Sunderland first acquired the confidence
of the Duchess of Portsmouth. She had asked him when in Paris to
take care of her financial interests in France. Two years later when
Charles decided to create her son the Duke of Richmond, the King
asked him to be responsible for the rather delicate negotiations.[4]
Like his friend the Duchess of Portsmouth, he was a compulsive
gambler, risking huge stakes at the tables, but he was not addicted
to whoring, the prevalent vice in that age. He was a connoisseur
of art and a collector of pictures, and was on the whole a consider-
ate husband, but among his circle of friends it was openly said
that Anne Sunderland was the lover of Henry Sydney, Sunderland's uncle. Sydney was only a year older than the Secretary of
State.

Louise, who adored political intrigues, was on the whole on
friendly terms with Henry Sydney,* and he visited her when in
London. Bishop Burnet describes Sydney as "a graceful man, and
one who had lived long in the Court where he had some adventures that became very public. He was a man of a sweet and caressing temper, who had no malice in his heart, but too great a love
of pleasure." As a young man of twenty-five, Sydney had been
attached to the household of the Duke of York as groom of the
Bedchamber, but he is alleged to have caused scandal by his too
ardent attentions to Anne Hyde, James's first Duchess. She was
probably flattered by his behaviour, but there is no real evidence
that she became his mistress. Sir John Reresby merely relates:
"She was kind to him and no more."

The Duke of York, however, though notoriously unfaithful to
his wives, resented Sydney's amorous disposition and abruptly
dismissed him from the Court. In 1679 he was appointed Ambassador to the States of Holland, and during the last two years of his
embassy succeeded in gaining the full confidence of Prince William

* Created Earl of Romney by William III.

of Orange. Sydney's correspondence whilst at The Hague is of importance, throwing as it does much light on the characters of the leading politicians of that era.

In Louise's household was a favourite negro page, possibly the one in Pierre Mignard's portrait of her in the National Portrait Gallery. One day two courtiers named Jarret and Duncomb mischievously decided to get the blackamoor drunk, giving the boy money, so that he might be tempted to relate some scandal about the Duchess of Portsmouth. When Charles heard of this further attempt to slight his mistress, he was furious and forbade the two offending men to appear at Court.

In March 1679, Charles II declared publicly in Council that he had never married any other woman but the Queen. When several Lords of the Country Party suggested that Monmouth might be legitimized, Charles said that he would rather see him hanged. He was firmly attached to the principle of the legitimate succession. When Danby was impeached, Charles II told the House of Lords that he had pardoned him, and would try to save him "ten times over". It was in vain. Many of the opposition, bribed by French gold, were resolved to ruin him. They wanted him to be imprisoned in the Tower. As Danby went down the river, he was greeted by a howling mob, holding up halters.[5]

On her knees Louise de Keroualle, Duchess of Portsmouth, tearfully implored her royal lover to work for a reconciliation with King Louis, who had not forgiven Charles for his part in promoting the marriage of his niece to William of Orange. During June the King and Louise started secret negotiations with Barrillon in her apartments in Whitehall. Sunderland favoured this policy, but his wife feared the influence of the Duchess of Portsmouth, and transmitted secret reports to Henry Sydney in Holland in which she told him that Sunderland was negotiating with Barrillon.[6]

John Evelyn was an intimate friend of Lady Sunderland, and had a high opinion of her, sending her religious books, but she had a biting and malicious tongue. Princess Anne, who disliked her, later referred to her as "the greatest jade that ever was".* "She goes to St Martins morning and afternoon, because there are not people enough to see her at Whitehall Chapel, and is half an hour after everybody is gone at her private devotions." Princess Anne was spiteful by nature. Lady Sunderland certainly possessed grace and

* 20th March 1687.

charm and manner, and was devoted to her hyper-sensitive brilliant husband. She took infinite trouble to make the gardens at their country seat of Althorp beautiful. Evelyn wrote: "The gardens were furnished with the choicest fruit in England and exquisitely kept, great plenty of oranges and other curiosities."

The Duchess of Portsmouth was on friendly terms with Arthur Capel, Earl of Essex, who may be described as a moderate working for an *entente* with Holland. Members of this group, which included Sir William Temple, a very experienced diplomat, were on the whole hostile to her. They were in favour of William of Orange as a rival to the Duke of Monmouth as Protestant leader, while they even considered William as a possible successor to Charles II if James were excluded.[7] As for the Duchess of Portsmouth, she was seldom consistent in her political role as intermediary between Charles II and Louis XIV. After a visit to England Henry Sydney confided in his Diary that "the Du. Por." [Duchess of Portsmouth] with whom he had an interview was as powerful as ever. She bade him tell the Prince of Orange that she was more his friend than he imagined.

During the summer of 1679 together with Henry Sydney, the Duchess of Portsmouth had interviews with Mr William Harbord, a Member of Parliament and a supporter of William of Orange's cause. He is mentioned in Barrillon's account books: "December 22nd, To the Sieur Harbord, 500 guineas, which makes £543.16s. sterling." One wonders whether the man was worth bribing. Yet at the same time Louise intrigued with the Duke of Monmouth, sending him her confidential *femme de chambre*, Mrs Wall. Sydney wrote: "Mrs Wall loves him above all things. He would have given her 500 guineas but she refused it." The Duchess of Portsmouth obtained the post of laundress (keeper of the linen-closet) to the King for Mrs Wall.

Lady Sunderland informed Sydney during May 1680 that the King had been ill.* "He is now very well again and I hope will continue so if he can be kept away fishing when a dog would not go abroad." In one of her letters when she was overjoyed that her friend had been granted leave by the King to visit England she asked him to bring £20 in money, "such wax lights as you sent me last, only that they may all be of the long sort, four to the pound . . . I hope you received my letter with the pattern of cloth the Duchess of Portsmouth bid me send you."

* He was sick with ague.

What worried Lady Sunderland more than anything else was her husband's passion for gambling. She confided to Sydney: "My Lord has fallen again to play to a more violent degree than ever, all day and night. It makes the horridest noise in the world; 'tis talked of in all the coffee-houses." His stakes at Basset were sometimes as high as £5,000 a night. She implored Sydney to write to Sunderland warning him against gambling, for it did him much harm with his enemies. She assured him, however, that her Lord "laboured like a horse, and like an honest man to his country".

How far Louise was sincere or consistent in her political allegiance can be realized when she on one occasion was bold enough to declare openly in favour of the Prince and Princess of Orange. Barrillon was exasperated, because she seemed to prefer English to French interests. He reproached her for currying favour with France's enemy Holland. The French Ambassador, however, was well aware of the deep unpopularity of both the Duchess of Portsmouth and Lord Sunderland. He told Louis XIV that the drunken bloods reviled them in the theatres.

There is a mysterious entry in Sydney's Diary on 9th October 1680, which reveals that Louise was indulging in intrigues with the Duke of Monmouth, although he was now in disgrace with his royal father. Charles had behaved with too much indulgence to his illegitimate son, and he had been repaid with gross ingratitude. "I was with the Duke of Monmouth," wrote Sydney, "I talked to him of all our affairs. In the evening I was with my Lord Shaftesbury. D.— and D—[sic] met." He is referring to the Duchess of Portsmouth and the Protestant Duke, as Monmouth was sometimes called.

Lord Sunderland wrote to Henry Sydney that the King told the Duke of Monmouth he would have him lay down his commission of General and that he must absent himself for some time from his dominions. Eventually the young Duke defied Charles by returning to England during November 1679 without his permission. He returned to his old lodgings in the Cockpit at Whitehall. When he tried to obtain an interview with the King, Charles refused to see him. There is in the Ellis Collection[8] an interesting letter believed to be authentic from the Duchess of Portsmouth to the Duke of Monmouth. It is certainly not in her large handwriting so it was presumably dictated. She wrote:

My Lord Duke,

I sent Mr Rumbold a gentleman of my house to your Grace, to let you know that I would be glad to speak with you, but if you were unwilling to come to my lodgings, thinking it might be to your prejudice, because at this time I am so hated by the common people. Then I would meet you privately anywhere else, but since you are not afraid to come to mee, I will speak freely and assure you, whatever you may think, I was not ye person who did ever presse the King to take away yr commission, or to send you beyond the sea. I will not deny you I did know of it, for then you would not think mee, as indeed I am, a woman very sincere, since the King loves mee so well as to tell mee everything he intends to do, and when he told mee of his resolution to take away your commission [as General] and to banish you, I must confesse in my judgment I did approve of it, for I have a great while thought you did the K's business much hurt, by countenancing such ill men as my Lord Shaftesbury, Lord Bedford, Lord Russell, and Mr Montague. I would not trust wholly to my own poor judgment, and did therefore desire ye King to ask the opinion of his ministers, Lord Essex, Lord Halifax and Lord Sunderland, all my very good friends . . . Had you not all this while very coldly and very unkindly dealt with me, I had made you ye greatest man in the kingdom, next to D of York, as you may see by what I have done by my Lord Sunderland whom ye King never had a good opinion of, till I recommended him. I have made Lord Halifax an Earl, upon his application to me. The King was pleased to make the Earl of Essex a commissioner of the Treasury . . . be as just to mee, as I have been to him, ever since I gave myself up to him . . . nobody shall come to Court or to any preferment, but those who will be my creatures. The King of England hath promised to support mee, and I am allyed to most of ye sovereign princes abroad, as you may see by my being so often obliged to be in mourning for them.

This letter is unsigned and dated 20th November 1679. In her characteristic way Louise referred arrogantly to her relationship with most of the crowned heads of Europe.

At the end of November, there suddenly appeared in London the Duke of Monmouth, who defied his father's commands by thus returning without his permission. The "Protestant Duke" was as popular as ever. In London, the church bells acclaimed him, and pamphlets announcing his return were sold in thousands in the streets. King Charles was furious, and ordered Monmouth to leave Whitehall. The young nobleman now found an ally in Nell Gwyn, who supped with "Prince Perkin", as she called him.

Though she seldom interfered in politics, she boldly interceded
on Monmouth's behalf with Charles II, imploring him to see his
wayward son, who had grown "pale, wan, lean, and long-visaged
merely because he was in disfavour."[9] Charles was very angry
with Nelly, and told her to be quiet. Barrillon wrote to the King
of France that he was astonished that Monmouth "every night
sups with Mistress Nesle, the courtesan who has borne the King
two children, and whom he daily visits". Monmouth soon withdrew to the country after appealing to the Duchess of Portsmouth
to use her influence with his royal father on his behalf. She frigidly
replied that she could do nothing for him so long as he was an
enemy to the King and to her.

It is evident that during the last five or six years of Charles II's
reign Louise was increasingly aware of her ascendancy at Court
and her power over the mind of her royal lover. She might be
referring to herself as a Queen when she arrogantly writes of the
obligation of going into mourning on the decease of various
sovereigns abroad. It must have given her great satisfaction that
the King of France addressed her as "*ma Cousine*".

It was on 16th June 1680 that Lord Shaftesbury, acting with
arrogant effrontery, and accompanied by seven Whig Lords:
Russell, Cavendish, Huntingdon, Grey of Werke and others, proceeded to the historic Westminster Hall. He then appeared before
the Grand Jury for the County of Middlesex in the Court of the
Kings Bench and presented them with an indictment against the
heir-presumptive to the throne, James Duke of York, as a Popish
recusant. As such he was liable to have two-thirds of his property
forfeited, and to various other penalties. To the Duchess of Portsmouth's horror, Shaftesbury then declared before the Grand Jury
that she should likewise be indicted as a national nuisance. The
Lord Chief Justice Sir William Scroggs included the indictments
on the list for the Grand Jury, tried various other cases, and then
cunningly dismissed the Jury, thus giving them no opportunity to
consider the accusations. For this action he was called to account
by the House of Commons before the end of the year. When
Henry Hyde, Earl of Clarendon complained of Louise's evil influence as the King's mistress, Shaftesbury merely said that she was
small game. He was hunting "tigers and birds of prey, not cony-
catching".

Fearful and apprehensive for her safety, Louise, never a woman
of high principles or courage, now temporarily opposed the policy

of Charles II. She openly went over to the side of the Exclusionists, those who favoured the exclusion from the throne of the Duke of York. James was very resentful and later described her defection as "a dog trick".[10] To explain her decision Louise declared that the Duchess of York had not treated her with the kindness and consideration that was her due. How far she influenced her friend Sunderland to become an Exclusionist is uncertain, but the minister's determination to support exclusion was no sudden conversion. We know that both the Duchess of Portsmouth and Lord Sunderland used their influence with Charles II during October 1680, that the Duke of York should once again be sent into exile—this time in Scotland.

Again and again we observe how Louise constantly had her way. Narcissus Luttrell related that she prevailed upon the King to remove Sir Job Charleton ("an old loyal Royalist") from his position as Lord Chief Justice of Chester, and to appoint Sir George Jeffreys, Recorder of London, in his place.* It is curious how Louise helped the advancement of Jeffreys' career.

A few months earlier John Dryden one dark evening in December 1679 had been attacked in Rose Alley, Covent Garden, by three ruffians who had beaten him very severely.[11] It was supposed that the attack had been instigated by the Duchess of Portsmouth in revenge for the poet's *Essay on Satyr*† at the time attributed to him, but this seems extremely improbable for Louise was far too refined to encourage such a dastardly affair. Nor would Dryden have cared to offend the King by attacking his chief favourite in a poem. The instigator of this crime was for a long time suspected to be Rochester, but Anthony à Wood, a contemporary authority, believed that it was the Duchess of Portsmouth, who resented the attacks on her in this poem. Professor J. H. Wilson in his work *The Court Wits of the Restoration* suggests that the actual attacker was the homicidal Earl of Pembroke, her brother-in-law. As Louise disliked Pembroke, it is difficult to imagine them collaborating together in this brutal affair.

The autumn of 1680 was a period of drama and uncertainty. Intense excitement reigned both in Parliament and the country as to the fate of James Duke of York who was in Edinburgh and vigilant while heated debates took place in the House of Commons.

* 30th April 1680.
† John Sheffield, Earl of Mulgrave, was the chief author of an *Essay on Satyr*, though others may have contributed to it.

On 4th November, when the Exclusion Bill received its first reading in the House, only three members, Laurence Hyde, who was brother-in-law of the Duke of York and younger son of the Earl of Clarendon, Sir Edward Seymour and one of the Secretaries of State, Sir Leoline Jenkins, dared to oppose it. It was Lord Russell who carried the Bill to the Upper House, attended by a vociferous number of his supporters, and also by the Lord Mayor and Corporation in state.

The Exclusion Bill is memorable because of the gladiatorial contest bitterly fought between Lord Shaftesbury for the Bill, and Lord Halifax who opposed it in speeches of fiery eloquence. It was mainly owing to Halifax's endeavours that the Bill was thrown out.

A contemporary wrote:

> Of powerful eloquence and great parts were the Duke's enemies who did assert the Bill, but a noble Lord [Halifax] appeared against it who that day in all the force of speech, in reason, in arguments of what could concern the public or the private interests of men, in honour, in conscience, in estate, did outdo himself and every other man, and in fine his conduct and his parts were both victorious, and by him all the wit and malice of that party was overthrown.[12]

Among those who took part during the debates was the Duke of Monmouth. According to Barrillon, "on this occasion he did not speak ill". At ten o'clock that night Lord Sunderland rose, and speaking with apparent sincerity declared that he voted in favour of the measure because he could see no other way of safeguarding the King's throne. When the Duke of Monmouth spoke about the dangers to his dear father, Charles II, who was present throughout the debates, was heard to say to his neighbour in a loud voice, "The kiss of Judas!" It was finally rejected by sixty-three votes to thirty, owing to some extent to the bishops supporting the principle of hereditary right.

On 19th November Dorothy, the Dowager Lady Sunderland, wrote to her brother Henry Sydney in Holland an interesting letter about Lord Halifax's great speech in the House of Lords on the Duke of York's behalf. She wrote to him that the great actors came to him as friends to tell him if he did speak against it, he would be impeached by the House of Commons in an address made to the King to remove him from his place of Privy Counsellor. He then answered boldly that neither threats nor promises would hinder him from speaking his mind. Despite Halifax's successful efforts on his behalf, James Duke of York never really liked him and resented his project to curb or limit his power* if he were to ascend the throne.

When Henry Sydney had an interview with William of Orange in November, he told the English Ambassador that he thought the exclusion of the Duke of York (his father-in-law) an unlawful and unjust thing. He would do nothing to contribute towards this, nor to advise the King to take such a course. In the Prince's opinion "everybody would be undone". "I left him very melancholy," wrote Sydney to the Secretary of State. It did not suit William's plans that the Protestant Duke of Monmouth should become Charles II's successor.

The letters in the correspondence of Henry Sydney[13] are very vivid, arresting and sometimes intimate. Dorothy Sunderland ends one of her letters to her brother with a postscript: "My dearest Sydney take this ugly scrible in good part 'tis so darke at noone that I can neither see nor feele, somethings lye heavye at my hart if you wear in my corner you should know all my secrets I durst trust you and love you very well."[14]

After the defeat of the Exclusion Bill, Lord Sunderland was constantly in the Duchess of Portsmouth's apartments in Whitehall. He worked in very close collaboration with her. However, at the beginning of February 1681 he was dismissed from his position as Secretary of State and succeeded by Lord Conway on 4th February. For a time Sunderland was completely out of favour with the King.

Ironically enough the Duchess of Portsmouth now became, for the time being, a favourite of the House of Commons. She went in her coach on 24th November together with Lady Sunderland, Lady Newport and Mrs Crofts to dine with a cousin of the Sunderlands in the Tower. The Dowager Countess of Sunderland told Henry Sydney that Louise had dined with her son a few days ago, and that after dinner the King came in as he used to do. That at least shows there had been no open rupture between Charles and Louise.

Louise was present at the trial of the venerable William Howard, Lord Stafford, an irascible man of sixty-nine, who was brought from the Tower on 29th November to Westminster Hall to face his trial for treason by his fellow peers. He was a Roman Catholic

* The so-called scheme of Limitations.

and a helpless victim for the evil, depraved men who had organized the reign of terror which had descended on England. Louise
was in her private box, and it was noticed that in her new role as
a favourite of the opposition party in the House of Commons that
she bestowed her smiles on them and handed sweetmeats to them,
hoping by this means to please them. Charles II was in his private
box with curtains, and Queen Catherine also present on this
important state occasion.

The Lord High Steward, Baron Finch of Daventry later created
first Earl of Nottingham by the King, presided at this trial, and
the prosecution was in the able hands of Sir William Jones, a
member of the opposition party, and other lawyers. It was a
deadly duel between a defenceless old man denied the aid of
Counsel, struggling to rebut the perjured statements of Titus
Oates, Dugdale and Turbeyville. The accused man was found
guilty by a majority of his peers—fifty-five votes to thirty-one—
and he was sentenced to death. Lord Thomas Bruce,[15] writing to
a correspondent many years later observed: "My poor Lord
Stafford who, I believe upon my conscience, would have trembled
at the sight of a naked sword, I know him so well." The King
seemed powerless to save him, though convinced that he should
allow justice, if it could be termed such, have its course. The old
man protested his innocence to the end but he went to the block
on Tower Hill with the howls and groans of the rabble ringing
in his ears.

It did Louise little good to try to gain the goodwill of the
Country Party, for Lord Shaftesbury attacked her in a venomous
speech in the House of Lords. "If," said he, "I must speak of
them [i.e. the 'chargeable' ladies at court] I shall say as the prophet
did to King Saul: 'What meaneth the bleating of the cattle?' ...
We must have neither Popish wife nor Catholic mistress, nor
Popish Councellor at Court, nor any new convert."[16]

On the evening of 12th December, as he looked out of the
window of his chamber, Evelyn saw a blood-red comet appear
in the skies, "like the blade of a sword". It recalled to his mind a
similar portent he had witnessed during the trial of the Earl of
Strafford in 1640—forty years before.

The rejection of the Exclusion Bill was a heavy reverse of fortune for Lord Shaftesbury, but he continued to attack Charles II,
maintaining in the Lords that it was essential for the safety of the
state that the King's marriage should be annulled. Charles would

then be free to marry a Protestant princess. Charles, eager to rush to the defence of his barren Queen, furiously protested: "I will not have such an insult passed on an innocent woman." When the second Earl of Clarendon (Laurence Hyde's elder brother) related some private, almost intimate details about Queen Catherine, her husband remarked humorously, "Odds fish! I do not altogether like Lord Clarendon being so intimate with my wife's concerns."

To mark his disapproval of the mean attack on the Queen, Charles went to her apartments for several hours after dinner, where he slept heavily. It was his usual custom to go to the Duchess of Portsmouth's chamber after dinner, but Louise did not grudge her royal lover spending some time with the Queen.

NOTES

1. Macaulay, *History of England*, I, p. 246.
2. Blencowe (ed.), *Diary of the Times of Charles II* by Henry Sydney.
3. *Ibid.*
4. J. P. Kenyon, *Robert Spenser, Earl of Sunderland.*
5. Sir Arthur Bryant, *King Charles II.*
6. Blencowe, *op. cit.*, I, pp. 84–7.
7. J. P. Kenyon, *op. cit.*
8. Add. MSS. 24938, fol. 24.
9. *Verney Family Memoirs.*
10. F. C. Turner, *James II.*
11. Luttrell, *Brief Relation of State Affairs.*
12. Robert Halstead, *Succinct Genealogies.*
13. Add. MSS. 32681, II.
14. 25th November.
15. *Memoirs of Thomas Bruce*, I, p. 51, where he discusses Lord Stafford's trial.
16. H. Noel Williams, *Rival Sultanas.*

ELEVEN

"MY DEAR LIFE"

There is no doubt whatsoever that Charles II loved Louise passionately. In the County Record Office at Chichester there are three
letters[1] to his mistress, written in his characteristic style. They are
all undated. One of the letters was written on a Saturday from
Newmarket, probably in 1680.

> I shall not be out of paine [he told her] till I know how my dearest
> gott to London and for that purpose I send this expresse to come
> away tomorrow morning to bring me word how you have rested
> after your journey. I will not trouble you with a long letter now,
> knowing how troublesome that is to one indisposed, and pray do
> not answer this yourselfe, except you are quite out of paine, all I will
> add is, that I should do myselfe wrong if I tould you that I love you
> better than all the world besides, for that were making a comparison
> where 'tis impossible to expresse the true passion and kindnesse I
> have for my dearest dearest Fubs.

That was Charles's nickname for his sweetheart, for she was now
getting rather plump. During 1682 he acquired a new yacht, which
he christened *The Fubbs* in her honour. Nothing gave Charles
greater pleasure than to sail in this yacht when he showed his skill
during rough weather, handling the sails and ropes like an ordinary seaman. John Gostling, Minor Canon of Canterbury, wrote
of the King's exhilaration during one of his last recorded sailings
round the North Foreland.

In other letters or notes to Louise, he calls her "my dear Life".
He wrote her: "There was a message from the Queen today to
desire the Ladys to dine att their table and to invite strangers and
there being a good deal of company I can't come till after dinner.
Adieu my Life."

The third note is even shorter and more hurried: "My dear
Life, I will come tomorrow either to dinner or immediately after,
but certainly I shall not mind the Queen when you are in the case.

I am yours." It is amusing to think of Charles inventing subterfuges when he wished to see his mistress.

It is unfortunate that there are no letters in existence from Louise to Charles II, for they might throw more light on her character.

As already mentioned, Louis XIV frequently corresponded with the Duchess of Portsmouth, and addressed her as "*Ma Cousine*". Copies of the French King's letters[2] to her and hers to him are in the County Record Office at Chichester.

Louise's letters to Louis XIV written with wheedling charm, were intended to flatter him. On one occasion she discovered that she had inadvertently offended Louis by writing on paper perfumed with ambergris. She was unaware that Louis loathed perfume. Put out of countenance, Louise apologized profusely— "I ask your humble pardon, Sir, and believe me, this is the only fault I could be capable of towards your sacred person." The original letters from Louis to Louise are in the French Archives.

On 18th February 1683 when Lord Sunderland was once again a Secretary of State, Louise wrote to the King of France, informing him of the good news. Louis replied: "*Ma Cousine*, I have learnt with pleasure of the continuation of the kind feelings you bear me. I am convinced that the choice he has just made in appointing Lord Sunderland to the post of Secretary of State will contribute very much to my perfect understanding with the King of Great Britain; since you are well aware of this minister's faithful attachment to the true interests of the King his master, and that he owes his re-establishment to some extent to your good offices."

In one of her letters Louise wrote tactfully to the French King assuring him that she hoped her son the young Duke of Richmond would one day put the sword, so graciously given by the King of France, at the service of His Majesty.[3] She corresponded with the French Minister of Foreign Affairs about the best means of persuading her son aged thirteen in 1685 to become a Roman Catholic. She was assured that nothing would give the King of France more satisfaction than to hear of the trouble she was taking to persuade her son to make this conversion. Louise held earlier ambitions—misguided though they were—that her son reared as a Protestant might possibly succeed his father as King. Since this letter was written after Charles II's death when James II had ascended the throne, it no longer mattered if Richmond were to change his religion. Indeed he would gain favour with James for doing so.

Although Charles II was often secretive and reticent, he confided in his devoted mistress "Fubbs" almost everything, even relating to her intimate details of his father's execution in 1649. Louise was very discreet, and never revealed what Charles confided to her.

Thomas Carte gives an account of an episode, which clearly shows that Charles II during the last six years of his life found it difficult to refuse his French mistress anything. In his life of James Butler, first Duke of Ormonde,[4] he tells us that Charles II, King of Spain, having on 31st August 1679 married Maria Louise, elder daughter of Henriette-Anne ("Minette") first Duchess of Orleans and the Duke of Orleans, the King of England wanted to send Ormonde's son the Earl of Ossory as his Envoy Extraordinary to congratulate the King of Spain on his marriage with his niece. A jewel was made by Langooste the Jeweller, which cost £13,000 and was intended as a present to the Queen of Spain. Charles II could not have chosen a more suitable envoy because Ossory was of fine character, much respected and beloved by his contemporaries. However, Lord Essex used his influence to prevent the journey. Ossory's premature death a year later was much lamented. Not long afterwards Charles II gave this valuable jewel to Louise. We know that she intrigued with her friends Lord Sunderland, Laurence Hyde and Sidney Godolphin to have the Duke of Ormonde removed as Lord Lieutenant of Ireland. It would seem that Lord Essex coveted this important post, and that the Duchess of Portsmouth tried to help him obtain it. But Charles did not always allow himself to be swayed by the wishes of his mistress, and on this occasion he was determined not to part with his Lord-Lieutenant.

Thomas Carte also relates that the Duchess of Ormonde was very reluctant to receive the King's mistresses. She would, for instance, "never wait on the Duchess of Cleveland", and as one might expect, Barbara never forgave her for that slight. The Duchess of Portsmouth, however, always expressed the greatest regard for the Duchess of Ormonde, and often visited her. The Duchess of Ormonde was very strict with regard to the behaviour of her grand-daughters. On one occasion during 1682 when Louise, who was at Windsor, wished to dine with her, the Duchess of Ormonde sent away her grand-daughters Lady Anne

Stanhope (afterwards Countess of Strathmore) and the Lady Emilia Butler to London for the day. Consequently Louise discovered when she arrived at Her Grace of Ormonde's country home near the Court at Windsor that only her formidable hostess and the Bishop of Worcester confronted her at table.⁵ The Duchess of Ormonde was not the only aristocratic lady at Charles II's court unwilling to receive the King's powerful French favourite. Important Whig families such as the Russells and the Cavendishes refused to conciliate her.

When Louise heard during 1680 that Madame de Montespan, Louis XIV's arrogant and voluptuous mistress, was no longer in favour, she experienced mixed emotions. Madame de Montespan had been extremely indiscreet, and had allowed her name to be involved in a celebrated criminal case. She had dabbled in black magic, desperately hoping by indulging in satanic rites and magic to keep the love of Louis XIV. Unlike Louise, Madame de Montespan could not restrain her mordant tongue. The King of France was sensitive as to his *gloire*. Nothing must be allowed to tarnish the image of his Majesty. Madame de Montespan had the mortification of seeing her rival the royal governess Madame de Maintenon, who was pious but hypocritical, supersede her in the King's affections. Madame de Sévigné wrote to her daughter on 18th September 1680: "I know not which of the courtiers tongues first blabbed it out, but Madame de Maintenon is now everywhere privately called Madame de Maintenant [the lady of today]".

Louise shuddered at the thought of the downfall of Madame de Montespan and a sense of insecurity overwhelmed her. Could she be ever certain that Charles might not tire of her? But she knew that the King was increasingly dependent on her. Although from motives of expediency and dissimulation, which she had learnt through hard experience, she might flirt with the opposition, she thought that she was binding the King by silken fetters to France.

Few people realize that the Duchess of Portsmouth was a magnificent patron of foreign artists in London, and possessing superb taste, as has already been stressed, did much to encourage *les beaux-arts* in England.⁶ It was owing to Louise's initiative that many French workmen were brought over to England, and to help them she established royal workshops. Charles Le Brun, whose name is associated with the celebrated Gobelin factory, was an artist, who designed for her ormolu mounts. She was a patron of Henri Gascar the French artist, who painted her, of Lely, Verelst, Wissing, Laguerre, Pierre Mignard, and to the more famous Sir Godfrey Kneller, successor to Sir Peter Lely. Simon Verelst had a fair conceit of himself. He once presented himself at Whitehall and said that he would like to talk for two or three hours to the King. Being refused admittance, he said, arrogantly: "He is King of England, I am King of painting. Why should not we converse together familiarly?"[7] It is easy to sneer at Louise and to refer contemptuously to her as a spy of France at Charles II's court, but her influence in artistic matters was extremely beneficial to England. The portraits of her by Lely and Gascar have particular charm. Louise was a woman of some sensibility, and although she possessed no creative talents, genuinely loved beautiful things. In this aspect of her character, she had much in common with her friend Lord Sunderland, a very cultivated nobleman, who took infinite trouble to collect fine portraits at Althorp in Northamptonshire. Louise visited him there on one or two occasions.

Jesse[8] relates that the gentle playwright Nathaniel Lee dedicated to the Duchess of Portsmouth his two plays *Sophonisba* and *Gloriana*. In his dedication, Lee addressed her in the extravagant language of that age: "I pay my adorations to your grace, who are the most beautiful, as well in the bright appearances of body, as in the immortal splendours of an elevated soul." Few people would have agreed with him about her elevated soul.

Among her more endearing qualities was her strong sense of family pride. If Louise were alive today, nothing would give her more pleasure and family pride than to realize that Goodwood House, bought by her son the first Duke of Richmond in 1720, is still the much loved home of her descendants. Although she only once visited this beautiful house, resplendently situated as it is within four miles of Chichester in an unspoilt part of Sussex, it has many associations with her son, and her grandson Charles second Duke of Richmond. Among its relics are the first shirt ever worn her son, which would have reminded Louise of the Duke of Richmond's boyhood. There, too, is the jerkin of old damask linen put on before the shirt.

There is a fine Kneller of the Duchess of Portsmouth at Goodwood, which seems to give the lie to those who maintain that she was no beauty. There she is in all her stately dignity, an aristocratic lady, who held her own with intelligence and dignity

9

in Charles II's ignoble court. The Kneller of Louise at Sherborne is a very impressive portrait. As Osmund Airy wrote: "She alone among Charles's mistresses had a conception of *la haute politique*."[9] For the last four years of the King's life she might be described as virtually Queen of England. There is a picture of her with her son, painted about 1675 by Henri Gascar,* but we already get the impression that Louise is putting on weight. Kneller's portrait of the first Duke of Richmond painted about 1690, shows that he was very handsome as a young man. Perhaps one of the most enchanting pictures at Goodwood is the Kneller of Anne, daughter of Francis Lord Brudenell and widow of Henry, second Baron Bellassis of Worlaby. Kneller painted her in a lovely satin blue dress, and we almost hear its faint rustling as she walks gracefully to her room to attend to her correspondence. She married the first Duke of Richmond in 1693,† and was to prove a devoted wife and mother. Her letters to her mother-in-law the Duchess of Portsmouth are of considerable interest, and will be discussed in a later chapter. The Duchess of Portsmouth was tenderly attached to her grandson the young Earl of March, who was destined to succeed his father as second Duke of Richmond in 1723. Her letters[10] to her young grandson reveal that she was capable of deep devotion to those few people she really loved.

The Duchess of Portsmouth's income in 1681 was as high as £136,000,[11] but she was extremely extravagant. High stakes were wagered at her basset-table, and Louise sometimes lost a small fortune, for instance five thousand guineas on one occasion. She, however, derived considerable revenue from the sale of royal pardons to offenders against the law. She found it profitable to employ a man named Timothy Hall, who acted as her agent in these matters, and the business was highly lucrative.[12] It is related that she refused a bribe of a hundred thousand pounds to procure the pardon of Lord William Russell condemned to death for participating in the Rye House Plot. The story, however, rests on doubtful authenticity. Anna Scott, Duchess of Monmouth, related that the Duchess of Portsmouth honestly thought that Queen Catherine was extremely fond of her.[13] The Duchess of Monmouth's opinion was that the truth was otherwise. She considered that Louise mistook the Queen's contempt for her for civility and compliment. On one occasion Mrs Temple (un-

* Born in Paris 1635, died in Rome 1701.
† As her second husband.

married ladies were referred to as such), who was in attendance
on the Queen, complained to her mistress about the Duchess of
Portsmouth. Lady Conway immediately went to Louise, and told
her about it. Louise burst into tears when she related the matter
to her royal lover. Charles then took the opportunity of mentioning to his wife that never again must she listen to anything
derogatory to the Duchess of Portsmouth. As a punishment the
Queen deprived Phyllis Temple of a quarter's salary.

It must not be supposed that Catherine did not resent her
husband's mistresses, particularly Louise. One day in late April
1681 high words passed between the King and Queen when
Charles remarked that she enjoyed more privileges regarding her
servants than any of her predecessors. Catherine then angrily
retorted that her mother-in-law Queen Henrietta had possessed
many more privileges, "but today the mistresses govern all!" The
King later referred to the matter in the apartments of the Duchess
of Portsmouth.

Yet Sir John Reresby relates that Louise at least had the good
taste to inflict her presence but rarely on Queen Catherine. One
day,* however, when the Queen was at Windsor about to have
dinner, the Duchess of Portsmouth as a lady of her bedchamber
entered her apartments. Catherine was unable to conceal her
embarrassment, and tears came involuntarily to her eyes.

It was very unwise for diplomats or politicians to offend Louise.
One one occasion the Dutch Ambassador, a rather unpleasant man
named Vanbeunengen, wishing to make mischief between the
King and his mistress† drew attention to her familiarity with the
French Ambassador Barrillon, who had access to her at most hours
of the day and night. This could hardly fail to annoy the King.
Louise was furious, and at once complained to Charles of the
Dutch Minister's want of respect for her. Vanbeunengen was
forced to make profuse apologies, and to explain that he had no
intention of offending a lady for whom the King showed such a
high regard. He even offered to go to Louise's apartments in
Whitehall to apologize.

The people resented Charles II's generosity to his French
mistress. Charles gave her a magnificent present of gold plate,
proudly exhibited in the shop of the goldsmith who had made it.
A mob at once collected in front of the shop, and yelled abuse at

* May 1684.
† And no doubt to sow trouble between England and France.

"Madame Carwell". It was unfortunate that he had not given it to their favourite "Mrs Nelly".

One thing is certain that despite the Duchess of Portsmouth's unpopularity among the people, it was hard for her enemies to oust her as the King's chief mistress. Owing to her cleverness, resourcefulness and tact, her position seemed supreme. That was her ultimate triumph.

NOTES

1. Goodwood MSS. 3.
2. *Ibid.*, 4, copies made by a French scholar, J. Lemoine.
3. Jeanine Delpech, *The Life and Times of the Duchess of Portsmouth.*
4. Thomas Carte, *Life of James Butler*, II, p. 421.
5. *Ibid.*, II.
6. Lady Russell, "The Real Louise de Keroualle", in *The Rose Goddess and other sketches of Mystery and Romance.*
7. Clayton, *English Female Artists.*
8. Jesse, *Memoirs of the Courts of the Stuarts*, III.
9. Osmund Airy, *Charles II*, p. 254.
10. Goodwood MSS. 8.
11. Accounts of the Secret Service Funds.
12. H. Noel Williams, *Rival Sultanas.*
13. *Diary of Mary Countess Cowper*, p. 94.

TWELVE

THE TURNING OF THE TIDE

> From hence you may look back on Civil Rage,
> And view the ruines of the former Age.
> Here a New World its glories may unfold,
> And here be sav'd the remnants of the old.
> But while your daies on publick thoughts are bent
> Past ills to heal, and future to prevent;
> Some vacant houres allow to your delight,
> Mirth is the pleasing business of the night,
> The King's prerogative, the people's right.[1]

In such a way did John Dryden address the King in an epilogue at the opening of the Playhouse at Oxford on Saturday, 19th March 1681.

The political situation at the beginning of this year seemed extremely ominous. Everybody talked of the imminent civil war. The mood of the rabble in the London streets was ugly, inflamed to madness as they were by the propaganda of Lord Shaftesbury, who understood the art of inciting them, like a conductor feels instinctively what his orchestra is capable of. His highly organized party the Whigs now controlled the electoral corporations throughout the country. It was war to the death between the King and Shaftesbury. The latter's "brisk Protestant boys" were mobilized, and they shouted anti-popish slogans at Wapping, Southwark and all over London. Then Charles II decided on a masterly stroke of policy, which was to confound his enemies. He ordained that Parliament, instead of meeting at Westminster should do so at Oxford, known for its loyalty to the Crown. Although the Whigs protested that Parliament should assemble at Westminster, Charles ignored their petitions.

The King arrived at Oxford on 14th March to receive a rousing welcome from his subjects. He stayed in Christ Church, while many of the courtiers were provided with accommodation in

Merton and Corpus Christi Colleges. There was a feverish air of excitement in her ancient streets. While Charles was opening Parliament on 21st March dense crowds lined the streets as the Duke of Monmouth accompanied by his friend Lord Grey of Werke rode over Magdalen Bridge. They were followed by a clamorous, ill-disciplined mob shouting anti-popish slogans.

At this critical juncture an attractively decorated coach was seen edging its way with difficulty through the streets. The crowd, imagining that it contained the hated favourite, "Mrs Carwell", the Catholic Duchess of Portsmouth, started to mob the coach and to hurl insults at its suspected occupant. However, the curtains were drawn aside to reveal the attractive countenance of Nell Gwyn, who cried to the people in her inimitable way: "Pray, good people, be civil: I am the Protestant whore."* This sally was greeted by laughter and merriment. No doubt both Louise and Nelly were in Oxford during these anxious days, but we do not know with which lady, Charles II found "the mirth the pleasing business of the night". Charles's Queen was also there to give solace to him in these troubled times.

The vital question was the future of the English monarchy. When Charles is attacked for cowardice in signing the death warrants of men whom he knew were innocent during the Popish Terror, it is fitting to remember that he steadfastly adhered to the legitimate succession, that James Duke of York should succeed him. But he was forced to agree to various expedients, that the abuse of power by a Catholic successor must be prevented.

John Evelyn wrote in his diary on 27th March: "The Parliament now conven'd at Oxford. Greate expectation of his Royal Highness's case as to the succession, against which the House was set.

"An extraordinarily sharp cold spring, not yet a leafe on ye trees, frost and snow lying: whilst the whole nation was in the greatest ferment."

It was on the same day that Charles's Council advised him to dissolve Parliament. On Monday 28th, the King took his seat on the throne in the Lords, crowned and robed. Black Rod was then sent to fetch the Commons. It was the appointed day for the introduction of a new Exclusion Bill, and many of the Whigs were in a truculent mood, thinking that the King was about to

* This story is absolutely authentic, but it is not certain that it occurred on this occasion.

capitulate to their wishes. To their surprise, however, Charles said a few terse words, then commanded the Lord Chancellor to dissolve them. Lord Thomas Bruce as a young man was present on this occasion, and he tells us[2] that the King in his amiable way turned to him, saying: "I am now a better man than you were a quarter of an hour since; you had better have one King than five hundred."[3] After dining, the King entered Sir Edward Seymour's coach, and made for Windsor.

A few days later a secret treaty was signed with France whereby it was agreed that Louis XIV was to pay about £400,000 spread over three years, provided that Charles pursued no action hostile to his interests abroad.

Towards the end of May, the Duchess of Portsmouth accompanied by a few friends, Philippe de Vendôme, the Grand Prior, Lord Ranelagh and Mrs Crofts were guests of Lord Sunderland at Althorp. Sunderland wrote Henry Sydney that they only stayed two days. Louise returned to Windsor to be present on the King's birthday, 29th May. Philippe de Vendôme was the grandson of Henri IV of France and his beautiful green-eyed mistress Gabrielle d'Estrées. He was a scoundrel, who was fond of bragging that he had not gone to bed sober, or without being carried, for thirty years. His relations with the Duchess of Portsmouth created a sharp scandal at court two years later, and his behaviour was such as to arouse jealousy in Charles II.

During late June Henry Sydney was back in England, and took the opportunity of supping with Louise at Windsor. She spoke kindly to him, but did not discuss politics, only making mysterious references to some black hens. Sydney was no longer Ambassador in Holland, but he kept his friend William of Orange closely in touch with affairs in England. He wrote: "I delivered a compliment from your Highness to the Duchess of Portsmouth, which she took extremely well, but it will do you little good, for she hath no more credit with the King." It seems that Louise was temporarily out of favour with Charles at this time, for he resented her intrigues with the Duke of Monmouth. Some of the ministers tried to persuade the King to get rid of Louise, "and think by it to reconcile themselves to the people".

The trial of Edward Fitzharris, an Irishman, in June 1681 for high treason, caused enormous interest. He was a tool of Lord Shaftesbury and of one of his associates William, Lord Howard of Escrick, who persuaded Fitzharris to accuse the King of popery.

Fitzharris had given false evidence against the Queen, asserting that a Portuguese diplomat had informed him that she was involved in a plot to poison the King. Charles realized that Fitzharris was lying, and charged the man with high treason.

In the course of the trial before the Lord Chief Justice Pemberton, the Duchess of Portsmouth's name was mentioned several times, which caused her grave embarrassment. On one occasion she had begged some kindness, for Fitzharris from the King, but she maintained at the trial that she was not acquainted with his affairs. Mrs Wall, Louise's confidential servant appeared as an important witness. The account in the State Trials[4] shows that Fitzharris expressly asked that the Duchess of Portsmouth should be allowed to give evidence.

MRS WALL:	She is not come because the Court is very full, but if the Court will send for her, she will come presently.
FITZHARRIS:	My Lord, I beg that my Lady Duchess of Portsmouth may be sent for.
MRS WALL:	She gave me a commission to say, if the Court would have her to come, she would so do.
LORD CHIEF JUSTICE:	We cannot send for her, if she please to come so; we have no occasion to send for her . . .
FITZHARRIS:	Will you send one of your footmen, Mrs Wall? I am a prisoner and have nobody to send. In the meantime, where is the porter?
MRS WALL:	Here he is.
FITZHARRIS:	How long is it since you paid the money to me from my Lady Portsmouth?
PORTER:	I cannot tell indeed, it is so long since.

If any money was paid by Louise to Fitzharris, it was doubtless convenient for the porter to forget the transaction.

Later her grace of Portsmouth appeared as a reluctant witness. Her evidence shows quite clearly that she was perfectly able to hold her own against Fitzharris. Her sharp intelligence saw to that. The following exchanges took place between the two:

FITZHARRIS:	I am sorry to see your Grace come here upon any such account, but I hope your Grace will excuse me, 'tis for my life.

| | I desire to know of your Grace whether I was not employed to bring several Papers to the King, and among the rest, the impeachment against your Grace ... I told your Grace, I knew one Master Everard, who knew all the intrigues and all the Clubs in the City, I could tell all the designs of my Lord of Shaftesbury and all that party. And your Grace did encourage me to go on and I did by your Grace's direction, and by your means, I come to speak with the King about it. |
| LADY DUTCHESS: | When must I speak? |

One of the Counsel for the Crown was Sir George Jeffreys, a friend of Louise's. He tried to put her at her ease.

SIR GEORGE JEFFREYS:	Now Madam; and will your Grace now be pleased to stand up.
LADY DUTCHESS:	I have nothing at all to say to Mr Fitz-Harris, nor was concerned in any sort of business with him. All I have to say is he desired me to give a petition to the King to get his estate in Ireland, and I did three or four times speak to the King about it. But I have not anything else to say to him;

After more evidence had been given, Louise said that she had not come to court to wrangle with Mr Fitzharris, but to say what she knew. Finally, she addressed him in her most arrogant manner, being careful to convey a touch of disdain.

| | |
| LADY DUTCHESS: | Mr Fitzharris, if I had anything in the world to do you good, I would do it; but I have not, and so can't see that I am any ways more useful here.[5] |

Then she turned and left the court.

In his own defence Edward Fitzharris persisted in declaring: "Though my Lady Portsmouth, and Mrs Wall and the rest, are pleased to say that I was not employed, nor received money for secret services, yet, 'tis very well known I did so."

Fitzharris was found guilty of high treason, and condemned to death, although he tried to save his life by turning King's evidence.

That September her Grace the Duchess of Portsmouth was indisposed whilst at Newmarket, and had to send for a doctor or two.[6]

Despite his reputation for indolence, Charles II sometimes acted with energy and decision. Sir Charles Lyttleton wrote on 2nd July that the King surprised everybody "that is not a Privy Counsellor by coming by 8 o'clock to Town".[7] That morning Lord Shaftesbury was apprehended at Thanet House in Aldersgate Street, whilst he was still in bed, by a sergeant at arms Mr Deerham, and examined by the Council. He was later committed to the Tower upon a warrant of high treason, sworn against him by four persons. Just over three months later it was rumoured that Shaftesbury would be set at liberty, if he were to promise to retire to his house in Dorsetshire.[8] John Dryden wrote of him with venom in "Absalom and Achitophel":

> Of these the false Achitophel was first,
> A name to all succeeding ages curst:
> For close designs and crooked counsels fit,
> Sagacious, bold, and turbulent of wit,
> Restless, unfixed in principles and place
> In power unpleased, impatient, of disgrace;

Lord Campbell, however, at least says in his favour that he never took bribes as a Judge, while Dryden's praise of Shaftesbury in his judicial capacity is overdone, for he was an indifferent Judge.

To gain his freedom, the Earl offered to go overseas and to spend the remainder of his life in Carolina in America, which he had helped to colonize, and where he possessed property. The King, however, was adamant that he must face his trial by his peers. The bill of indictment against the prisoner was rejected by a grand Jury in London. The indictment rested on a statute of Edward III. He was accused of "compassing and imagining the death of the King and of designing to raise an insurrection at Oxford among other offences".

It so happened that Charles II was walking in the Mall one day with John Dryden when he remarked: "If I were a poet (and I think I am poor enough to be one), I would write a poem on Lord Shaftesbury's escape from justice in the following manner." This gave Dryden the idea to write his famous satirical poem "The Medal",[9] in which he attacks Lord Shaftesbury.

Ev'n in the most sincere advice he gave,
He had a grudging still to be a Knave.
The frauds he learnt in his fanatique years
Made him uneasy in his lawfull years.
At best as little honest as he cou'd;
And, like white witches, mischievously good.

On 17th November—the anniversary of the accession of Queen Elizabeth—the customary Pope-burning pageant took place in the murky London streets. Never has our capital in its long, turbulent history witnessed a stranger procession. Charles Bertie wrote to Lady Rutland: "All our streets shine with Popes and bonfires, and our bells are solemnly jangled to express all possible respect to her memory [Queen Elizabeth's]. My girl is just now come in from seeing the Popes and the show, and her tongue does so run with the story that she puts an end to this."[10] The excitement of the bawling mob in the sepulchral darkness increased as a bellman walked in the procession and exclaimed in a loud and mournful voice, "Remember Justice Godfrey". Next came an effigy of the murdered magistrate carried aloft. He wore a chamblet coat and about his neck was the linen cravat with which he was strangled. He is seated upon a white horse and supported by a Jesuit to keep him from falling.[11] Next came an effigy of the Pope, carried in a scarlet chair of state, wearing a magnificent scarlet gown lined with ermine and richly embroidered with gold and silver lace. About His Holiness his attendant devils "wonderfully soothing and caressing him". Imagine the weirdness of the scene, macabre and terrible as it undoubtedly was, with the flambeaux held by link-boys, and the gesticulating puppets, who followed them. How our television producers today would glory in such a spectacle! Then the Whig Lords, members of the Green Ribbon Club, on the balcony of the King's Head Tavern with their periwigs slightly aslant and half-drunken with wine puffing at their pipes as they shout encouragement to the mob below.

The French Ambassador Paul Barrillon had expressed a desire to see the show in 1679, and had watched it with English friends from the Palgrave-Head tavern. If the mob had known of his presence, they would surely have torn him to pieces.

During the early months of 1682, the Duchess of Portsmouth, who had been unwell, wished to visit her native country, so as to take the waters of Bourbon. She now felt that her position at court was so secure that a temporary separation from the King would not matter. It had given Louise enormous satisfaction to learn during December 1681 that Charles had made their young son the Duke of Richmond, now aged nine, Master of the Horse. The duties were to be administered by deputies. His father also created him a Knight of the Garter.

Louise was very clever, if an opportunist. She now realized that with the defeat of the Exclusionists it was inevitable that James Duke of York would succeed the King if he were to die. She needed ample money for her journey to France, and it occurred to her that she might be able to arrange a business deal with James whereby she could exchange £5,000 of her income from the hereditary excise for £5,000 of his from the Post Office. During March 1682 the Duke was in temporary exile in Edinburgh. The Duchess of Portsmouth wrote to him, putting this suggestion. James, although he had not forgiven Louise for "her dog trick" in siding with the Exclusionists, was anxious to return to London. He now behaved with unusual astuteness.[12] He was well aware that his income from the Post Office was a parliamentary grant, and he could not alienate it except by act of Parliament. Nor was he anxious to help his brother's mistress. However, he pretended that he agreed to her project, but wrote that it was not possible to complete the transaction unless he were to come to London. Louise therefore used her influence with Charles to have his brother recalled. Sir John Reresby relates that the King spoke freely in the Duchess of Portsmouth's apartments, that he was the last man in his own kingdom to have either law or justice, and that his case was hard. During the next few months the Duke of York once in England found that an extraordinary reaction had occurred in his favour. He also found various pretexts for not continuing to negotiate with Louise concerning his financial affairs.

So as to pay for her journey to France, the Duchess of Portsmouth used in advance a quarter of her pension, which was about to fall due at the end of March. Both the King of England and Barrillon wrote to Louis XIV on 16th March requesting him to grant her the same privilege enjoyed by the Duchess of Cleveland at Versailles, namely the right to sit on a *tabouret* when she went to pay her respects to the Queen. Barrillon wrote the French King:

I turned the conversation to another subject, when he spoke about her with that your Majesty should withdraw the domain of Aubigny from the Crown to give it to her. But I made him hope that your Majesty would give her other marks of kindness. The truth about her is, that she has shown great, constant, and intelligent zeal for your Majesty's interests, and given me numberless useful hints and pieces of information. She believes that the King of England wishes to further your Majesty's interests. The enemies of the Duchess of Portsmouth give out that she is going to France to settle there.[13]

Barrillon, too, served his King devotedly and with ability, but this cynical, unscrupulous man is not a sympathetic character. Yet he had a more agreeable side to his nature. He had a real love of and feeling for literature, and numbered La Fontaine among his intimates. He was a great friend of Madame de Sévigné's and once wrote to her: "Those, who like you better than I do, love you far too well."

While Charles travelled to Newmarket, Louise embarked on 4th March in a yacht at Greenwich. She was accompanied by her son aged ten, and a considerable suite attended her. She landed at Dieppe.

Never has a favourite of a reigning monarch been received with more acclaim and honours than the Duchess of Portsmouth at the French court. Her visit to France resembled more a triumphal progress of a Queen rather than that of a favourite of Charles II. The English Ambassador, Lord Preston, leased for her a magnificent house in Paris. Her extravagance and her ostentation caused an enormous sensation. It was rumoured that at the beginning of her visit she had lost as much as a hundred and five thousand *écus* at the gambling tables.[14] La Keroualle, who some remembered as the poor, despised girl without a dowry, was now treated like a queen. Never had she looked more resplendent, with her jewels sparkling on her dresses and in her ears, as she attended the *fêtes* at Saint-Cloud. Perhaps she recalled the shy maid of honour, who had once waited on the Duchess of Orleans. Now the courtiers vied with one another to overwhelm her with compliments on her superb taste.

Saint-Simon wrote of her: "When, on a high holiday, she went to visit the Capucines in the Rue Saint-Honoré, the poor monks, who were previously told of her intention, came out to meet her in procession, bearing the cross, the holy-water, and the incense, as if she had been a Queen, which made her strangely embarrassed, since she did not expect so much honour."

Towards the end of April Louise left Saint-Cloud for Aubigny to visit her estates in the country, which she now saw for the first time. Then she joined her sister the Countess of Pembroke at Bourbon in the middle of May. Henriette de Keroualle was nearly as extravagant as her elder sister, being especially fond of jewellery. No doubt she confided to Louise how unhappy she was being married to Philip, Earl of Pembroke. We must hope that the Duchess of Portsmouth derived more benefit for her health than Madame de Montespan, who on one occasion during 1676 had wittily complained to Madame de Sévigné that Bourbon, instead of removing a pain from her knee, had given her toothache. Louise stayed at Bourbon for about three weeks, and then departed for Paris.

At court she saw for herself the ascendancy Madame de Maintenon had acquired over the mind of Louis XIV. She reflected how transitory is the fate of mistresses of monarchs. Madame de Sévigné now recorded: "Everything is under her dominion, all her neighbour's [Montespan's] chambermaids are hers. One kneels to offer her the pot of paste, another brings her gloves, yet another puts her to bed. She bows to no one, and I believe that in her heart, she laughs at this tyranny." No greater contrast could be found than the flamboyant Montespan with her craze for gambling, and the serpent-like, intellectual Maintenon, formerly the royal governess. Louise probably calculated that Madame de Maintenon's career as reigning favourite might not last more than a few years. If so, that would explain why she did not pay sufficient court to the new favourite. Madame de Maintenon would remember Louise's apparent neglect and hold it against her some years later.

All her life Louise was haunted by the memory of the enchanting Duchess of Orleans. Remembering the days of obscurity when she attended her mistress in the beautiful gardens at Saint-Cloud. She was now all the more delighted by the homage and flattery of the French courtiers, although she saw through the insincerity of their compliments.

The Duchess of Portsmouth stayed for over four months in France, and did not return to London until the end of July. Her journey had been a triumphal progress, and her influence and power at Charles II's court were never more pronounced than in the period 1682–1685. Barrillon spoke of "the homage paid her by Louis XIV being like sunshine, gilding and glorifying an insignificant object".[15] What gratified Louise more than anything was the King of France's tribute to herself, that he had the fullest confidence in her judgment, and that no blunder could be committed so long as she was his medium.

Henceforward she worked in close harmony with the Duke of York. It was owing to Louise's influence that Lord Sunderland was restored to his former position as a Secretary of State at the end of January 1683. Barrillon wrote Louis XIV on this occasion: "Lord Sunderland will share her [Louise's] devotion to your Majesty's interests, with which those of the King of England are, and always must be, closely identified."

Though her enemies were to make one more desperate attempt to ruin the Duchess of Portsmouth, her position was so powerful that they failed to achieve their purpose.

NOTES

1. *Poems of John Dryden*, I, p. 258.
2. *Memoirs of Thomas Bruce, Earl of Ailesbury.*
3. Sir Arthur Bryant, *King Charles II.*
4. Cobbett, *Complete Collection of State Trials*, VIII.
5. *Tryall and Condemnation of Edward Fitzharris.*
6. Luttrell, *Brief Relation of State Affairs.*
7. *Hatton Correspondence.*
8. *Ibid.*
9. *Poems of John Dryden*, I, p. 255.
10. H.M.C. Rutland, II, 60; Sir Arthur Bryant, *op. cit.*
11. Sir George Sitwell, *The First Whig.*
12. F. C. Turner, *James II*. Perhaps the Duchess of York advised him concerning this transaction.
13. Forneron, *Louise de Keroualle.*
14. Jeanine Delpech, *The Life and Times of the Duchess of Portsmouth.*
15. Barrillon, 18th October 1682.

THIRTEEN

LOUISE'S TRIUMPH

When the new Moroccan Ambassador named Hamet was received at court towards the end of January 1683, it was the Duchess of Portsmouth who queened it. She was hostess at a magnificent banquet where sweetmeats and other delicacies were served. An orchestra played music. The guests sat at a long table, each lady between two Moors. Evelyn, who was present, tells us that Nell Gwyn was also there, "concubines, and cattell of that sort, as splendid as jewels, and excesse of bravery could make them". Two natural daughters of the King, Lady Lichfield★ and Lady Sussex, sat between the Moors. Sir John Reresby informs us in his memoirs, "that the Ambassador's present consisted of two lions and thirty ostriches, at which His Majesty laughed and said he knew nothing more proper to send by way of return than a flock of geese". The Ambassador took his leave of the Duchess of Portsmouth with courtly grace, praying that God would bless her and the prince her son, meaning the Duke of Richmond now aged eleven. Evelyn relates that the Ambassador during his stay often rode in Hyde Park where he and his retinue displayed their expert horsemanship "flinging and catching their lances at full speed, and managing their spears with incredible agility".

That spring there arrived in London Philippe de Vendôme, Henri IV's illegitimate grandson. He was a witty, handsome, dissolute French nobleman of twenty-eight, having been born in 1655. Consequently he was six years younger than Louise. Barrillon in his correspondence with Louis XIV always refers to Philippe de Vendôme as "*Le grand Prieur*" (the Grand Prior). This was the highest national rank conferred by the order of the Knights of Malta.

Philippe de Vendôme was an evil, depraved man, who boasted of the numbers of women he had seduced. Saint-Simon, writing

★ A daughter of the Duchess of Cleveland.

many years later in 1715, relates that the Grand Prior was openly unfaithful and that he prided himself on being the most sophisticated and the cleverest of deceivers. Saint-Simon certainly disliked him, calling him "liar, swindler, thief, frivoller, dishonest man, even to the marrow of his bones". However, the Duke of Orleans, later Regent of France, admired him, possibly because he was himself as dissolute. Such a man as the Grand Prior, possessing all the courtly graces, and with his false and insincere manners, knew well how to flatter women, who it must be admitted found him attractive. Ladies in the Stuart Age were as partial to rotters as they are today.

No doubt Philippe de Vendôme had heard of the great wealth amassed by the Duchess of Portsmouth and the Countess of Pembroke in England. He therefore came to London on the pretext of visiting his aunt the Duchesse Mazarin. Philippe was son of the Duke de Vendôme and Laura Mancini sister of Hortense Mazarin. The Grand Prior lost no opportunity to pay court to Louise, and it was soon evident to the watchful, prying courtiers that she was much attracted to Vendôme. Louise could not conceal that she had fallen in love with this nobleman.

She was now a woman of thirty-four, and she knew that Charles at fifty-three, overcharged with sensuality and sex, was not so virile as of old. For the first time she felt the need of a younger man. Vendôme pleaded with her with his eyes, and when he saw that she responded started to woo her with his lying, lascivious ways. There were stolen meetings, in her apartments in Whitehall arranged by the indispensable Mrs Wall, and Louise felt a warmth and a tenderness for him which had lain dormant in her. To the courtiers she had often appeared frigid, because she had found it necessary to conceal her instincts. Louise's enemies exulted in her infatuation for Vendôme, because they hoped to make it the means to ruin her. On her part Louise had suffered so much in spirit from Charles's infidelities that it made it easier for her to become for a brief spell the Grand Prior's mistress.

I think that this was the only occasion when Louise was unfaithful to Charles II, for she was no wanton by nature. A careful study of Barrillon's correspondence with Louis XIV in the Quai d'Orsay convinced me of the truth of this. The French Ambassador with his cold, precise legal mind, was well aware of Louise's intrigue with the Grand Prior, and believed that she enjoyed intimate relations with the Grand Prior. He wrote to the King of France that prudence should have made "Madame de Portsmouth" oblige Vendôme to return to France.[1] Barrillon, vigilant and uneasy, saw that Charles II was annoyed by Louise's friendship with the Grand Prior. The King was no fool, and he occasionally showed signs of ill-temper and jealousy. "His bad temper does not last long," wrote Barrillon. Yet the Duchess of Portsmouth's friends were not without anxiety. Even Lord Sunderland, who was also a friend of Vendôme, confided in Barrillon about the suspicions of the King of England. Despite his fears that the Duchess of Portsmouth might be ruined by her indiscreet behaviour, Sunderland took particular care to be on amicable terms with Monsieur de Vendôme, whom he invited to dine at his house. There was a good deal of gossip at court. The Lord Privy Seal told Sir John Reresby that he lamented the interest that the Duchess of Portsmouth had with the King. He thought that she was not only betraying him as to his councils, but in his bed, since she was certainly lying with the Grand Prior.[2]

It is related by Bishop Burnet that Charles II on one occasion entered Louise's apartments to find Philippe de Vendôme making love to her. It is usually supposed that Charles condoned the sexual frailty of his mistresses, but he was capable of acute jealousy. He now asked Lord Sunderland to tell the French Ambassador that the Grand Prior must be forbidden to visit the Duchess of Portsmouth. Consequently Philippe de Vendôme did not appear in her apartments for four or five days, but later resumed his visits.

In an interview with Barrillon, the King told him of his desire to rid himself of the odious presence of the Grand Prior. He asked the French Ambassador to tell Vendôme to leave the kingdom, a delicate and difficult message for a diplomat to convey to such an important person as the Grand Prior.[3] However, Barrillon used all the arts of persuasion to induce this unwelcome guest to depart from England. The Grand Prior remained obdurate declaring that he would only leave when the King gave him the express order to do so by word of mouth. He now requested Barrillon to demand for him an audience. Charles with extreme reluctance agreed to see Vendôme. Once admitted to the King's presence, he attempted to justify himself in his emotional way, but Charles refused to listen to his excuses.

After several days further reflection, Charles sent Lieutenant Griffin, an officer of the Guards, to intimate to Vendôme that unless he left within two days, he had orders to arrest him and put him on a packet, which was to sail for Calais. The Grand Prior, however, found various pretexts for staying on in England. He had the effrontery to tell Barrillon that if he was allowed to remain in England, he would agree to retire to the country. Louise now begged Barrillon to reveal this proposal to the King, but Charles remained adamant. At all costs Louise wanted to avoid a scandal.

By this time she was no longer deluded as to Vendôme's real character. She was terrified lest he might try to compromise her, or to publish the letters which had passed between them. Until he left England she was nervous in case the Grand Prior should make a scene in public. The Duke of York, Lord Sunderland and Lord Rochester (Laurence Hyde*) all encouraged the King to be resolute and to get rid of Vendôme. Lord Halifax told Barrillon that these high persons would lose much honour for being involved in this affair.

It must have been an enormous relief to Barrillon when the Grand Prior left England at 4 o'clock one afternoon at the end of November. As Barrillon told Louis XIV, Vendôme hoped to derive great advantages and prestige from a liaison with the Duchess of Portsmouth.

Her enemies had conceived ardent hopes that Louise would be ruined by her affair with the Grand Prior, but they were doomed to disappointment. It is probable that Charles chiefly blamed the Frenchman, and knowing as he did that he, the King, had wronged Louise on various occasions, he was inclined to be indulgent. The real truth is that he was so dependent on "his dearest Fubbs" during his last years that he could forgive her anything.

Louis XIV, who felt grateful to the Duchess of Portsmouth for her work as an agent of his foreign policy, helped her at this difficult juncture. He commanded the Duc de Vendôme, the elder brother of the Grand Prior, to inform him that he could return to the Court of France, where he would meet with a better reception than his bad conduct in England had led him to expect.[4] He sent Colbert de Croissy with a special message to the Grand Prior that if ever he said anything derogatory about the Duchess of Portsmouth, he would incur his resentment. So, the scandal was hushed up and Louise could breathe freely.

* Created Earl of Rochester in 1682. John Wilmot, second Earl of Rochester, had died two years before.

When it was proposed that Princess Anne, James Duke of York's younger daughter, should marry Prince George of Denmark, Louise used her diplomatic gifts to further the match. The Duke of York asked Louise's advice concerning the suggested marriage and charged her to ascertain whether or not Louis XIV would favour the match.[5] The King of Denmark, knowing how valuable were the Duchess of Portsmouth's good offices, sent her his miniature set in diamonds. Evelyn was not unduly impressed with Prince George. He describes him as "having the Danish countenance, blonde, of few words, spoke French but ill, seem'd somewhat heavy, but reported to be valliant". The marriage took place on a glorious summer day, 28th July 1684.

Barrillon observed towards the end of 1683 that the influence of the Duchess of Portsmouth was as strong as ever with the King of England, and that he even caressed her in public. Bishop Gilbert Burnet wrote: "His fondness broke out in very indecent instances, and he caressed her in the view of all people, which he had never done on any occasion or to any person formerly."

By the beginning of 1683, the King was rid of his vindictive enemy Lord Shaftesbury. During the preceding November, hearing that Charles again intended to arrest him, Lord Shaftesbury settled his estate, so that his family would inherit it, if he were to die. A fugitive from justice, he secretly left Thanet House, and lay concealed and disguised for some time among his friends in various parts of the City of London. Eventually, he was apprised by one of his intimates, Lord Mordaunt, of a suspicious meeting in the apartments of the Duchess of Portsmouth. Lord Shaftesbury then remarked: "My Lord, you are a young man of honour and would not deceive me: if this has happened, I must be gone tonight."[6] Cleverly disguised he managed to escape overseas where he died in Holland on 21st January 1683 in the arms of his faithful companion, Wheelock. With the death of this dangerous opponent the King's triumph over his enemies was almost assured.

The Rye House Plot, which occurred during the spring of 1683, was a dastardly attempt by an old Cromwellian officer, Captain Richard Rumbold, and other fanatics to kill Charles II and the Duke of York. Rumbold's home was the Rye House at Hoddesdon, near Ware in Hertfordshire. It lay on the direct road between London and Newmarket where the King attended the spring horse matches. It was planned that as the coach, which contained Charles and his brother passed Rye House, it should be obstructed by a hay-cart, thus giving the assassins the opportunity to shoot the royal brothers with their muskets.[7] By an act of providence, however, owing to the carelessness of a royal groom, who had set fire to the stables, thus causing a disastrous fire, Charles decided to leave Newmarket a week earlier than he had intended. In such a way were the murderous designs of the conspirators frustrated.

Later investigations revealed a second plot concocted by the Whig Lords, William Russell, Essex, Algernon Sydney and others, who had planned to seize Whitehall and to promote a general insurrection throughout the country. The principal conspirators were arrested. Charles, heavy in heart, was well aware that the Duke of Monmouth was also implicated. One summer day as he was setting his watch by the sun dial in the Privy Garden at Whitehall, he turned to young Lord Thomas Bruce, who was in attendance, telling him to go to Toddington in Bedfordshire to arrest his son Monmouth.[8] Bruce, knowing that his master still loved Monmouth, despite his bitter feelings, remarked that the order was a difficult one to fulfil. He made various ingenious excuses, which both knew to be fallacious. He told his master that Lady Henrietta Wentworth's* house at Toddington was surrounded with vast ponds and that there were many vaults underground by which he might escape. If he were to raise a militia-troop, Monmouth would hear of it and make his escape. Marvelling at his invention, Charles turned his dark eyes on Lord Thomas with a look of gratitude, and told him to come back for orders another time.

Among the conspirators who were tried at the Old Bailey on Friday, 13th July, was Lord William Russell. He was found guilty of high treason. Russell had powerful friends who tried to intercede for him with the King. He was told that the pardoning of Lord Russell "Would lay an eternal obligation upon a very great and numerous family, and the taking of his life would never be forgotten". Charles then said: "All that is true; but it is as true, that if I do not take his life, he will soon have mine."[9] Charles was inexorable. Russell was beheaded by Jack Ketch. The most despicable of the accused men was Lord Howard of Escrick, who turned King's evidence, thus saving his life. Arthur Capel, Earl of Essex, whom the Duchess of Portsmouth had known well,

* Mistress of the Duke of Monmouth, whom he tenderly loved.

cut his throat in the Tower with a kind of Roman stoicism. Charles might have spared his life, for he maintained "that my Lord of Essex needed not to have despaired of mercy, for I owed him a life". Arthur Capel's father had died on the scaffold for Charles I.

As for the Duke of Monmouth, he presented to a committee of the Privy Council gathered at the Duchess of Portsmouth's apartments a letter so cleverly worded that it was said to be written by Lord Halifax. In this letter to the King, Monmouth wrote: "I was not conscious of any design against Your Majesty's life, yet I lament the having had so great a hand in that other part of the said conspiracy." It is related that Queen Catherine, who had been fond of the young Duke, interceded for him. Charles informed Monmouth that it was only her intercession which had persuaded him to forgive the offence.[10] That the Duchess of Portsmouth also added her pleas to the Queen's is at least improbable. Barrillon informed Louis[11] that the King of England has spoken of the Duke of Monmouth with all the bitterness possible to Madame de Portsmouth and told her that he believed him capable of the blackest crimes and the worst actions.

One day in early January 1684, Charles II drew Barrillon aside, and told him confidentially: "The Duchess of Portsmouth and her son, the Duke of Richmond are the persons above all others in the world, whom I love the most. I would be deeply obliged to the King of France if he were to agree to reconvert the estate of Aubigny into a duchy for her, with the reversion to her son and his future issue."[12] The Ambassador received the King's request rather coldly. He had been embarrassed by her indiscreet behaviour with the Grand Prior, and his private opinion was that Louise did not merit such a high honour. He wrote on 21st January: "Is not this outstepping all bounds? As an English Duchess, she has by courtesy the same honours in France as a French Duchess. But that does not satisfy her. She must have them in virtue of letters patent, and as a right sit on a *tabouret* whenever she may go to pay her respects to the Queen at Versailles."[13]

The French Ambassador wrote his master that "Madame de Portsmouth" had herself spoken to him. Lord Sunderland, no doubt under an obligation to Louise, argued that such a concession would attach her all her life to the interests and service of the King of France. Barrillon assured Sunderland that in matters of such consequence he did not wish to hold light hopes, thus laying himself open to reproaches.

The Duke of York, who was outwardly at least on friendly terms with Louise, used his influence in favour of this project. The French Ambassador was at last forced to admit that if His Majesty (the King of France) were to decide to agree with "Madame de Portsmouth's" suggestion, he was persuaded that great advantages for his service could be derived in England. Louis XIV did not hesitate. Letters patent were issued to revive the Duchy of Aubigny. It was a triumph for the Duchess of Portsmouth.

Since the Duke of York had helped her over the Duchy of Aubigny affair, Louise used her influence on his behalf that he should be reinstated as Lord High Admiral in March 1684.[14] Though her power was great in the last year of the life of Charles II, Forneron exaggerates when he writes "that she held so completely England in her hands, that she was the real Sovereign". Such a sweeping statement is absolutely untrue. Charles was now content that his brother should chiefly manage affairs, for he was tired and his natural indolence made him happy that some of the burden should be taken off his shoulders. James performed many duties, but "with great haughtiness", according to Sir John Reresby. Bishop Burnet also wrote: "The King had scarce company about him to entertain him, when the Duke's *levées* and *couchées* were so crowded that the antichambers were full. The King walked about with a small train of the necessary attendants when the Duke had a vast following . . ." There are reasons for believing that Louise was jealous that James was closeted for long hours with the King.[15] Sometimes she regretted that she had been the means of bringing him back from Scotland to the chief place in Charles's Counsels. Towards the end of her royal lover's life she was intriguing that James should again be banished to Scotland. She used all her powers of persuasion on her royal lover to accomplish this aim. Except for the King's premature death, it is likely that James would have faced a further term of exile.

New Secretaries of State were careful to cultivate the favour of the Duchess of Portsmouth and not to offend her. When Sir Leoline Jenkins owing to bad health resolved to retire from his position in 1684, a Cornishman, Sidney Godolphin,* succeeded to the vacant position. There is no doubt that Louise helped

* 1645-1712. Created a Baron in 1684.

Godolphin to attain this promotion. The ancient and beautiful former ancestral home of the Godolphin family* where Sidney Godolphin was born lies near Helston in Cornwall. Charles wittily said of Godolphin that "he was never in the way and never out of it". Pepys also liked him, "finding him a very pretty and able person, a man of very fine parts".[16]

When Charles, second Earl of Middleton, was appointed a Secretary of State in 1684, he took good care to ingratiate himself with the Duchess of Portsmouth. He wrote to Lord Sunderland: "I shall deal no more for the last Lord Rochester's [Laurence Hyde's] lodgings if it is true that the Duchess of Portsmouth has a mind to have them. You may tell her this from me and that I had wrote to you at Winchester, but had never heard of her interest till within these two days. You may also propose as from yourself that if she'll allow me to go into them now, if she can get Mrs Crofts afterwards for me I shall be willing to change."[17] Lord Middleton subsequently became a Secretary of State to James II during his final exile at Saint-Germain.

When Louis XIV commanded the Marquis de Preuilly to sail up the Channel without bothering to send a notification to Charles II, it was Louise, who tactfully explained to the King that this was not a sign of want of respect or friendliness. The best course for Charles was to pretend that this action had been agreed to by the two kings.[18] It was Louise who persuaded Charles to concur without murmuring about the capture of Luxembourg by Louis.[19] Moreover, Charles was never duped by Louis. Louise, as has been stressed, possessed enormous influence, but Charles was the master.

During November 1684 Louise fell dangerously ill, and the King was usually to be found in her apartments. Barrillon and the other ambassadors made constant inquiries about her state of health. Louise feared lest she might die and her son, since he was a foreigner, would not be able to inherit the money she had invested in France. She therefore through Barrillon requested King Louis XIV to issue letters of naturalization to her son Charles Lennox, Duke of Richmond. Louis did not hesitate for one moment to grant her request.[20] Louise, carefully looked after by Charles's doctors, recovered her health. The King murmured sweet endearing words into her ears, and her hold over him seemed as strong as ever. Lord Ailesbury writing many years

* Now owned by Mr and Mrs Schofield.

later, states that Charles was tiring of Louise during the last few months of his life, and would have liked to have got rid of her. Even if this were true—and it is doubtful—Louise was so essential to him as his intermediary with the French King, that he could not do without her.

When Louise's brother-in-law the Earl of Pembroke died, Henriette de Keroualle, Countess of Pembroke decided to retire to France. Louise had quarrelled with Pembroke, accusing him of making no provision for her sister when she was with child in 1675. She had threatened to complain to the King about it. This interference had infuriated Pembroke, who declared that he would set her on her head at Charing Cross unless she kept quiet.

Henriette was now eager to return to her native land, taking with her her ill-gotten possessions. She was nearly as avaricious as her sister. She had acquired so many valuables that it was found necessary to charter several ships to convey them to France. She possessed a pearl necklace worth twenty thousand francs with earrings, drops and clasps, a miniature of Charles set in brilliants, and a resplendent bed of crimson Genoese velvet, hung with brocade, with a pattern on a white mound. Chests on the ships were laden with silk moire, with Indian stuffs flowered with silver, and Welsh flannel with cabinets and looking-glass frames. She took a hundred pounds of best wax tapers, and also a large number of tallow ones. This lady seems to have possessed a special fancy for expensive gloves. During 1682 Lesgu, a shopkeeper of Paris and Jaquillon Laurent his wife sold her "twenty-eight pairs of openwork white gloves, with orange and amber scent, and one pair of gloves costing thirty-three livres trimmed with ribbon, gold and silver at the arms, and herring-boned in gold and silver on the back of the hand".[21] Lady Pembroke also owned beautiful Chinese lacquer cabinets and other rare Japanese curiosities.

John Churchill's fiery wife, Sarah, knowing how unwise it was to offend the Duchess of Portsmouth, once wrote her: "If you remember Madam how few days past, when you ware heare, that I did not doe all I could, to have the pleasure of seeing you, you will forgive my not writing all this time. I am sure nobody can be more sensible of the kindness you have shown me than I am, nor wishes more than I doe to serve you . . ."

When the Duchess of Portsmouth returned from her travels, she certainly kept the customs officers busy opening her boxes at the ports. A typical entry in the Treasury Books reads: "Treasury warrant to the Customs Commissioners to direct the Customs Officers at Rye to open the Duchess of Portsmouth's goods in her presence, if she lands there on her return from France."[22] Another entry goes: "Henry Guy to Mr Hewer to the Customs Commissioners to have opened at the Duchess of Portsmouth's lodgings in Whitehall a package marked D.P. for which Dr Taylor her Grace's Commissioner will pay the customs." Dr Taylor was Louise's steward or man of business, who banked money received and gave receipts.

The Duchess of Portsmouth sometimes brought back consignments of wine from France, as this entry records: "Henry Guy to the Customs Commissioners to deliver to Mr Whitly at Whitehall for the Duchess of Portsmouth, some wine, *etc.* on board Captain Clement's yacht at Greenwich."[23]

On 24th November 1684—the Queen's birthday—there was a splendid display of fireworks on the Thames before Whitehall, where castles and forts, the arms of Charles II and those of Catherine of Braganza, were represented in fire, a glorious display never seen before.[24] Several mock skirmishes took place on the water that night, and to see its surface aglow with many fires was both curious and beautiful. It was said that the show cost as much as £1,500. Afterwards there was a ball where the ladies of the court and the young gallants danced in the great hall. Evelyn wrote that "the Court had not been seene so brave and rich in apparel since Charles II's Restoration".

That winter there were clear indications that Charles II's splendid health was failing, He had some trouble with one of his legs, which prevented him walking three or four hours a day. This was his usual custom. Instead of consulting his doctors, he went to his laboratory where he unwisely treated it with drugs, such as mercury. Wellwood later declared that Charles's death was caused through his lack of exercise because of the wound in his leg. It was noticed that his post-prandial slumbers were becoming more regular and that he now lived very quietly.

NOTES

1. Correspondance Angleterre, CIL, fol. 183.
2. *Memoirs of Sir John Reresby*, p. 299.
3. Correspondance Angleterre, CL, fol. 468.

4. Forneron, *Louise de Keroualle*.
5. Correspondance Angleterre, CXLIX, fol. 401; Barrillon to Monsieur Colbert.
6. John, Lord Campbell, *Life of Lord Shaftesbury*, I, p. 370.
7. Hesketh Pearson, *Charles II, his life and likeness*.
8. *Memoirs of Thomas Bruce, Earl of Ailesbury*, I, p. 75.
9. Lady Rachel Russell, *Letters*.
10. Lillias Campbell Davidson, *Catherine of Braganza*.
11. Barrillon, 24th April 1684.
12. Barrillon to Louis XIV, 14th January.
13. Forneron, *op. cit.*
14. Barrillon wrote the news to Louis XIV on 19th March.
15. F. C. Turner, *James II*.
16. *Diary of Samuel Pepys*, 10th February 1668.
17. Dorothy Middleton, *The Life of Charles second Duke of Middleton*.
18. Forneron, *op. cit.*
19. Osmund Airy, *Charles II*.
20. Correspondance Angleterre, CLI, fol. 230.
21. Forneron, *op. cit.*
22. Calendar of Treasury Books, VII, Part i, p. 500.
23. *Ibid.*, Part ii, p. 729.
24. *Memoirs and Correspondence of John Evelyn*, III, p. 121.

FOURTEEN

CHARLES THE SECOND'S DEATH

In his memoirs written many years later when he was in exile,
Lord Ailesbury refers wistfully to the last days of Charles II, as if
it was a kind of golden age.[1] As Lord Thomas Bruce, a young
Lord-in-waiting, he idolized Charles II, and the King was the
inspiration of his early life. He wrote: "We breathed nothing but
peace and happiness, and God knows that was the last year [1684]
of our enjoying my good and great King and master."

Bruce began his last week of waiting on the afternoon of
Monday, 26th January 1685. Charles had been slightly indisposed
and prevented from taking his customary walks in the Park or
Arlington Gardens owing to a small sore on one of his heels. So,
in order to get some air he went in a *calèche*, attended by the
faithful Bruce. He recollected that Charles II had an excellent
appetite during these last days, "and one thing very hard of
digestion—a goose egg if not two". On the evening of Sunday,
1st February John Evelyn was present in Whitehall Palace, and
strongly disapproved of what he saw:

> I can never forget [he wrote] the inexpressible luxury and profane-
> ness, gaming and all dissoluteness, and as if were total forgetfulness
> of God (it being Sunday evening) which ... I was witness of the
> King sitting and toying with his concubines, Portsmouth, Cleve-
> land and Mazarin, a French boy singing love-songs in that glorious
> gallery, whilst about twenty of the great courtiers and other dissolute
> persons were at basset round a large table, a bank of at least two
> thousand in gold before them.

Cleveland and Mazarin were no longer concubines, while Louise
was by this time rather a beloved companion than a mistress.

After dining the King pursued his usual habit of going to the
Duchess of Portsmouth's apartments where he amused himself
conversing with the people who were there. The King was in a
most gracious humour that evening, so that those present could

hardly remember having seen him in so charming a mood. At the customary hour Bruce lit him to his bedchamber. As he handed the candle to the page of the back stairs, it went out. He thought it an ill-omen, for he shook his head.

Bruce's account of the King's last illness is the best contemporary one, because it is written with such transparent simplicity, sincerity and honesty; there is a strange beauty when he describes events, though his prose is sometimes clumsy. It was an anxious night for the King's attendants. Bruce found it difficult to sleep, and noticed that the King was rather restless. The scene is rendered very vivid for us. "Several circumstances," Bruce wrote, "made the lodging very uneasy—the great grate being filled with scotch coal that burnt all night, a dozen dogs that came to our bed, and several pendulums that struck at the half quarter, and all not going alike, it was a continual chiming."

It was the morning of 2nd February. In the room adjoining the King's bedchamber Robert Howard, one of the royal grooms, asked Lord Thomas Bruce how the King had slept. Bruce informed him that he had turned sometimes in his sleep. "Lord," remarked Howard, "that is an ill mark, and contrary to his custom." Charles on rising had been unable to say one word to his attendants. Pale as ashes, he had gone to his private closet. It was a bitter February morning, and Bruce sent Will Chiffinch the first page of the back stairs with a message to his master, begging him to return to the bedchamber.

As Charles was being shaved by his barber, he fell back into Bruce's arms in a fit, his mouth foaming "and screwing horribly upwards towards a white, pupilless eye".[2] Bruce in an agony of apprehension immediately ordered Dr King, the royal physician, to bleed King Charles, which he did without delay. The King lost fifteen ounces of blood. Charles was put to bed. Bruce then hurriedly went to fetch the Duke of York, who arrived with a shoe on one foot and a slipper on another.

In his account Bruce never mentions the Duchess of Portsmouth at the King's bedside, though Lord Macaulay relates that "during a short time, the Duchess of Portsmouth hung over him with the familiarity of a wife".[3] Since Queen Catherine and the Duchess of York were about to enter the room, the favourite mistress was forced to retire. Macaulay almost certainly used Bishop Gilbert Burnet's contemporary account, which is sometimes prejudiced and unreliable. It is extremely likely that Louise out of decency never appeared in the royal bedchamber on that terrible morning. We know that Charles's little Portuguese Queen knelt at the end of his bed, rubbing his feet. When the devoted Bruce approached his master for a moment, Charles was able to take his hand and whisper: "I see you love me dying as well as living."

The royal bedchamber was crowded almost to suffocation with fourteen doctors, and courtiers. The remedies applied were barbaric and absurd. The patient was often bled, and hot iron was applied to his tortured head. The doctors prescribed for the King manna and cream of tartar in thin broth and barley-water together with a little light ale made without hops. Nothing was denied him except rest and privacy. The King bore his sufferings with infinite fortitude, though he complained that he felt as if a fire was burning within him.

The Duke of York was constantly at his brother's bedside, and since he feared an insurrection ordered that the ports should be closed. He was anxious lest any news of the King's illness should reach the Duke of Monmouth. Beyond the barred gates of the Palace of Whitehall, the silent, tearful multitude waited anxiously and tensely, for Charles was much beloved, despite his grave faults.

On the morning of Thursday, 5th February, Charles seemed much better, and some of the doctors were even of the opinion that His Majesty was out of danger. John Drummond wrote to William Douglas, Duke of Queensberry: "The King continues to grow better and better, how the recovering so violent a deceas must needs be by slow steps and degrees ... he had Jesuites powder twice given him in the night ..." From Whitehall on that murky February day came the cheerful chime of the Church bells: "About seven this morning he began to talk of the way he took his disease very cheerfully to the unspeakable joy of all present."[4] That evening, however, a relapse occurred, and the doctors were obliged to abandon all hope of his recovery.

The Protestant prelates, including William Sancroft, Archbishop of Canterbury, an honest, modest and pious man, and Thomas Ken, Bishop of Bath and Wells, gathered round the King imploring Charles to take the last rites of the Protestant Communion. Sancroft urged him in his low voice. "It is time to speak out, for your Majesty is about to appear before a Judge who is no respecter of persons." The King seemed unresponsive. It was known that Ken was Charles's favourite Bishop, and it was now decided that he should be their spokesman. Bruce related that Ken's voice was "like to a nightingale for the sweetness of it, so he was desired by the rest to persuade the King to hearken to them". Charles thanked them in a faint voice with his customary courtesy but said there was time enough.

Meanwhile Louise, who was grief-stricken on hearing of Charles's grave illness was closeted with the French Ambassador Barrillon in her apartments. At this juncture she did not think of her own interests, though fully aware that her royal lover's death would entail her loss of power and influence. She took the fat, astute Barrillon aside, and said in a low voice, confidentially to him: "*Monsieur L'Ambassadeur*, I am now going to tell you a secret, although its public revelation would cost me my head. The King of England is in the bottom of his heart a Catholic, and there he is surrounded with Protestant Bishops! There is nobody to tell him of his state or to speak to him of God. I cannot decently enter his room. Besides, the Queen is now there constantly. The Duke of York is too busy with his own affairs to trouble himself about the King's conscience. I conjure you to go and tell him that the end is approaching, and that it is his duty to save without loss of time, his brother's soul."⁵

What were the motives of the shrewd Bretonne in making this strange request to Barrillon? She was a sincere Roman Catholic, and believed that to abandon her lover's soul to heretics was a crime. Possibly, too, she wished to curry favour with the Duke of York, for she knew that James was about to succeed his brother. Barrillon hastened back into the sick chamber, and requested the Duke of York to accompany him into the Queen's room. There he told him in great secrecy of the King's need to see a priest. The Duke, plunged in deep thought, said to Barrillon: "You are right, there is no time to lose. I will hazard everything rather than not to do my duty on this occasion." He hurried back to the royal bedchamber. Kneeling by the King's bed, he whispered in his ear: "Do you desire to see a priest, Sire?" The craning courtiers heard the King say in a faint voice "Yes, with all my heart.' Charles begged his brother to do nothing which might endanger himself.

It was a dramatic scene that night in the ancient Palace of Whitehall. The Duke of York, heavy with lack of sleep and obviously under strain from long hours of vigil, told the French

Ambassador that the King had consented to see a priest. A difficulty now arose. Among the Queen's Portuguese priests gathered together in a small closet there was nobody who could speak a word of English, except Father John Huddleston, a Benedictine Monk, born at Faringdon Hall, near Preston,* who, when he was residing in the family of Thomas Whitgreave at Moseley Hall in Staffordshire had saved Charles II's life after the Battle of Worcester. As a token of gratitude the King had preserved Huddleston's life by allowing him to remain at Whitehall during the Popish Terror. The old man was now smuggled by Will Chiffinch, disguised in cassock and wig, to a side door of the bedchamber.[6]

It was now almost eight o'clock in the evening and the flickering candles lit up the pale features of the dying King. The Duke of York then ordered all the courtiers to leave the room, except for two Protestants, John Earl of Bath, a boyhood companion of the King's and the French born Louis de Duras, Earl of Feversham, whose loyalty could be relied on. He led Huddleston to his brother saying: "Sire, here is a man who saved your life and is now come to save your soul."

"He is very welcome," said the King. One account of the King's death relates that on seeing the reverent Father, the King cried out: "Almighty God! What good planet governs me, that all my life is wonders and miracles! When, O Lord, I consider my infancy, my exile, my escape at Worcester, my preservation in the Oak with the assistance of this good Father, and now to have him again to preserve my soul."[7] As Charles's senses were rapidly becoming dimmer, one may conjecture how Charles summed up sufficient strength to say such words.

What is certain is that Charles expressed a desire to die in the Catholic faith. When Huddleston was ready to give the King extreme unction, he tried to rise from his bed, saying: "Let me meet my Heavenly Father in a better posture than in my bed." Huddleston gently bade him to stay still.

When his sons came to take their leave of their father, Charles spoke with special affection to the Duke of Richmond, though he never once mentioned the Duke of Monmouth. His three natural sons by the Duchess of Cleveland, the Dukes of Grafton ("the sailor prince"), Northumberland and Southampton, all asked their father's blessing. So did the Duke of Saint Albans, Nell Gwyn's son. The King implored his brother to take care of

* 1608–1698.

Robert Spencer, second Earl of Sunderland by Carlo Maratti (*by
courtesy of the Earl Spencer and Courtauld Institute of Art*)

Louise de Keroualle, Duchess of Portsmouth, by Sir Godfrey Kneller
(*from Goodwood House by courtesy of the Trustees*)

Louise, "I have always loved her," he said, "and I die loving her. And do not let poor Nelly starve," he added. When the Queen was forced to retire to her apartments, no longer able to endure the harrowing scenes, she sent a message to her husband by Lord Halifax, begging for his forgiveness. Charles returned the answer: "Alas! Poor woman! She ask my pardon? I beg hers with all my heart." Charles died just before 11 am on Friday, 6th February.

The Hon. John Drummond wrote to the first Duke of Queensberry, "He died as he lived the admiration of all men for his piety, his contempt of this world, and his resolutions against death."[8] Musing on the King's premature death a month later, Madame de Sévigné wrote:[9] "he was but in the prime of life, and yet to be obliged to quit everything in the midst of enjoyment, and to be hurried to death (of which he had never taken any thought) from the lap of riotous pleasures and debauchery." There she was wrong, for papers found in Charles's strong box after his death prove that Charles had given some thought to religion, though he was not religious.

The death of Charles was a terrible blow for the Duchess of Portsmouth, and she now gave herself up to an agony of grief. Both the Duchess of Portsmouth and Nell Gwyn attempted to decorate their horses and coaches in mourning for Charles, although this privilege was really confined to the royal family.[10] Deserted by the fickle courtiers, Louise now lost all claim to political importance. When the new King James II visited her within an hour of his brother's death to assure her of his protection and friendship, she did not attach much faith to his protestations of good will. The truth is that James disliked her, and she knew it.

Lord Ailesbury wrote in his memoirs: "The King [James] had a true English spirit, and I knew well that the French lady and her creature the French Ambassador, Monsieur Barrillon were looked on very coldly."[11] James could never forgive Louise for her intrigues with the Duke of Monmouth when he was temporarily in exile in Brussels and Scotland. Ailesbury considered that Louise and Barrillon were in reality James's secret and most vindictive enemies. Though the new King might at times look on Barrillon coldly, he confided in him more freely than with some of his ministers.

Louis XIV was indignant when he heard at the beginning of March that James had taken away from the thirteen-year-old Duke of Richmond the post of Master of the Horse and given it to his loyal friend George Legge, Earl of Dartmouth. Louis wrote to his Ambassador: "I have learnt with surprise that the new King of England had deprived the Duke of Richmond of the office of Master of the Horse, notwithstanding the manner in which the late King recommended this son of his to his brother."[12]

James was obliged to pay Louise several visits in the course of which he explained as tactfully as possible (and he was not known for his tact) the reasons why he had deprived young Richmond of this office. He considered that he lacked experience and was too youthful for it. Louise patiently listened and accepted James's explanations. James's action was, however, deeply resented by her son, who later left England in high dudgeon.

After Charles II's death there arose the customary rumours, so prevalent in that age that the King had been poisoned. Typical stories were that the hated Duchess of Portsmouth had poisoned him in a cup of chocolate, and that something had been put into his favourite dish of eggs and ambergrease. It was even reported that the Queen had poisoned him in a jar of dried peas. It was whispered abroad in the coffee-houses that the late King's tongue had swelled to the size of a neat's tongue, and that a cake of deleterious powder had been discovered in his brain.[13] It seems incredible but some gullible people believed these rumours. The probability is that Charles died from chronic granular kidney disease, accompanied by uraemic convulsions and coma.[14]

Louise's main object at this time was to return to France as soon as possible, and to settle her financial affairs. She told Barrillon that a mark of esteem from King Louis would be of great benefit to her, and that she would by this means secure incomparably better treatment in England. She was well aware of her unpopularity, and that people accused her of selling England to France with the assistance of Lord Sunderland.

James told her that he was anxious that the Duke of Richmond should become a Catholic, and that if she agreed to it, he would do everything in his power for the boy.

The most powerful of James's ministers was his brother-in-law Laurence Hyde, Earl of Rochester,* who had consistently supported the new King during the Exclusion crisis. He had been appointed Lord Treasurer on Charles's death. Since Rochester seemed well disposed to her, Louise was much gratified.

Her income consisted of a pension of three thousand guineas

* Brother of Anne Hyde, first Duchess of York.

per annum granted to her by James II, and the King allowed Richmond two thousand guineas per annum. Besides these sources of income Louise enjoyed two thousand a year from the confiscated estate of Lord Grey of Werke, afterwards created Lord Tankerville by William III, who had been involved in the Rye House Plot. When her son the Duke of Richmond came of age, she would no longer benefit from the two thousand for it would belong to him. So, the Duchess of Portsmouth returned to France in August 1685 with an English estate worth £5,000 a year. Besides this income, she had invested large sums of money in France, and possessed valuable personal property such as furniture and jewellery. She had besides 200,000 francs in gold which she had received on the death of Charles II. Before leaving England, she was at least able to pay off her debts. Louise was no easy mistress to her servants and quarrelled with them about financial transactions. One of her servants named Mrs Ellin Oglethorpe had been unlucky enough to incur her displeasure. When Louise was in France in 1686, Mrs Oglethorpe wrote to her:

> And the incouragement of your parting kindnesse was your telling me, that though you should dye in the journey you would take care that I should be paid ... Madam, you know that when you were pleased to withdraw your favours from me that you did not only forbidd your servants, but even my friends and acquaintancies and all people else, that had expectation or dependence upon your favour not to see me under payment of your displeasure. I have paid out expenses for your grace from my own pocket ... It is not nyne months agoe since I paid a bill of sixty-six pounds for things that Monsieur Carwell and the Duke of Richmond had ...

Mrs Oglethorpe ends her letter: "I thanke God that I never can forgett that I have been obliged to the Duchess of Portsmouth for my all."

Although she was mainly to live in France for the remainder of her long life, the Duchess of Portsmouth visited England on several occasions. On 28th May 1688 Mrs B. Strickland wrote to the Duchess of Albermarle: "The Duchess of Portsmouth is come into England, and looks as well as ever."[15]

Whilst she was still in England, the Duke of Monmouth on 11th June 1685 together with some supporters landed at the port of Lyme in Dorset. Monmouth was very popular in the West of England. Men ran to and fro in the crowded streets crying "A Monmouth! A Monmouth! the Protestant religion!" Louise had so often indulged in political intrigue with Monmouth that she must have watched events with keen interest that summer. She would have heard of the Battle of Sedgemoor when the rebel forces under Monmouth were utterly routed. He was captured in a ditch disguised as a shepherd and brought to London where he was later executed on Tower Hill. Knowing how deeply his father had once loved him, Louise would have been saddened by his fate. What she thought of the Bloody Assizes when her friend Sir George Jeffreys, now Lord Chief Justice, condemned many of the rebels to death, we do not know. It is easy to condemn the inhumanity of the Bloody Assizes—and no doubt there was much sadistic cruelty. Yet those who judge the events of the seventeenth century by the moral stands of the twentieth are for the most part mistaken and lacking in historical perspective.

NOTES

1. *Memoirs of Thomas Bruce*, Earl of Ailesbury, I, p. 85.
2. Sir Arthur Bryant, *King Charles II*.
3. Macaulay, *History of England*, I, p. 429.
4. Earl of Moray, H.M.C. Buccleuch, II, p. 212.
5. Correspondance Angleterre, CLIV, fol. 110.
6. Sir Arthur Bryant, *op. cit.*
7. *The Phenix or a revival of Scarce and Valuable Pieces.*
8. H.M.C. Buccleuch, II, p. 212.
9. On 7th March 1685.
10. F. C. Turner, *James II*.
11. *Memoirs of Thomas Bruce*, Earl of Ailesbury, I, p. 103.
12. Forneron, *Louise de Keroualle*.
13. Macaulay, *op. cit.*, I, p. 440.
14. Raymond Crawford, *Last Days of Charles II*.
15. H.M.C. Buccleuch, I.

FIFTEEN

LOUISE'S RETURN TO FRANCE

Louise, Duchess of Portsmouth was destined to survive her royal lover by nearly fifty years, and to outlive almost all her contemporaries. The character of this clever Bretonne, who has often been unfairly maligned, can be seen at its best in her close family relationships, for instance her letters to her grandson Charles, later second Duke of Richmond, reveal that she had a warmer heart than hitherto suspected. During the fourteen years Louise had reigned as Charles II's mistress she had formed extravagant habits. Now, deprived of his support she seemed unable to adapt herself to altered circumstances. That was her tragedy.

On arriving in France, Louise was dismayed to discover that her sister Henriette, now a widow, was with child, and obliged to acknowledge that she had privately married Timoléon Gouffier, Marquis de Thois, Governor of Blois. During February 1683 Louise had attempted to persuade Louis XIV to take steps to prevent this marriage, but the French King had not wanted to interfere in this affair.[1]

Louise had many enemies in France, and no doubt they were ready to take the opportunity of sowing mischief between her and King Louis. She was unwise enough during 1686 to speak too freely and disrespectfully of Madame de Maintenon—now the secret wife of the French King. Her indiscretion was reported to Louis XIV, who instructed Monsieur de Louvois to send her an official letter (*lettre de cachet*) banishing her from the court to the country. In this time of need her old friend dapper little Monsieur Honoré de Courtin, former French Ambassador in London, proved a true friend. It happened that he was visiting his intimate friend Monsieur de Louvois one evening, and noticed the *lettre de cachet* on the minister's desk. Speaking with emotion he reminded Louvois of Madame de Portsmouth's enormous services to France. His intervention certainly was instrumental in persuading

Louvois not to send this document. Instead, he gave an immediate account of the episode to King Louis, who himself threw the *lettre de cachet* on the fire.[2] In future the Duchess of Portsmouth was warned not to talk so freely. She had an interview with the King of France in the course of which she defended herself strongly against her accusers.

"Madame", Elizabeth Charlotte, Princess Palatine and Duchess of Orleans, the intelligent second wife of Philippe Duke of Orleans, liked and admired Louise. She saw her often at Saint-Cloud and said of her: "She is the finest lady of her kind that I have ever met; she is extremely polite and interesting in her conversation." The Duchess of Portsmouth told Elizabeth Charlotte that the late King Charles II was in the habit of saying: "My brother when he becomes king will lose his kingdom through excess of zeal for his religion and his soul for a lot of ugly trollops, for he has not sufficiently good taste to like beautiful ones."[3] Elizabeth Charlotte was familiarly known as Liselotte. Her letters, which have recently been edited and translated by Maria Kroll, show that she possessed literary ability. Her dislike of Madame de Maintenon amused her contemporaries. She referred to her as "the old whore".

Louise's political friends and associates such as Henry Sydney, later created Earl of Romney by William III, and Robert Spencer, Earl of Sunderland, did not forget her when she departed from England. They kept up a correspondence.

There is a letter[4] from Henry Sydney to her among the Goodwood MSS in his elegant handwriting, but it seems to have been written in February 1685, perhaps before Charles II's death when Louise still lived in her sumptuous apartments in Whitehall. He wrote:

> 'Tis a hard matter for me to expresse the joy I have when I heare that I am att any time in your thoughts. I must needs say you ought in gratitude not absolutely to forget me, for I am sure no man could be more concerned for you, nor more faithfull to your service when I have been without intermission. There is no letter (I beleeve) that you will receive this post, but will be filled with the relation of the fine entertainment that was on Monday att your lodgings. I am told that you intend to be here in May, which is the best news I have heard a great while and I hope nothing will happen to change such good intentions.

Despite his opposition to the Duke of York during the Exclusion crisis, Sunderland had managed to acquire the royal favour of James II when he succeeded his brother as king. This was partly owing to his great administrative ability, and partly owing to his conversion to the Roman Catholic religion, which had notably pleased the King and given infinite satisfaction to James's Catholic Queen Mary of Modena. He had succeeded Lord Halifax as Lord President and again became a Secretary of State. There are two letters in French from this artful politician to the Duchess of Portsmouth, both written in August 1688. One of these written on 13th August is full of chatty news, just the sort of letter to interest Louise. He told her that John Churchill (now Lord Churchill) had been appointed Captain of the Guards. He refers to her old rival Madame Mazarin (Hortense): "She has been at Tunbridge, but she has not stayed more than a day, for she was so bored." He tells Louise that he is very impatient to hear that she has arrived safely in Paris. He wishes her much happiness and begs her to take care of herself.[5]

The second written from Windsor on 26th August thanks her for all her kindness to him. He informs her that the King intends to go to Winchester for several days, but without the Queen. "She is enjoying herself very much here." Over two months before, James's Italian Queen Mary of Modena had given birth to an infant Prince of Wales—James Francis Edward Stuart in St James's Palace, much to the consternation of many of James's Protestant subjects.

There is an earlier letter from Henry Rumbould, who was a member of the Duchess of Portsmouth's household, and who apparently looked after her affairs in London after she had returned to France. It is written on 4th August 1687 at a time when James II and Mary of Modena were contemplating a progress all over the West Country. Rumbould wrote to the Duchess: "The King and Queen goe towards the Bath on Thursday next, the King intends to make a greatt progresse all over the West country, somethinks the Queene will goe to St Winifreds well before shee comes back."[6] Mary of Modena had restored the Shrine of St Winifred at Holywell, since it had once been a pre-Reformation centre. For her it was a vital pilgrimage, because she longed for a son.

Celia Fiennes writing during the reign of William and Mary mentions her travels to St Winifreds Well when she was shown nine large stones at the bottom of the basin, "which are red marks said to be the blood of St Winifred". She saw "abundance of the devout papists on their knees all round the well; poor people are deluded with an ignorant blind zeale," she adds rather patronizingly, "and are to be pitied by us that have the advantage of knowing better . . . They tell of many lameness's and aches and distempers which are cured by it."[7] So charming did Mary of Modena make herself to the people of Bath that it remained a stronghold of Jacobitism for many years.

During May 1688, Louise once again came to London. Her object was to attend the wedding of her niece Lady Charlotte Herbert, only daughter of Henriette by her first husband the dipsomaniac Earl of Pembroke. She was married to John ("Jacky"), the wealthy son of the infamous Judge Jeffreys, whose early career had been helped by Louise. "On Tuesday, the 17th July, at Bulstrode," wrote John Verney, "the Lord Chancellor's son (aged 15, body low of stature, but a fine scholar) was married to the daughter of the last Earl of Pembroke by [the Duchess of] Portsmouth's sister, and some say they were again married after the Romish manner the latter end of the week."[8]

Earlier Louise was present in London during June* when the Queen gave birth to an infant Prince of Wales. No doubt she listened to the absurd and malicious warming-pan stories, publicized by the King and Queen's enemies, that a substitute baby had been placed in the Queen's bed in St James's Palace. Perhaps Louise was unwise enough to say something critical or derogatory of the Queen, which was immediately repeated to Mary of Modena. They had never liked one another.

After reigning for three years James II had alienated a large portion of the nation by his rash and arbitrary actions. His too precipitate attempt to restore England to the ancient faith was ill-advised and tactless. During these sullen summer days when the politicians incessantly intrigued, and the very air was full of treachery, Louise recalled the melancholy prediction of Charles II that his brother would only last on the throne three years.

William of Orange on his part lost no opportunity of plotting and intriguing against his uncle. The birth of an infant prince to the King and Queen was a great disappointment to William, because in the natural course of events James Francis Edward Stuart would take precedence over his half-sister Mary, William's wife. His own ambitions were thwarted by the embarrassing

* On Trinity Sunday, 10th June.

birth of a Prince of Wales. Three weeks, however, after the birth, a secret invitation was sent to William to come to England with an army to vindicate the constitutional rights of the English people. This invitation was signed by six leading politicians: Charles Talbot, Earl of Shrewsbury, the Earl of Danby,* the Duke of Devonshire, Henry Compton Bishop of London, Edward Russell and Louise's friend Henry Sydney.

It is necessary to discuss the revolution, but briefly. On 5th November William of Orange landed in Torbay. In the early hours of 11th December, the King was compelled to send his devoted Queen and the Prince of Wales to France. The two people who were mainly responsible for arranging their escape were foreigners—Francesco Riva, an Italian, who was keeper of Mary of Modena's wardrobe, and the Comte de Lauzun, a quixotic Frenchman. James was also forced to flee to France.

Louis XIV behaved generously to the royal exiles, allowing them the use of the Château of Saint-Germain. The French King expressed admiration for Mary of Modena, praising her fortitude in adversity, her dignity as Queen, her passion for her husband and her spontaneous charm and grace. "See what a queen ought to be," Louis said of her.

The Duchess of Portsmouth wished to pay her respects to the exiled Queen, but Mary of Modena snubbed her by making various excuses. Lauzun told her that the Queen could not see anybody before she was settled at Saint-Germain. It was reported to Louise that James's Queen had resented her insinuations about the birth of the Prince of Wales. Louise at once protested that she was innocent of any offence, and that her remarks had been misinterpreted. Later she was received on 10th January 1689 by the Queen at Saint-Germain, together with Madame and all the princesses of the blood royal. After they had all been allotted chairs and stools, the Queen asked Louise to be seated together with her favourite lady-in-waiting and intimate friend the Countess Vittoria Davia Montecuccoli, later created Countess of Almond by James II. Dangeau thought that this favour granted to the Queen's friend was extraordinary, because she was not of royal blood. The Duchess of Portsmouth at least had the satisfaction of being received by the exiled Queen and she hoped that it would restore her prestige with the French.

Louise was anxious about her financial affairs, and always ready

* William III created him Duke of Leeds.

to intrigue and to play a double game where it served her interests; she wrote in French to her friend Henry Sydney on 8th March 1689 to ask him to speak on her behalf to William of Orange—now established on the throne of England as William III. She did not fail to remind William that she had used her influence with Charles II to further his marriage with the Princess Mary, the King's niece. She had done her utmost to exclude the Duke of York from the throne. She wrote to Sydney:

> I know all the kindness with which you have spoken of me, Monsieur, and I am infinitely obliged. You know how all my life I have forwarded your interests and those of your friends. On my side I have not changed in the least and no one could be more concerned about everything that affects you than I am. I trust that my absence will not impair your feelings for me and that you will be pleased in so far as you are able, in good faith to protect my interests. You know that they are so closely attached to those of the Duke of Richmond that they cannot be separated. I do not doubt that the memory you have of him whose son the Duke has the honour to be, will help you to continue all the more strongly to give us your friendship, which I prize so highly for both of us.[9]

William III, however, saw no reason why he should help the Duchess of Portsmouth, who had acquired lavish wealth and possessions in England. On William's accession her pension in England was stopped. Yet Louis XIV constantly behaved generously to her, giving her an allowance of £12,000 in June 1689, and also allowing her son a pension of £20,000 in September.

Dangeau[10] relates that in January 1689 the Duchess and her son Richmond were accused of having spoken badly of the English court at Saint-Germain, but that Louis XIV took their part, declaring them incapable of doing so.

Louise survived almost all her contemporaries. On 14th November 1687, Nell Gwyn died at her house, 79 Pall Mall, at the early age of thirty-seven. It is curious that she should die on the same day and month as Louise, who survived her almost forty-seven years. Nell was buried in the beautiful church of St Martin-in-the-Fields.

Her former rival Barbara Duchess of Cleveland was treated rather badly by her lovers in her old age. After her lawful husband Roger Earl of Castlemaine had died in 1705 she married a scoundrel named Robert Fielding, usually called Beau Fielding, who failed to inform her that he had a wife living. Two years later

their marriage was declared void. She died in October 1709* in a
house in Chiswick Mall, today known as Walpole House because
of its later associations with Sir Robert Walpole. For some time
she had suffered from dropsy, which had "swelled her gradually
to a monstrous bulk". There is a legend that Barbara still haunts
her old home in Chiswick Mall. On moonlight, stormy nights
her ghost can be seen at a window, supplicating somebody or
other to give her back her lost beauty.[11]

After the death of Charles II, Hortense Mancini, Duchesse
Mazarin had lived in a house in Kensington Square and later in
Chelsea. Even in later life her beauty remained unimpaired. She
died on 2nd July 1699, heavily in debt and attended by her
devoted friend Saint-Evremond.

Louise's father died in 1690, and a year later she was greatly
shocked to hear that a fire had destroyed her apartments where
she had lived for so many years in the Palace of Whitehall. Evelyn
refers to this in his Diary:

> This night a sudden and terrible fire burnt down all the buildings
> over the Stone gallery at White-hall to the water-side, beginning
> at the apartment of the late Dutchesse of Portsmouth (which had
> been pull'd down and rebuilt no lesse than three times to please
> her) and consuming other lodgings of such lewd creatures, who
> debauch'd both King Charles 2, and others, and were his destruc-
> tion.[12]

In France, Louise's son the Duke of Richmond served with some
distinction in the French Army, and Louis XIV showed him
marked favour. Aged only seventeen, the King gave him a company in a cavalry regiment. When his uncle James made prepara-
tions to invade Ireland, in order to be restored to his kingdom,
Richmond asked permission to accompany the expedition, but he
was deemed too young. This bred in Charles II's handsome son a
kind of frustration, and he became discontented and rebellious.

By temperament Richmond was unstable, and he shifted his
political allegiance according to his whims. Like his mother, he
seldom pursued consistent policies.

Dangeau relates in his Journal that the Duke of Richmond left
France without saying a word to anybody on 4th February 1692.
Somebody had encountered him near Abbeville. His mother
spoke very bitterly about the folly (*sottise*) and no doubt ingrati-

* In her sixty-ninth year.

tude of her son, whom she thought intended to join William of Orange. She told Louis XIV that she was in despair.[13] Not unnaturally the French King was very angry with Richmond, though he was fair enough not to blame the Duchess of Portsmouth for her son's defection. Dangeau relates that the Duke, now almost twenty, had written on 14th February to a French gentleman, Monsieur de Barbezieux, that he wished to return his commission of Captain of Cavalry to King Louis. He was about to proceed to a country (England) where he would enjoy a far higher rank and more revenues than he would have in France. He would, however, always retain sentiments of great respect for the King of France, and decidedly pro-French inclinations.

On arriving in England, the young Duke hastily declared himself a Protestant, and his re-conversion to the Anglican Church took place in Lambeth Palace on Whitsunday, 15th May 1692.[14] At first William was mistrustful of Richmond, suspecting that he was aware of a secret journey to England made by the Jacobite Duke of Berwick, James II's illegitimate son.* Later during November 1693 Richmond took his Seat in the House of Lords. The dour, austere William seems to have been impressed by the young nobleman. He made him one of his aides-de-camp. As a soldier, Richmond showed plenty of courage, serving with distinction at the battles of Steinkerque and Nerwinde. In his portraits by Sir Godfrey Kneller, the Duke much resembled his father Charles II. John Macky describes Richmond as "a gentleman good-natured to a fault, very well-bred, with many good things in him, an enemy to business, very credulous, well-shaped, black complexion much like King Charles not thirty years old."[15] His dark eyes also reminded one of his father the late King. His portraits give an impression of indolence, but he was very graceful in his movements, and possessed attractive manners.

In early January 1693 when he was not quite twenty Richmond married a very attractive young widow aged about twenty. She was Anne, widow of Henry, second Baron Bellasis of Worlaby. Richmond's wife was the daughter of Francis, Lord Brudenell, son and heir of the Earl of Cardigan. The new Duchess of Richmond was to prove a loyal, devoted wife. Her correspondence with her mother-in-law the Duchess of Portsmouth is of great interest, and it reveals that she was on excellent terms with her.

* By Arabella Churchill.

Louise's friend Paul Barrillon Marquis de Branges with whom she had so often negotiated in London, had now returned to France. Madam de Sévigné tells us that he did not accompany the exiled James II to Ireland. He had been superseded by Avaux, who had been appointed French Ambassador at James's court. It was considered that Avaux had a far more intimate knowledge of the affairs of Holland than Barrillon, the former Ambassador in London. Madame de Sévigné, an intimate friend gives us a little picture of Barrillon in his later life: "He is rich, fat and old as he says, and views without envy M. d'Avaux's brilliant station. He loves to be surrounded with his friends and family in peace and tranquillity, which satisfies him." He always treated Louise with marked respect, despite the fact that she now lacked importance.

Among Louise's correspondents was Lady Sophia Bulkeley, who had known her in London. Lady Sophia was now a lady-in-waiting to Queen Mary of Modena at Saint-Germain. In her letter she refers to the death of the Queen's only brother Francesco d'Este, Duke of Modena, who died in 1694. There is also an interesting allusion to the death during December 1694 of William III's Queen, Mary II, merely called "the princess" by the Jacobite Lady Sophia. She wrote to the Duchess of Portsmouth: "You see Deare Madam there is nothing to bee done butt to come to see the Queen [Mary of Modena] when you find yourselfe well enough to doe soe without any inconvenience to yourselfe ... I am very sorry to hear my deare Dutchesse is any wayes troubled with her collick or with any other indisposition noebody living wishing your grace more happynesse than I am sure I do."[16] She adds in a postscript that there was great consternation and affliction in England, for Queen Mary II was much beloved. Louis XIV ordered that there should be no mourning on this occasion.

Lonely and forlorn, the Duchess of Portsmouth lived for a while in a magnificent mansion on the Quai des Théatins in Paris, now numbers 3 and 5 on the Quai Voltaire. After the luxurious life she had been accustomed to in London, she made no effort to acquire economical habits. Under the beautiful chandeliers, she tried to forget the emptiness of her life and the boredom enhanced by too much leisure. She gambled incessantly, and sometimes lost money, which she could ill afford. In London she had led an active life as Charles's chief mistress, now she brooded for hours on her changed fortunes.

Louise never married, nor did she resume her intrigue with the

Chevalier Philippe de Vendôme when she returned to France. She had no doubt discovered his real character. However, she became infatuated with another charming rotter. For a time she became a mistress of the debauched Henri de Lorraine, Duke d'Elbeuf, a man much younger than herself.[17] Saint-Simon wrote of him: "A liar, a cheat abandoned to vice, he spent his youth as a scourge to every family through his lewd behaviour to women and his frequent boast of favours he had not received." Henri de Lorraine was married to a niece of Madame de Montespan.

In her later life Louise lived much on her estates at Aubigny. It is generally supposed that she only thought of accumulating wealth for herself, but Louise had a social conscience and was distressed by the poverty and misery of the people on her estate. She wrote on 2nd April 1692 to the Count of Pontchartrain, Controller-General of Finance in her queer handwriting, informing him of their plight.

> The extreme misery of the people and peasants in the country surrounding Aubigny, which is my Duchy, makes me, Monsieur, plead urgently with you to have pity on the unhappy condition to which they are reduced, as much by the poll-tax and the high rate of requisitions that they have to meet yearly as the misfortune of a frost which this year hit them all. They are so crushed, and so little able to pay that they are abandoning the township and the land. Monsieur, I venture to implore you to request M. de Céraucour, Governor of Bourges, to exempt old soldiers this year, and to agree to reduce their poll-tax, for the countryside will be absolutely ruined, if you are unable to do me this kindness . . .

She asks him to pardon her bothering him about this matter, but she is assured of his kindness.[18]

During the summer months the Duchess of Portsmouth usually moved to the Castle of La Verrerie, situated in the countryside near Aubigny. It was characteristic of her to order that a river should be diverted because she could not sleep owing to the noise. The Duchess of Portsmouth continued to be extravagant, despite her reduced income. It was foolish on her part to live too luxuriously, for she got into debt and no longer a woman of power and influence, found herself pursued by her creditors. When threatened with distraint in 1699, Louis XIV remained a constant friend. In September he ordered that all her law suits should be suspended for one year. When that period elapsed, her creditors issued fresh writs against her. She was obliged to appeal to the King for further help. Louis never wavered in his support of the Duchess of Portsmouth and in driving away her creditors.

When William Bentinck, Earl of Portland, William III's intimate friend and favourite was entrusted with a splendid embassy to France in 1698, Louise wrote to him, asking him to put in a word on her behalf with William. She was now anxious to visit England, so as to plead her case before William. Portland replied politely in French that it was hardly a propitious time for her to visit England. To William, Portland wrote with some enthusiasm about the charms of Saint-Cloud, so familiar to the Duchess of Portsmouth, where he had been entertained by Monsieur, Louis XIV's brother: "Your Majesty would be pleased with the situation, the beautiful natural waters, the fine views, and the great variety there is in the place."[19] Portland had been reluctant at first to undertake this embassy, for he feared not without reason that he would be altogether supplanted by his enemy Arnold Joost van Keppel, Earl of Albermarle, in William's affections.

Portland wrote to King William during April: "The Duchess of Portsmouth bothers me to ask Your Majesty for leave for her to go to England; I can no longer refuse it."[20] Louise continued to pester William with letters, and he was tardy in giving permission to her to come to England. Louise's sister Henriette de Thois was also eager to return to England on business. Portland wrote to his master that if he did not wish the Duchess of Portsmouth to come to England again he would prefer not to tell her himself. It would be better if one of her friends in England were to write to her.

When she eventually landed in a yacht at Dover on 12th August she was met by her son the Duke of Richmond, who had hurried there, travelling by night.[21] She lost no time in presenting a petition asking for the grant of a pension of £8,000. She later stayed at her son's house in Sussex, where she took the opportunity of becoming acquainted with his wife Anne. The two ladies got on very well together. Four years earlier Anne, Duchess of Richmond, had given birth to a daughter, christened Louise in honour of her grandmother. The christening took place in St James's Church, Piccadilly. Lady Louise Lennox married James, third Earl of Berkeley, who had a distinguished naval career, and became First Lord Commissioner of the Admiralty during the reign of George I.

The Duchess of Portsmouth's elder grand-daughter was very partial to practical jokes. On one occasion she succeeded in rousing the anger of Jonathan Swift, as he relates in *Journal to Stella*.

> I dined with Lady Betty Germain, and there was the young Earl of Berkeley and his fine lady. I never saw her before, nor think her near so handsome as she passes for. Nothing makes me so excessively peevish as hot weather. Lady Berkeley after dinner clapt my hat on another lady's head, and she in roguery put it upon the rails. I minded them not but in two minutes they called me to the window, and Lady Carteret showed me my hat out of her window five doors off, where I was forced to walk to it and pay her and old Lady Weymouth a visit with some more bell-dames . . .*

Despite her agreeable stay in the peaceful Sussex countryside with her son and daughter-in-law, the Duchess of Portsmouth felt rather baffled and frustrated. When she returned to France during February 1699, she derived very little comfort from the assurance of a pension of £1,000.[22] She continued to correspond with her friend Henry Sydney, Earl of Romney. He wrote her on 9th March 1700: "When Madame one confesses a fault and askes pardon for it, I thinke one is most commonly forgiven, that is now my case, for I owne that I have not been so punctual in writing to you, as I ought to have been, but I assure you Madame it hath not proceeded from want of friendship or respect, for that I shall never be failing of towards you, but this winter hath been so tiresome and vexacious, that it hath made one forget sometimes the duty, that one owes to ones friends, which shall be more for the future." He assured her that whenever possible he would put William III in mind of the great esteem and regard the Duchess of Portsmouth had ever possessed for him, reminding the King "how extremely you depend upon his protection, which I hope may put your affairs in a better way than they have been alate."[23] Sydney, however, was getting rather senile, and could do little to help her.

It was on Friday, 16th September 1701 that James II in great piety died at Saint-Germain. Before his death a dramatic scene occurred in the King's bedchamber, when King Louis of France declared that he would recognize his son as King of England. This

* On 6th June 1711.

Charles Lennox, first Duke of Richmond, in 1690 at the age of 18, by
Sir Godfrey Kneller (*from Goodwood House by courtesy of the Trustees*)

Anne Brudenell, first Duchess of Richmond, by Sir Godfrey Kneller (*from Goodwood House by courtesy of the Trustees*)

Charles Lennox, second Duke of Richmond, as the Earl of March and Darnley, by Dahl (*from Goodwood House by courtesy of the Trustees*)

momentous decision was to be fraught with ruinous consequences for France. Resentful of Louis's attempt to foist a Catholic King on them, the English organized a coalition against the French King, together with Holland and Austria. This was only one of the causes of the War of the Spanish Succession which erupted on 15th May 1702.

The exiled King of England was not long survived by his nephew William III. During early March 1702, he was riding at Hampton Court when his horse stumbled on a molehill. William was thrown on his right shoulder, and broke a collar-bone. Owing to the delicate state of his health, William later died at Kensington Palace, to be succeeded to the throne of England by his sister-in-law Queen Anne.

NOTES

1. *Journal du Marquis de Dangeau*, I, p. 117.
2. *Mémoires de Saint-Simon*, XI, pp. 345–6; also reported in *Journal du Marquis de Dangeau*.
3. Orleans Correspondence, II, 94.
4. Goodwood MSS. 5.
5. *Ibid.*
6. *Ibid.*
7. *Through England on a sidesaddle in the time of William and Mary being the Diary of Celia Fiennes*.
8. *Verney Family Memoirs*.
9. Blencowe (ed.), *Diary of the Times of Charles II* by Henry Sydney, p. 307; Jeanine Delpech, *The Life and Times of the Duchess of Portsmouth*.
10. *Journal du Marquis de Dangeau*, II, p. 287.
11. Charles G. Harper, *Haunted Houses, Tales of the Supernatural*.
12. *Memoirs and Correspondence of John Evelyn*, III, p. 302, 10th April 1691.
13. *Journal du Marquis de Dangeau*, IV, p. 18, 4th February.
14. Lady Russell, "The Real Louise de Keroualle".
15. *Memoirs of the Secret Services of John Macky*.
16. Goodwood MSS. 5.
17. Jeanine Delpech, *op. cit.*
18. Letter preserved in the French National Archives b[7]. Mentioned by Forneron, *op. cit.*, also quoted in Delpech, *op. cit.*
19. Nesca A. Robb, *William of Orange*, II.

20. Calendar of State Papers, Domestic, William III, Volume IX, 1698.
21. *Ibid.*
22. Jeanine Delpech, *op. cit.*
23. Goodwood MSS. 5.

SIXTEEN

HER LATER LIFE

The first Duke of Richmond bought Goodwood* at a cost of £4,100 in 1697 for use as a hunting-lodge, having signed an agreement to buy the property two years before. On one occasion when the Grand Duke of Tuscany came on a visit to William III, the King took him to Goodwood to stay with the Duke.[1] They enjoyed fine hunting in the neighbourhood, particularly with the Charlton pack of hounds. Monmouth when he was alive had a special affection for Charlton, and had enjoyed splendid sport there together with his friend, Lord Grey of Werke, keeping a couple of packs of foxhounds at Charlton. In ancient records—such as the Domesday Book—Goodwood is invariably written Godinwood. So it remained until the reign of Elizabeth I when it was known as Godingwood. It was changed to Goodwood while Charles II was king. The house familiar to the first Duke of Richmond was Jacobean.

As she grew older, the Duchess of Portsmouth was often an unhappy woman, and it was a consolation to her to correspond with her son, her daughter-in-law Anne, and her grandchildren. The Duke and Duchess of Richmond had three children, Louise, Anne and Charles Lennox, born on Charles II's birthday, 29th May 1701. Louise was particularly interested in Charles Lennox, who was later to succeed his father as second Duke in 1723. There is a quaint letter[2] from Lady Anne Lennox, aged about nine, in her childish handwriting to her grandmother the Duchess of Portsmouth. She probably stood in considerable awe of Louise. It concerns a riding accident which had unfortunately befallen her father. She wrote her:

* Original house largely rebuilt by Thomas Percy, ninth Earl of Northumberland.

Madame, when I first heard of Papa's sad accident I could hardly
write to him I was so frighted as I belleve he found so tru that he
coud never read my letter it was so sadly wret, the next time Mama
sent letters for France indeed she never told me. So I hope your
grace will forgive my not writing soonner, pray dear Madam don't
lett Papa goe out without a grate many footmen and make him
come home soonner at night and to be sure he will obey your grace
sence he expected we should obey him, I am glad to hear Papa will
be soon att home, but think tis long before your grace gets a time
of seeing us.
    I am
        Madame Yre Graces most dutefull and obedeant servant
                    Anne Lenos.

In 1723 Lady Anne Lennox married William Anne Keppel,
second Earl of Albermarle, son of William II's Dutch favourite
Arnold Joost van Keppel, first Earl of Albermarle, who came with
his master to England in 1688 as a page of honour. They had
fifteen children. Louise's daughter-in-law refers to Lady Anne's
childhood in one of her letters: "Lady Anne is extreamly proud
of Yr Graces naming her in your letter, she has almost left off
making faces, but I feare theire return for she begins to bleed att
nose againe wch first occasioned them and I apprehend will make
her very leane. She has certainly very pretty little features and
would be much handsome if Ld Duke would give me leave to
pull her eye-brows for they meeting gives her a cloudy looke . . ."
Though Louise was interested in the activities of all her grandchildren, Charles Lennox, Lord March was her favourite. The
Duchess of Richmond wrote her mother-in-law that Lord March
presented his humble respects and assured your grace he is perfectly sensible of all your favours and kind expressions towards
him. "Though he is excessively wild and rattled-headed," added
his fond mother, "he is of a very good nature and gratefull
temper." There he resembled his father, who shared Charles II's
amability.
    When misunderstandings arose between the Duchess of Ports-
mouth and her son the Duke of Richmond, Anne Richmond
stoutly defended her husband against what she considered were the
calumnies of his enemies. It had been reported to Louise that her
son led a debauched life, and that he caroused at night until the
early hours of the morning. She wrote to reproach him. In her
relations with her mother-in-law, the Duchess of Richmond

needed considerable tact. She feared lest she had offended her mother-in-law. She added, however, "I shall thinke myself the most unfortunate creature alive if I should prove the unhappy occasion of Yor Graces being offended with my Lord Duke; but all that I can doe on my part is to assure you, that I shall always behave myself as becomes his wife."

There were further recriminations. Letters were delayed or lost in the post. The Duchess of Richmond was again obliged to defend the conduct of her husband, and she did so in a most spirited way. She wrote the Duchess of Portsmouth: "Madame, I hope you will give me leave to say how very much the Duke of Richmond was troubled at the letter he received by Mr Wilton and at the same time permission to asure your Grace that he has in somethings bin much misrepresented and injured in. For I doe protest with all the truth imaginable, that since I have had the happiness to know His Grace, he had never bin from me twice after nine o'clock at night (wch is far from leading a debauch'd life)." She wrote her mother-in-law that all who knew the Duke wondered that one so young was so regular in his way of life and discreet in his habits. Naturally she had to admit that her husband had to be in the best company.

Men of the greatest quality in the early eighteenth century were accustomed to drink to excess and it was impossible for her husband to avoid too much indulgence in wine. "All those that are so handsome as His Grace will have enemies uppon the account of envie," she confided to Louise. It was his enemies who spread abroad the rumours that Richmond was a drunkard and debauched. "No man has it in his power," Anne Richmond assured her mother-in-law, "to make himself so considerable in the world as he has, being master in his person and understanding of all fine qualities and esteemed so by all sides here . . ." Despite the loyalty of his wife, most of Richmond's contemporaries thought that he mixed in bad company, and that he was a rake. Jonathan Swift sneered at him as "a shallow coxcomb". The Duc d'Aumont—a cultured French friend of the Duke of Richmond's in London wrote during February 1713, to the Duchess of Portsmouth that he was as convinced as her of her son's good heart. "I do not know how to prevent myself from telling you," he added, "that bad companions often spoil the best intentions."[3] He had just dined with Richmond, and Lord Bolingbroke in London. Since Harry St John, Lord Bolingbroke, was known as a mercurial, convivial companion it cannot be wondered at that Richmond sometimes drank too deeply.

When her son, Lord March, had a riding accident, though he mercifully escaped any injury to life or limb, the Duchess of Richmond wrote to Louise to implore her to use her influence with the Duke of Richmond to promise that Lord March should not ride for a year or two.

> For indeed, Madam, as he is very young, weake and extremly rattled-headed his liffe upon those horses will be in ye greatest of dangers ... Hunting being a qualification not necessary to make a fine gentleman. I thinke a fond mother may reasonably aske this favour especially for an only son, wch yor Grace by experience knows to be a dear treasure besides the danger of it when a youth gives himself up to these kinds of sports. It certainly makes them neglect their Booke and Learning, which is of much greater consequence than any devertions can prove ...

If only her mother-in-law could obtain her son's promise, it would allay a thousand dreadful fears.

The Duke of Richmond, like his father, was also a keen horseman, which made him inclined to humour Lord March's fondness for riding and hunting. His mother thought that Lord March was very tall for his years, "which makes him excessively weake in his lims, a fault I hope will mend when he has don growing and begins to spread". The Duchess of Portsmouth wrote to her son to persuade Lord March to give up riding for a time.

From 1701 onwards Louise was much troubled by her financial affairs. During that year the ancient manor house of the Keroualles, overlooking Brest was included in the evictions which the creation of arsenals, store-rooms and munition-dumps would necessitate for the King's fleet. Substantial financial compensation had to be paid the owners. Louis XIV now decided that the States of Brittany were responsible for these sums. The States of Brittany, however, attempted to contest these valuations,[4] but the Duchess of Portsmouth managed to win her case. She applied to the Comptroller-General of Finances, and obtained an Order of the Council granting her 56,122 livres, payable by the Exchequer of the States of Brittany.

In 1708 her financial affairs were in such a deplorable state that Louise was obliged to pledge some of her possessions against loans. It is difficult to feel much sympathy for Louise, for she was

usually wasteful and extravagant. She spent much time writing
to Desmarets, now Controller-General of Finances, imploring his
assistance. These letters in her large sprawling handwriting can
be seen among the French National Archives.[5] She wrote to
Desmarets from Paris on 20th March, complaining about the
behaviour of a Sieur Nicole "who is acting disgracefully towards
me since, for four months I have not succeeded in dragging
[*tirer*] one *sou* out of him for my expenses. He has my beautiful
tapestry, and he is using and spoiling it completely."[6] Louise was
certainly unfortunate in some of her agents, who took advantage
of the fact that she was a woman.

In the same spirit as she now pleaded her dire distress to Desmarets, she had formerly written to his predecessor Chamillard on
2nd April 1701: "In heaven's name, Monsieur, have enough kindness and pity for my sad circumstances to be willing to grant me
the payment of fifteen thousand *francs* that the King commanded
that I should have at present."[7] What these supplicating letters
cost Louise in subduing her pride we can only conjecture. In the
summer of 1708 she continued to remind Desmarets that her
pension was overdue.

During the autumn of 1709 Louise was once again living on
her estates at Aubigny. She wrote to Desmarets on 5th October:
"Monsieur, I find myself in such straitened circumstances, that I
am constrained to implore your help and your friendship. I come
here in the hope of finding some peace and quiet; but the misery
all around is so dreadful that nobody can find a single *sou*, there is
nothing with which to buy a single seed for the sowing; and if
you don't take pity on me, my fields will not be sown at all."[8]
She begs him in her dire distress to let her have her pension. It was
in 1709 that Louise's mother the Comtesse de Kerouaille died,
having survived her husband many years.

The people of France were now suffering terrible hardship on
account of the ruinous wars inflicted on them by Louis XIV,
Louise's friend in adversity. These were the years when a soldier
of genius John Churchill, later Duke of Marlborough command-
ing the allied forces defeated the French in such decisive battles at
Blenheim (1704) and Malplaquet (1709). During 1708 there was
a famine in France, mostly caused by a very poor harvest.[9] In
Brittany corn was fetching five times its normal price. The old
King, saddened by the sufferings of his subjects, did what he
could to relieve their plight. Special taxes were raised to assist the

poor, and during a six-months' period his own contribution was £1,400.

There are several letters from the Duke of Marlborough to the Duchess of Portsmouth among the Goodwood MSS. One wonders how Marlborough engrossed in his enormous responsibilities could possibly find time to write to her. Writing in French on 9th July 1709, two months before the Battle of Malplaquet, Marlborough apologized for not doing so more promptly. He is now encamped before Tournay. The Duchess of Portsmouth has requested him to send her some bottles of wine. "In truth, Madame," Marlborough wrote, "good wine of this kind is so rare at present in England that I fear that the best I have been able to find for my own use is not really worth the trouble of sending you." However, if the Duchess still wished him to send the wine, he would be happy to do so.

Louise continued to correspond with the Duke of Marlborough and wrote him on 3rd June 1712. The Duke's reply was courteous, for he was glad to learn of the satisfactory state of her health. "It is a long time since I have offered my very humble services to you," he wrote. There is a postscript with a suitable compliment from Sarah Duchess of Marlborough, who had known Louise during the early days at Charles II's court.

There are so many allusions to the indifferent health of the Duchess of Portsmouth in the letters of her contemporaries, that one wonders how she managed to survive to the age of eighty-five. The truth is that Louise took good care of her health. When she was a lady of power and influence politicians would often refer to this matter. Henry Savile wrote to the Marquess of Halifax on 8th March 1683: "The Dutchess of Portsmouth has sore eyes, for which she has been let blood this morning. The Dutchess has a cold, for which I hear she intends to keep her bed today."

Queen Anne died in August 1714, and was succeeded by the Hanoverian George I, one of the worst Kings who ever sat on the throne of England. The Duke of Richmond, who had ceased to be a Whig during the Queen's reign, almost certainly became one again at the accession of George I, for he was created a Lord of the bedchamber during October 1714, and later a Privy Councillor of Ireland.

An amusing story is related by Catherine Sedley,* Countess of

* Daughter of Sir Charles Sedley.

Dorchester, James II's celebrated mistress. She had much of Nell Gwyn's impudent wit, but lacked her unique charm. Happening to meet the Duchess of Portsmouth and Elizabeth Villiers, Countess of Orkney, William III's mistress, in London after the accession of George I, she exclaimed impulsively: "Fancy we three whores meeting like this!" a remark which would hardly have endeared her to Louise.

Louise's loyal friend King Louis XIV died on 1st September 1715, three days before his seventy-seventh birthday. Few people mourned for him, for the people of France felt crushed and in despair, oppressed by an empty treasury and a mountain of debts.[10] Very different had been the death of Charles II—a much loved King. Saint-Simon wrote about Louis's decease that the people gave thanks to God with a scandalous exuberance. He was succeeded by his great-grandson Louis XV, then only five years old. Philippe, Duke of Chartres and Orleans, son of Elizabeth Charlotte, Duchess of Orleans, at once became Regent of France, although Louis XIV had detested him, and had dreaded his rise to power. He possessed the intellectual tastes of a Renaissance prince, but he was very dissolute. When his mother complained about his choice of ugly women Philippe replied: *"Bah! Maman, dans la nuit tous les chats sont gris."**

So far as Louise was concerned, she had no cause to complain about the Regent. He realized the value of her past services to France, for he agreed to augment her pension from 12,000 francs to 20,000 francs, and then to 24,000 francs.[11] Louise left for Aubigny in the summer of 1718 in a more contented frame of mind.

Louise no longer had much faith in pensions and she very shrewdly wanted it changed into a government debenture. As a French woman she was an expert in striking hard bargains. With her customary persistence she managed to persuade the Regent to sign an order:

M. Pierre Gruyn, the Keeper of the Royal Treasury, is hereby ordered to pay in ready money to Madame Louise Renée de Penancoët de Keroualle Duchess of Portsmouth and Aubigny, the sum of 600,000 livres, which have been accorded to her by the King, to be employed in buying a life-annuity, payable out of his Majesty's Exchequer, and to replace the pension of 24,000 livres which was partially granted her by the late King and partially by his present

* "All cats look grey in the dark, Mother!"

Majesty, in consideration of the great services she has rendered
France, and to enable her to support her rank and dignity. Signed
on 28th October 1721.

Philippe d'Orléans.[12]

Louise lived now for the most part in the Château of Aubigny,
very seldom going to Paris. When urgent repairs were needed to
make the Château habitable, for the roof was falling in, and the
chapel was in a ruined state, Louise instead of meeting these heavy
expenses out of her own income, appealed to the Crown. She
argued with some skill that it was the Crown's responsibility to
maintain the Château. Since it was a royal appanage, it would
revert to the King if her descendants became extinct. Since Louise
was always more than ready to claim her seigneurial privileges, if
it benefited her financies, it was reasonable to expect her to take
on her responsibilities, rather than to attempt to evade them.
However, the Crown agreed to her overtures.

She was deeply saddened by the death of her son at Goodwood.
The Duke of Richmond died on 27th May 1723, his wife Anne
having predeceased him a year before. He was at first buried in
Henry VII's chapel, Westminster Abbey, but his body was later
removed to Chichester Cathedral a few miles distant from Goodwood. He was succeeded by his only son, Charles Lennox, who
was now a young nobleman of twenty-two. The new Duke has
been described as having had a defective education,[13] and he may
have possessed a sluggish intellect, although he was very well
informed. Lord March during his father's life-time had served as
Captain in the Royal Regiment of Horseguards. He had also
represented Chichester and Newport as MP.

Lord March married the eldest daughter of a distinguished
cavalry officer, Lord Cadogan, who had fought under Marlborough. An amusing story is related how the marriage came
about. The first Duke of Richmond was as crazy about gambling
as his mother. On one occasion he won an enormous sum of
money from Lord Cadogan, who was unable to pay his debts.
His wife, however, was a Dutch heiress. The Duke of Richmond
and Lord Cadogan now agreed that the gambling debt should be
cancelled, provided Cadogan were to give his eldest daughter,
Lady Sarah Cadogan, in marriage to Lord March. A marriage
ceremony was then solemnized between the young nobleman
now aged eighteen and Lady Sarah, who was scarcely thirteen.
The heir to the Richmond fortunes was not exactly impressed

with his bride, for he was heard to mutter: "Surely you are not going to marry me to that dowdy." The Lord March, accompanied by a tutor went off to the Continent on "the grand tour," and Lady Sarah returned to her mother. Three years elapsed.

On his return to London, Lord March decided to go one evening to the opera, for he was in no hurry to visit his young bride. Looking around him, Lord March noticed a beautiful young lady in a box, surrounded by several admirers. His curiosity aroused, he turned eagerly to his companion: "Who is that lovely young creature?" he asked him.

"You must be a stranger in London," said the man, "not to know the reigning toast of the Town, the beautiful Lady March!"[14] Lord March lost no time in claiming his wife, and the marriage turned out very happily. It was truly blessed, for the Richmonds had many children. The eldest Lady Caroline born in 1723 was a favourite of the Duchess of Portsmouth, and stayed, together with her parents, with her great-grandmother in Aubigny.

Among the Goodwood MSS is a collection of letters[15] from the Duchess of Portsmouth to her beloved grandson. These are all written in French and nearly all are dated. It is evident that one of Louise's few consolations now left to her was this correspondence with her grandson. In 1723 Louise was already an old woman, aged about seventy-four. Living quietly in the French countryside as she was, her chief interest for the remainder of her life was centred on her grandson and his family. Writing on 25th June 1723, a month after the death of the first Duke of Richmond, Louise confides to her grandson her grief. She always addresses him as "*Mon Cher Milard*", and ends her letters "Duchesse de Portsmouth". How eagerly she awaited news of him and his "*aimable duchesse*" (as Louise referred to Sarah, the new Duchess of Richmond). Louise very rarely mentions political events, for she was naturally now more concerned with intimate family affairs. In a letter, however, written in December 1723 she referred to the death of the Regent, the Duke of Orleans.

As she grew older, Louise became very pious and religious, no doubt regretting the sins of her early life. "It is necessary for me to submit to the will of the Lord" she told her grandson. She confesses to him the cruel shock it has given her to hear of his illness during 1725. On 23rd January 1728 the Duchess of Portsmouth wrote to her grandson to tell him how distressed she was that Sarah, Duchess of Richmond, had sustained a miscarriage.

Four years before her death, she still remembered to send tender messages to her great-granddaughter Caroline. Writing on 15th October 1730 she congratulated the Duke of Richmond on the birth of one of his sons, and expressed her delight that Charles and Sarah were about to visit her in France during the spring. In 1743—nine years after his grandmother's decease—the Duke of Richmond built Carne's Seat, a Stone Temple named after an old servant and friend of Louise de Keroualle.[16]

In 1725 the Duchess of Portsmouth was saddened by the death of her younger sister Henriette, Marquise de Thois, who had so often irritated her. She died in her house in the Rue de Varennes in Paris on 12th May.

The history of Louise, Duchess of Portsmouth, is nearly ended. Voltaire, who met her in Paris when she was about seventy, tells us that she retained her beauty even in her old age. He described her: *"Avec une figure encore noble et agréable, que les années n'avaient point flétrie."**

When the Duchess was eighty-one she was seriously ill, and when she was recovering the Curé of Aubigny wrote her grandson a reassuring account of her illness, how she was given seven or eight baths, and bled in the arm and in her feet. "She has been given almost thirty remedies," he wrote the Duke of Richmond.[17] He considered that she possessed a very strong will to recover from such an illness.

During the last few years of her life, Louise occupied herself in performing charitable deeds in her town of Aubigny. She founded a hospital for nuns, who passed their time in caring for the sick and educating the youth. In March 1732 the old lady enjoyed the visit of two English travellers, Mr G. Shirley and Mr Cross at her home at Aubigny, and she was very agreeable to them. Shirley wrote to the Duke of Richmond: "We found her Grace ye good old lady you described her to be; she was very good and obliging and made us very happy for a week."

During October 1734, Louise now aged eighty-five visited Paris, so as to consult her doctors. She died in that city on 14th November. She was buried in the Church of the Barefooted Carmelites, where there was a chapel of the des Rieux, her mother's ancestors. On the death of his grandmother Charles Lennox, Duke of Richmond, succeeded to the dukedom of

---

* With a face still noble and pleasing, that the years had never withered.

Aubigny in France.* In her will signed on 13th February 1731 she made her grandson her universal legatee. She did not forget any of her servants, leaving them legacies in her will, and others to benefit were her nephews and nieces, the children of her late sister the Marquise de Thois. She also bequeathed money to the poor of Guiler (or Guylar), a village near Brest, and made special provision for the poor of Aubigny. Even just before death Louise remained a typical Bretonne, fearful lest she had forgotten any of her servants. Her memory was remarkable, considering her great age. She died a true Catholic, requesting that a mass should be said every day for a year for the repose of her soul.

It has been written about Louise de Keroualle that luxury and riches were the grand objects of her life. Motives of self-interest, self-preservation and self-aggrandisement dominated her, though she was capable of kindness and generosity to her friends. She certainly succeeded in achieving her ambitions, though in her later life, deprived of the powerful support of Charles II, she was careless, and even stupid at times in the handling of her financial affairs. To found a noble house is no mean achievement, and it was natural for Louise to be proud of her own and Charles II's descendants, the Dukes of Richmond.

In an age which is remarkable for the brilliance of its women, Louise lacked the cultured distinction of such figures as Madame de Sévigné, Madame de Montespan and the Duchesse Mazarin. She had no imaginative sympathy for ideas. Her mind was rather sluggish, and lacking literary ability she found it difficult to express herself in her letters, which she almost always wrote in French. She did not share Charles II's tastes for poetry, nor do we hear of her reading the dramas of Molière or Racine with pleasure. Yet she was not frivolous. At the height of her power and influence, Thomas Otway, a dramatist of genius, dedicated his fine dramatic tragedy *Venice Preserved* in 1682 to the Duchess of Portsmouth. In his dedicatory letter he paid tribute to her generosity.

Nor must it be forgotten that she was a magnificent patron to foreign artists. Wissing, Gascar, Laguerre, Lely, Pierre Mignard, Verrio and Verelst were among those who worked for her.

By birth she was an aristocrat, and at Charles II's court when

* He died in 1750.

she was *Mâitresse en Titre* she behaved like a great lady. By temperament, unlike many of her rivals, she was chaste rather than wanton. She was almost always faithful to Charles II except for one affair with a fellow-countryman. When the King wanted charm of conversation, peace of mind, delicacy and refinement, he retired to the apartments of the Duchess of Portsmouth.

Her real strength lay in her subtle understanding of Charles's peculiar needs. It has never been fully stressed that she played her part in giving him comfort and support, while he was beset by the anxieties and vicissitudes during his reign. The King listened to her opinions, but he usually followed his own counsel. Sometimes she irritated him, occasionally she exasperated him, but she had the good sense to refrain from violent tempers. She possessed social tact, and marked ability for diplomacy. When negotiating she displayed a Bretonne persistence and obstinacy, which usually prevailed.

In a critical period in our history she assumed the role of intermediary between two great Kings Charles II and Louis XIV. Though she acquired an enormous ascendancy at the King's court, particularly from 1681 onwards, it is wrong to suppose that Charles II was ever a puppet in her hands. He was far too clever a man and skilled in kingcraft to be the dupe or slave of his most important mistress.

NOTES

1. Lady Russell, "The Real Louise de Keroualle".
2. Goodwood MSS. 6.
3. Goodwood MSS. 5.
4. Forneron, *Louise de Keroualle*; Delpech, *The Life and Times of the Duchess of Portsmouth*.
5. Many of them have been included in Forneron, *op. cit.*
6. French National Archives, b⁷, 543.
7. Add. MSS. 18675, fol. 74, B.M.
8. French National Archives, b⁷, 543; Delpech, *op. cit.*
9. Vincent Cronin, *Louis XIV.*
10. D. G. P. Gooch, *Louis XV, The Monarchy in Decline.*
11. *Journal du Marquis de Dangeau*, XVII, 20th June 1718.
12. MS. Bibliothèque Nationale, t.50417; Forneron, *op. cit.*
13. *Dictionary of National Biography.*

14. The story is told by Lady Russell in "The Real Louise de Keroualle".
15. Goodwood MSS. 8.
16. Goodwood—a pamphlet the copyright of Goodwood Estate Co.
17. Lady Russell, *op. cit.*

Genealogical Tree showing the family connectic

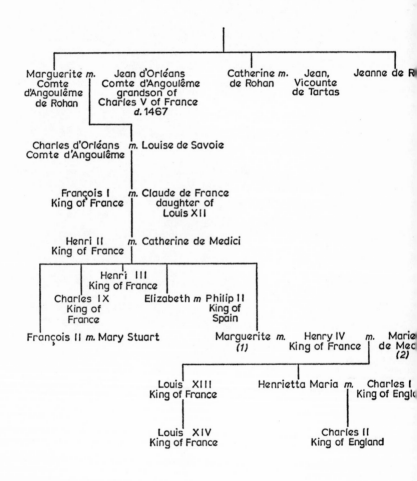

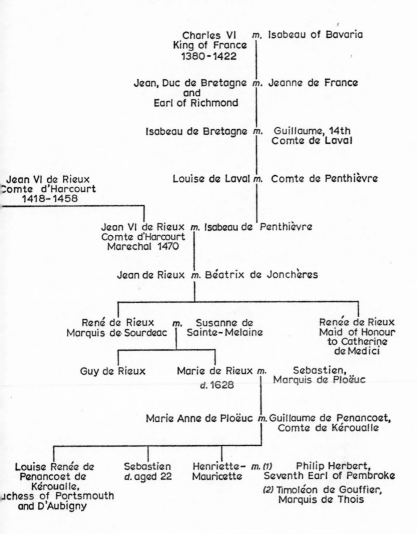

Charles VI *m.* Isabeau of Bavaria
King of France
1380-1422

Jean, Duc de Bretagne *m.* Jeanne de France
and
Earl of Richmond

Isabeau de Bretagne *m.* Guillaume, 14th
Comte de Laval

Jean VI de Rieux
Comte d'Harcourt
1418-1458

Louise de Laval *m.* Comte de Penthièvre

Jean VI de Rieux *m.* Isabeau de Penthièvre
Comte d'Harcourt
Marechal 1470

Jean de Rieux *m.* Béatrix de Jonchères

René de Rieux *m.* Susanne de   Renée de Rieux
Marquis de Sourdeac   Sainte-Melaine   Maid of Honour
                                            to Catherine
                                            de Medici

Guy de Rieux   Marie de Rieux *m.*   Sebastien,
                  d. 1628   Marquis de Ploëuc

Marie Anne de Ploëuc *m.* Guillaume de Penancoet,
                          Comte de Kéroualle

Louise Renée de   Sebastien   Henriette- *m. (1)*   Philip Herbert,
Penancoet de   *d.* aged 22   Mauricette   Seventh Earl of Pembroke
Kéroualle,
uchess of Portsmouth   *(2)* Timoléon de Gouffier,
and D'Aubigny   Marquis de Thois

BIBLIOGRAPHY

MODERN

Airy, Osmund, *Charles II* (1904)

Bevan, Bryan, *I was James II's Queen, The Story of Mary of Modena* (1963)

Bevan, Bryan, *Nell Gwyn* (1969)

Bryant, Sir Arthur, *King Charles II* (1931)

Bryant, Sir Arthur, *Restoration England* (1934)

Campbell, John Lord, *The Lives of the Lord Chancellors and Keepers of the Great Seal of England*, Volume III

Campbell Davidson, Lillias, *Catherine of Braganza, Infanta of Portugal and Queen-Consort of England* (1908)

Cartwright, Julia, *Madame. A Biography of Henrietta-Anne, Duchess of Orleans* (1894)

Christie, John, *The Life of Lord Shaftesbury (Anthony Ashley-Cooper)*

Clayton, *English Female Artists* (1876)

Collins Baker, C. H., *Lely and the Stuart Portrait Painters* (1912) Volume I

Crawford, Raymond, *The Last Days of Charles II*

Cronin, Vincent, *Louis XIV* (1964)

Dasent, Arthur Irwin, *Nell Gwyn* (1924)

Dasent, Arthur Irwin, *The Private Life of Charles II* (1927)

Delpech, Jeanine, *The Life and Times of the Duchess of Portsmouth* (1953), translated from the French

Elsner, Hebe, *Catherine of Braganza* (1967)

Erlanger, Philippe, *Louis XIV*, translated by Stephen Cox (1970)

Forneron, *Louise de Keroualle, Duchess of Portsmouth 1649–1734* (1887)

Gooch, Dr. G. P., *Louis XV, The Monarchy in Decline* (1956)

Haley, K. H. D., *Anthony Earl of Shaftesbury* (1968)

Harper, Charles G., *Haunted Houses, Tales of the Supernatural* (1907)

Hartmann, Cyril Hughes, *Charles II and Madame* (1934)

Hartmann, Cyril Hughes, *The Vagabond Duchess, The Life of Hortense Mancini* (1927)

Hopkirk, Mary, *Queen over the Water* (1953)
Imbert-Terry, H. M., *A Misjudged Monarch (Charles II)* (1917)
Jesse, J. H., *Memoirs of the Court of the Stuarts* (two volumes)
Kenyon, J. P., *Robert Spenser, Earl of Sunderland* (1958)
Lane, Jane, *Titus Oates* (1966)
Macaulay, Thomas Babington, *The History of England* (1862) Volume I
Middleton, Dorothy, *The Life of Charles, second Earl of Middleton 1650–1719* (1957)
Norman, Charles, *Rake Rochester* (1955)
Ogg, David, *England in the Reign of Charles II* (1934)
Oman, Carola, *Mary of Modena* (1962)
Pearson, Hesketh, *Charles II, His Life and Likeness* (1960)
Pollock, Sir John, *The Popish Plot*
Robb, Nesca A., *William of Orange* (1962) Volumes I and II
Russell, Lady, *The Rose Goddess and other sketches of mystery and romance, including the Real Louise de Keroualle* (1910)
Sackville-West, V., *Daughter of France, the Life of Anne Marie Louise d'Orleans, Duchesse de Montpensier* (1959)
Saunders, Beatrice, *John Evelyn and his Times* (1970)
Schofield, Seymour, *Jeffreys of the Bloody Assizes* (1937)
Scott, Lord George, *Lucy Walter, Wife or Mistress* (1947)
Sheppard, J. E., *Old Royal Palace of Whitehall* (1902)
Sitwell, Sir George, *The First Whig, an account of the parliamentary career of William Sacheverell, the origin of the two great political parties and the events which led up to the Revolution of 1688* (1894)
Turner, F. C., *James II* (1948)
Williams, H. Noel, *Rival Sultanas* (1915)
Wilson, John Harold, *Nell Gwyn Royal Mistress* (1952)
Wilson, John Harold, *The Court Wits of the Restoration*

MANUSCRIPT AND DOCUMENTARY

Additional MSS, British Museum
Calendar of State Papers, Charles II (1670–1685)
Calendar of State Papers, Domestic William III (1698) edited by E. Bateson
Calendar of Treasury Papers, Charles II
Correspondance Angleterre, the despatches of the French Ambassadors, in Archives de la Ministère des Affairs Etrangères, Paris
Goodwood MSS, County Record Office, Chichester

Harleian MSS, British Museum
Hatton Correspondence (Camden Series) Volumes I and II
Historical Manuscript Commission. Buccleuch (H.M.C. Buccleuch)
Historical Manuscript Commission. Rutland (H.M.C. Rutland II)
Orleans Correspondence, II
Public Record Office, Chancery Lane
Venetian State Papers 1671–1675
Verney Family Memoirs, Volumes I and II

CONTEMPORARY

Bruce, Thomas, Earl of Ailesbury, *Memoirs*, published by the Roxburghe Club
Burnet, Bishop Gilbert, *History of his owne time*
Carte, Thomas, *Life of James Butler, first Duke of Ormonde*, Volume II
Christie, D. (ed.), *Letters addressed to Sir Joseph Williamson*, Camden Society, Volume I
Cobbett, *Complete Collection of State Trials*, Volume VIII (1810)
Cowper, Countess, *Diary of Mary Countess Cowper, Lady of the Bedchamber to the Princess of Wales* (1714–1720)
Danby, Earl of, *Copies of Extracts of some letters written to and from the Earl of Danby, with particular remarks upon some of them.* Printed by John Nicholson at the Queen's Arms in Little Britain
Dangeau, Marquis de, *Journal*, Volumes I, II, IV, XIV, XVII
Davis, Charles E., *The Bathes of Bathes Ayde in the Reign of Charles II as illustrated by the drawings of the Kings and Queens Bath*
Dryden, John, "Absalom and Achitophel" in *Poems of Dryden*, ed. James Kingsley, Volume I (1958)
Elizabeth Charlotte, Duchess of Orleans, *Letters from Liselotte Elizabeth Charlotte Princess Palatine and Duchess of Orleans*, translated by Maria Kroll (1970)
Evelyn, John, (ed.) William Bray, *Memoirs and Correspondence of John Evelyn*, Volumes I–V
Fayette, Madame de la, *Vie de Madame Henriette*
Fiennes, Celia, *Through England on a side-saddle in the time of William and Mary, being the Diary of Celia Fiennes* (1888 edition)
Halstead, Robert, *Succinct Genealogies, a Memoir of Henry Mordaunt, Earl of Peterborough*
Luttrell, Narcissus, *Brief Relation of State Affairs*

Macky, John, *Memoirs of the Secret Services of John Macky*. Published from his original manuscript as attested by his son

Marvell, Andrew, "Britannia and Ralegh"

Montpensier, *Mémoires de Mademoiselle de Montpensier*, Volume IV

Oates Plot Trials Collection, printed for Robert Paulet at the sign of the Bible in Chancery Lane (1679)

Russell, Lady, *Letters of Lady Rachel Russell, from the MSS in the Library at Woburn Abbey* (1809)

Saint-Evremond, (ed.) Maizeaux, *Oeuvres*, Volume III

Saint-Simon, *Ecrits inédits*, E.16 (Hachette)

Saint-Simon, *Mémoires*, particularly Volume XI

Savile, George, Marquis of Halifax, *A Character of Charles II, and Political, Moral and Miscellaneous Thoughts and Reflections* (1750)

Sévigné, Marchioness de, *Letters*, (ed.) Spurs and Swift, Volume I–XIV

Sydney, Henry (ed. Blencowe), *Diary of the Times of Charles II by Henry Sydney, including his correspondence*. Two volumes (1843)

The Phenix or a Revival of Scarce and Valuable Pieces from the Remotest Antiquity down to the Present Times. A true relation of the late King's death (London 1707)

Tryall and Condemnation of Edward Fitzharris Esq., for High Treason at the Barr of the Court of King's Bench at Westminster on Thursday 9th June, in Trinity term, 1681. Printed for Francis Tytor and Thomas Basset, Booksellers in Fleet Street (1681)

Tuke, Richard, *Memoirs of the Life and Death of Sir Edmondbury Godfrey* (1682)

Voltaire, Siècle de Louis XIV (Paris Charpentier edition 1856), *Age of Louis XIV* (Everyman edition)

Wilmot, John, Earl of Rochester, *Complete Poems*, ed. David M. Vieth

Wilson, John Harold (ed.), *The Rochester-Savile Letters 1671–80*

Wood, Anthony à, *Life and Times*, Volume II

INDEX